REDWOOD
LIBRARY
NEWPORT
R.I.
WITHDRAWN
D1212025

Sibyl, Dame of Sark

By the same author

ENID BLYTON

Sibyl, Dame of Sark

a biography

by

BARBARA STONEY

HODDER AND STOUGHTON
LONDON SYDNEY AUCKLAND TORONTO

Copyright © 1978 by Barbara Stoney. First printed 1978. ISBN 0 340 21750 2. All rights reserved. No part of this publication may be reproduced or transmitted in any form or by any means, electronic or mechanical, including photocopy, recording, or any information storage and retrieval system, without permission in writing from the publisher. Printed in Great Britain for Hodder and Stoughton Limited, Mill Road, Dunton Green, Sevenoaks, Kent, by Willmer Brothers Limited, Birkenhead. Hodder and Stoughton Editorial Office: 47 Bedford Square, London WC1B 3DP.

CT
788
.H369
S76
1978

6
.H2849St

137102

Foreword

by Michael Beaumont, Seigneur of Sark

"The Seigneur of Sark plays a prominent part throughout and is a personage of considerable importance. He is, as it were, the pivot or centre, round which turn all the affairs of the Island . . . the greater number who have written about Sark have made strange mistakes in the matter, and have presented the Seigneur in a somewhat singular and sensational light."

So wrote the Rev. J. L. V. Cachemaille, Vicar of Sark, just over a century ago and the situation has not changed over the years. It was probably because my predecessor and grandmother, Dame Sibyl Hathaway, held the title as a woman in a very male-dominated world that she attracted more than the usual number of "strange mistakes in the matter".

Shortly after my grandmother's death a member of the family approached Barbara Stoney and asked her to consider writing a biography with a view to putting the real Dame Sibyl Hathaway on record. She contacted close relatives, particularly those connected with Sark, to determine their feelings and get their approval and made it clear that if she were to go ahead the biography would be based on her own researches, not biased by individual sensitivities. We were impressed by her obvious abilities and sincerity and readily gave our blessing.

There were some who asked the question, why a biography when an autobiography had been written as recently as 1961. But a biography can often be more revealing than an autobiography and in the case of my grandmother the revelations were more than even the family had anticipated, particularly with regard to historical accuracy. Furthermore there was no doubt about these revelations as Barbara Stoney's research was exceedingly thorough and every point of possible doubt was checked then rechecked from different sources. In retrospect we should not have been surprised, as my grandmother was always somewhat lax with regard to detail which did not interest her, nor did she consider it of great importance.

JUL 1 7 1978

It was people who interested her, their welfare on one level and entertaining them on another, and on this latter level the detail of Sark's history, or her own, would be bent to suit the listener, but entirely without intent to deceive, her sole purpose being to add to the entertainment value.

The interest shown in Sark and its hereditary Seigneurs (or Dames in the case of female descent) is due, certainly in part, to the island's unique heritage of law and custom. A full treatise would be quite out of order here, but a few words on the system as it is today may assist in understanding Dame Sibyl's singular position.

The Seigneur (or Dame) holds the island on perpetual lease from the Crown for a small rente and he has certain obligations all originally designed to maintain a settled community for its defence in time of war. For Sark the Crown is represented by the Lieutenant Governor in Guernsey and it is to him that the Seigneur is responsible for the appointment of the island officials and through them the maintenance of law and order and general well-being. Legislation is through the island parliament known as the Chief Pleas, presided over by the Seneschal and the members are the heads of the forty hereditary landholdings together with twelve elected Deputies. The Seigneur has one vote, as do the other members, and a veto applicable for twenty-one days only.

Legislation affecting non-residents in any way and laws affecting taxation have to be submitted to Her Majesty in Council for approval and foreign affairs, international agreements and EEC regulations affecting the island are handled directly by the Home Office.

The powers and privileges given to the Seigneur under the Royal Charter of 1565 and Letters Patent of 1611 were common in the Channel Islands in their day, but have all become extinct, except in Sark, which gives the island and its Seigneur a unique position in today's world. Though for all the uniqueness of the feudal system it may well be that Sark, and hence its feudal overlord, is best known through the banning of motor cars in the island, which has nothing whatever to do with its feudal basis.

There has been very little change in Sark since Dame Sibyl's death. The basic population remains stable at around five hundred persons and although tourism has increased steadily to an annual figure of some 75,000, this is not noticeable except in the shopping area. The constitution, law and custom of the island are fundamentally as she left them and I am certain that the problems reaching the Seigneurie today would be instantly recognisable to her.

J.M.B., 1978

Acknowledgments

Any attempt to have chronicled Dame Sibyl's ninety very full years of life would have been well nigh impossible without the generous cooperation of a large number of people. Special mention must be made, however, of her youngest and only surviving daughter, Mrs. Jehanne Bell, whose great help and encouragement throughout my researches has been invaluable. With her husband, the late Henry Parkin Bell, she has guided me painstakingly through some of the intricate laws of Sark with which she is so familiar and provided me with much useful island and family information. I am also indebted to Michael Beaumont, the present Seigneur of Sark, for writing the Foreword to this book, allowing me access to files and photographs at La Seigneurie and, with his wife, Diana, assisting me in so many other ways. Without the help, too, of Dame Sibyl's sister, Mrs. Doris Verschoyle, the early years would have been particularly difficult to chart and I am extremely grateful for her kindness to me and for the loan of many letters and other personal documents. Other members of the family whom I would also like to thank for their kind assistance include: Richard Beaumont, Dame Sibyl's only surviving son; Mrs. Enid Beaumont; David Beaumont; Colonel and Mrs. Harry Cantan; Peter and Patricia Cantan; David and Sally Ward-Jones; Mrs. Jane Rink; Mrs. Denis Parker; Miss Caroline Bell; Major-General W. d'A. Collings; Miss May Bonamy Collings; Miss Theodora Astley Cooper; Miss Lilian Palmer; Mr. and Mrs. Geoffrey Collings; Eric Lukis; Mrs. Jemma Kemmis Betty; Air Commodore W. G. W. Prall.

For interviews, correspondence, photographs or other assistance I am particularly grateful to: Mrs. Monica Adams; Basil S. Allen; Mrs. Audrey Arden; the late Mrs. Dina Baker; John and Mary La Trobe Bateman; Mrs. Ann Blakemore (who also lent me her late husband's unpublished book on Sark); the late Mrs. Cecile Bouget; Mrs. F. E. Brousson; Commander and Mrs. W. A. J. Campbell; Mr. and Mrs. Ernest Carré; Mr. and Mrs. Henry Carré; Greffier Hilary Carré and Mrs. Carré; Mr. and Mrs. Philip Carré; Mr. and Mrs. Willy Carré; Mr. and Mrs. Edwin Chapman; Miss Ethel Cheesewright; The Honourable the Lady Clitheroe; Dr.

Charles Cruickshank; Mrs. H. P. Davey; Mr. and Mrs. G. J. Dewhurst; A. Robert Dickinson; Raymond O. Falla; Mrs. May Falle and family; Mrs. Sheila Falle; Mrs. Elizabeth Le Feuvre; Mr. and Mrs. John Le Feuvre; Mr. and Mrs. John Guille; the late Louis A. Guillemette; Mrs. Harriet Hamon and the late Philip Hamon; Mrs. Edith Hamon; Mr. and Mrs. John Hamon; Jim Hamon; Mrs. M. Hartmann; Dr. N. S. Hewitt; Mrs. Monica Herry; the Reverend Fred Holmes; Mrs. Ruth Horan; the Reverend Philip Ellard-Handley; Theodore Hofler; Seneschal Bernard G. Jones and Mrs. Jones; Miss Celia Johnson; Mrs. D. Jowitt; Miss Sylvia Lamb; the late Mrs. M. Lavallée; Comtesse Susie Lippens (especially for permission to quote from her personal correspondence); Mr. S. D. Knox; Hubert Lanyon (in particular for his loan of a wartime diary and other notes); Mrs. Nina Larking; Vernon Luff; the late Mrs. Olive Mackie; Canon P. M. Martin, Chancellor of Wells; Philip Martel; Mrs. Hilda Mount; Hubert F. Nicolle; Mr. and Mrs. Douglas Norris and family; Miss Edith Page; Peter Pawson; Mrs. G. Pennington; Mr. and Mrs. E. C. Perrée; Mrs. Minnie Perrée; Mr. and Mrs. Philip Perrée; the late Brigadier P. J. T. Pickthall; Miss Ann Pickthall; Lieutenant-Colonel J. C. Preston; Mrs. Peggy Ravenshaw; J. Malcolm Robson; Miss Rosemary De Sausmarez; Mrs. Dorothy Scott; Elmo E. Shaver (especially for his loan of personal correspondence and permission to quote from it); Dr. and Mrs. R. B. Usher Somers; Mrs. R. Stratton; Mrs. R. O. Symons; Denys Tollemache; Mr. and Mrs. Cyril Wakley; Mr. and Mrs. W. J. Wakley; John York; Sidney Young (whose collection of scrapbooks has proved extremely useful); Peter Zwart.

I am also grateful for the help I have received from the Home Office; Public Record Office; Imperial War Museum; British Library, Bloomsbury and Press Library, Colindale; BBC Written Archives; BBC Sound Archives. Particularly helpful to me in Guernsey were the staffs of the Office of the Lieutenant Governor, Bailiff's Office, Greff Office, Guille-Alles Library and the *Guernsey Press*.

I would also like to thank the *Guernsey Press* and the *Jersey Evening Post* for permission to quote from files and William Heinemann Ltd. for their cooperation in allowing me to quote from Dame Sibyl's autobiography, *The Dame of Sark*.

I am indebted to Maureen Roberts for her clerical assistance and to Helene Read for the translation of German war documents. Last, but by no means least, my gratitude goes to my husband for his great understanding and encouragement throughout the many months I have been working on this book.

Contents

	page
Part One: Prelude	13
Part Two: La Dame de Serk (1927–1939)	77
Part Three: Occupation and Aftermath (1939–1954)	127
Part Four: Conclusion	199
Appendix One: Letters Patent of 1565	249
Appendix Two: Suggestions for Constitutional Changes Made by the Dame of Sark in 1969	253
Appendix Three: Queen Dismisses Petitions to Unseat the Dame of Sark	255
Bibliography	259
Index	263

Illustrations

	facing page
John Allaire	48
Marie Collings	48
The Rev. William Thomas Collings	48
The young Sibyl	48
The Collings family	49
Sibyl's father, dressed for a "spree"	49
Sibyl on her honeymoon	64
Dudley Beaumont	64
A skiing holiday at Mürren	64
At rest and work in Cologne	65
Family group 1923	65
La Dame at her Seigneurie desk	176
With Lord Sackville, Lieutenant Governor of Guernsey	176
With Edward, Prince of Wales	176
German officers at the Seigneurie	177
Prisoners of war repairing La Coupée	177
A visit from Colonel Graf von Schmettow in 1963	177
Charlie Perrée drives Princess Elizabeth and the Duke[1]	192
A meeting of Chief Pleas	192
With David Niven and Jehanne	193
A visit from Princess Anne[2]	193
The Seigneurie becomes a postage stamp[3]	193

CREDITS

1 Radio Times Hulton Picture Library
2 The Guernsey Press Co. Ltd.
3 Department of Postal Administration, Guernsey

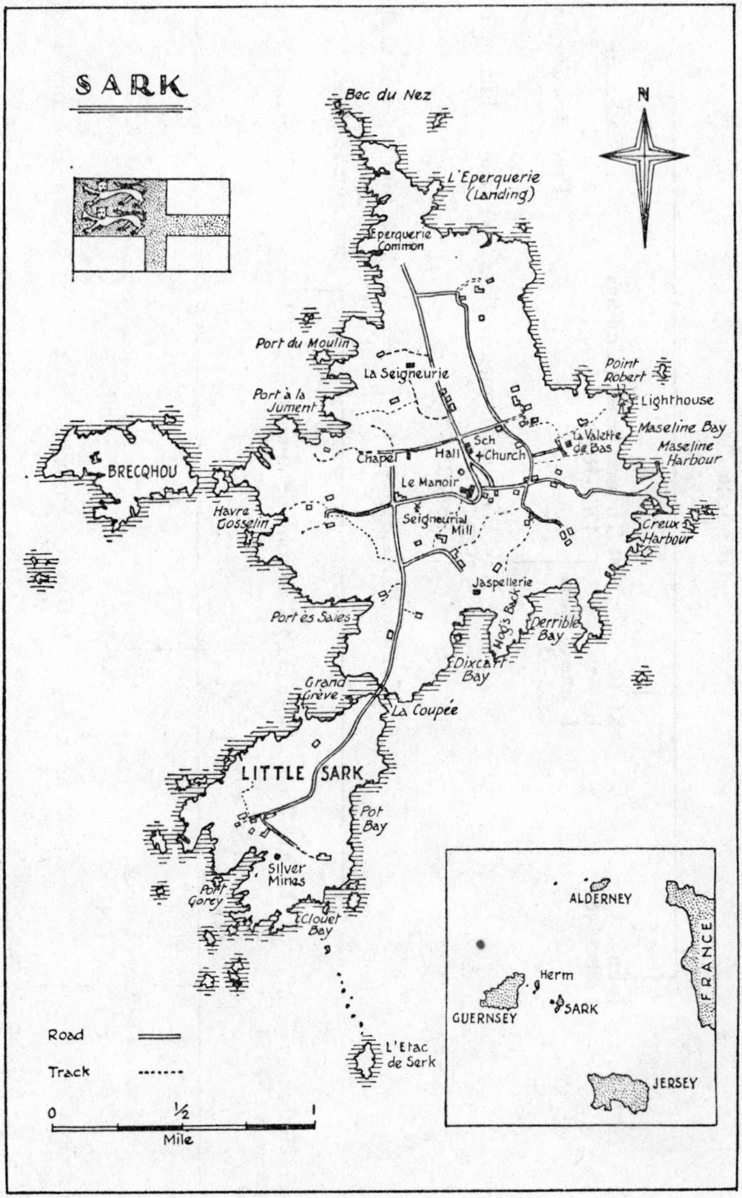
SARK
Bec du Nez
N
L'Eperquerie (Landing)
Eperquerie Common
Port du Moulin
La Seigneurie
Point Robert
Lighthouse
Port à la Jument
Maseline Bay
Maseline Harbour
La Valette de Bas
Sch
Hall
Church
Chapel
BRECQHOU
Le Manoir
Havre Gosselin
Seigneurial Mill
Creux Harbour
Jaspellerie
Hog's Back
Derrible Bay
Port ès Saies
Dixcart Bay
Grand Grève
La Coupée
LITTLE SARK
Pot Bay
Silver Mines
Port Gorey
Clouet Bay
L'Etac de Serk
Road
Track
0
½
1
Mile
ALDERNEY
FRANCE
Herm
GUERNSEY
SARK
JERSEY

SIBYL, DAME OF SARK – Family tree

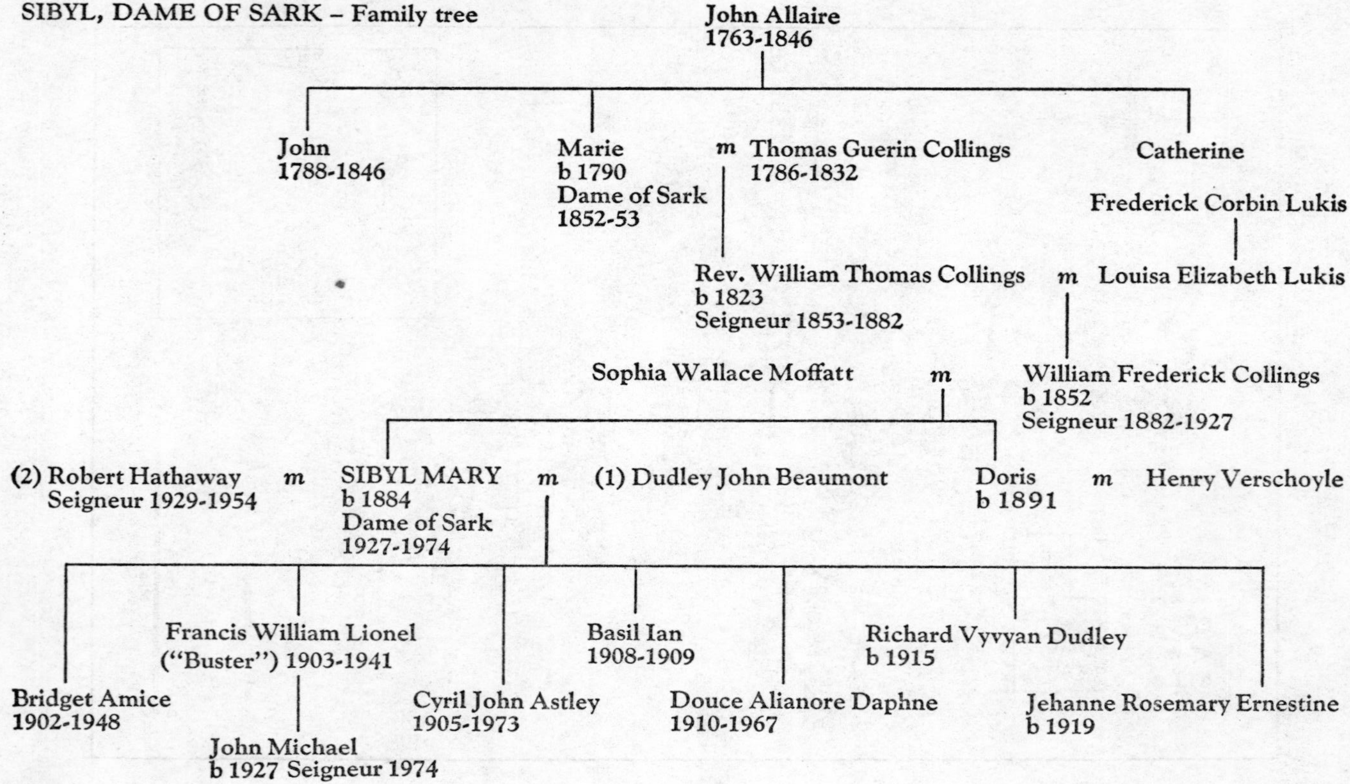

Part One

Prelude

Chapter 1

"Je n'ignore pas qu'en devenant Dame de Serk je me charge d'une grande responsabilité. Je ne suis qu'une femme parmis vous, mais de coeur je suis un 'vrai Serquais' et avec l'aide de Dieu je ferai tout mon possible pour le bien et la prospérité de l'île."

THIS WAS THE promise made by Sibyl, Dame of Sark, at the first meeting of the Chief Pleas, the island's governing body, after she had succeeded to the Seignory on her father's death in 1927. For the following forty-seven years, until she died in July 1974 at the age of ninety, she remained firmly in control of this small, beautiful Channel Island, with its distinctive character, feudal traditions and ancient laws, her earlier life having schooled her to surmount any obstacles encountered along the way – including her own personal griefs and disappointments.

Sark is the smallest independent state in the British Commonwealth – a mere 1,200 acres of fertile plateau set upon great cliffs rising more than three hundred feet above the sea. The poet Swinburne, who was captivated as many others have been by the island's rugged coastline, wooded valleys and wild flowers, once described it as a "small sweet world of wave-encompassed wonder", and certainly over the years it has acquired a fame which might seem out of all proportion to its size.

With the other Channel Islands of Jersey, Guernsey, Alderney, Herm and Jethou, Sark lies nearer to the coast of France than to the country to which it owes its allegiance and much of its customs and language is of Norman origin, although relics have been found of Roman and even earlier occupations. Its first recorded history was the foundation of a monastery in AD 565 by the Welsh Saint Magloire and sixty-two monks from Britain, Normandy and Brittany. This peaceful settlement flourished until Norse pirates brought it to an end several centuries later, pillaging and destroying most of the buildings and slaughtering the inhabitants. With the other Channel Islands, Sark then came into the possession of the Duchy of Normandy and passed eventually to the British Crown in 1218. During the next hundred or so years the island enjoyed a period of relative peace and prosperity until the outbreak of the Hundred Years War between England and France. It then changed hands several times as both sides laid claim to it and in 1372 was so devastated by the French that it soon became an uninhabited wilderness of decaying buildings and scrubland. It was not until the middle of the sixteenth century that Helier de Carteret, Seigneur of St. Ouen in Jersey, set about bringing this unhappy state to an end, and in the process became the island's first Seigneur.

In 1563, when England was once again at war with France, Helier de Carteret became concerned over Sark's unprotected and strategic position in the Channel and proposed to an English Government Commission, who happened at that time to be investigating Channel Island defences generally, that he be granted Sark as an adjunct to his own fief of St. Ouen. In return he promised to establish upon it a permanent settlement and guarantee its future defence. This offer was accepted but it was not until two years later, when the war was over, that Helier, his wife, Margaret, and a small party of tenants from St. Ouen, landed on the overgrown and rabbit-infested island, bringing with them food, livestock, tools and building materials. They cleared ground and planted corn and vegetables, living meanwhile in any of the ruined monastic buildings that still afforded shelter. Later the same year, following yet another threatening French claim to the island, Helier used the occasion of a visit to London to seek legal confirmation of his position and this was granted in the form of Letters Patent from Queen Elizabeth I, under the Great Seal of England (see Appendix) on 6th August, 1565. The terms of these stipulated that he should have Sark "settled, dwelt in or occupied by forty men at least" within two years, such men being loyal subjects of the Crown of England. Another condition was that he or his "heirs or assigns" should not "give, sell or alienate all his whole estate" without permission from the Sovereign.

One of Helier's first actions on his return was to divide Sark into forty parcels of land – "tenèments" – thirty-nine of which he leased out cheaply to settlers from Jersey, Guernsey and England, with the condition that each tenant should build himself a house and provide a man with "musket, ammunition and provisions" for the island's defence. On the remaining portion – which included the site of the old chapel of the priory of St. Magloire, in the centre of the island overlooking the stretch of sea between

Sark and his native home in Jersey – he built his "Seigneurie" known as "Le Manoir".

So successful did his small community become that in 1572 the Queen showed her recognition of his achievement by creating Sark a Fief Haubert,* separate from St. Ouen, and presenting it to Helier and his heirs in perpetuity. The Queen further showed her appreciation by sending him, as a contribution towards the island's defence, six brand-new pieces of ordnance from the Tower of London, with fifty cannon balls for each and two hundred pounds of powder.

The de Carterets continued as Seigneurs of the island for 155 years until, owing to family debts, Lord John Carteret was forced to seek Royal permission to sell the fief that had been granted to his ancestor. Sark then changed hands several times until Susanne Le Pelley bought it in 1730, with the money gained from her late husband's privateering ventures – privateering in those days being a highly profitable source of income for many Channel Islanders. The family of Susanne Le Pelley had lived on Sark since Helier de Carteret's time in a house called Le Perronerie, which was sited in the north-west of the island, and she decided to make this her home rather than Le Manoir which, up to that time, had always been the official "Seigneurie". More than a century later, one of her successors mortgaged the island's estates to yet another privateer, John Allaire, and it was as a result of this transaction that Sibyl – his great-great-grand-daughter – eventually became Dame of Sark and the island's twenty-first Seigneur.

John Allaire was said to have come from a respectable Jersey family but he was known throughout the Channel Islands as a debaucher with an evil temper, who had made a vast fortune from his exploits during the Napoleonic wars as a renegade privateer. Officially he sailed under the English flag with Letters of Marque granted by George III, entitling him to "apprehend, seize and take ships, vessels and goods belonging to France and other enemies", distributing the spoils according to certain specified terms. There appears to be little doubt, however, that if it suited him, he would run up the French flag, capture an English ship and transport the illegal booty to Jethou – the small island he owned off the coast of Guernsey. French being then the common language of the Channel Islands, his crew would not have aroused suspicion and Jethou was safe enough from in-

* A Fief Haubert is the highest form of land tenure whereby the holder owes personal allegiance to the Crown alone.

B

truders – the treacherous rocks and tides around it being sufficient deterrents to any inquisitive stranger wishing to land, let alone run the risk of meeting John Allaire or his crew – for mercy was not, it appears, one of the qualities either possessed.

Both the old granite house on Jethou and another Allaire property in Guernsey – "The Mount" – were rumoured to have been haunted by victims of John Allaire's callousness and many tales have been told of his wicked deeds. It was in an upstairs room at The Mount that an old woman is alleged to have visited John to plead for her son, sentenced to death for sheep stealing, and to have been angrily pushed aside by him and his drunken companions, causing her to fall downstairs and break her neck. From that time onwards it was claimed that in the dark night hours her body could be heard falling from stair to stair.* Disregard of yet another plea for mercy is also said to have resulted in a curse being put upon the privateer and all his descendants by a woman he had once left to drown, having heartlessly ignored her cries for help, after pillaging and eventually sinking the ship she was aboard. But this "Allaire Curse", as it became known to the family, appears to have had little effect upon John himself, for he lived to the age of eighty-three, having by that time amassed an enormous fortune. His son, John, however, never lived to enjoy his inheritance. He committed suicide less than three weeks after his father died, in July 1846 – the Guernsey newspapers of the time reporting that he took his own life following "acute depression" over his father's death.

A letter written soon after the suicide, by John Allaire's grandson – the Reverend William Thomas Collings – shows something of the wealth the privateer had acquired and also conjures up a vivid picture of the house on Jethou where John and his son had been living. The Reverend William Collings evidently visited the island on his mother's account – Marie Collings (née Allaire) having been too overcome by the deaths of both her father and brother, within three weeks of each other, to make the journey herself. He and his companions found, he wrote: "lots of money in Louis d'or guineas, notes and sovereigns and bags of two franc pieces . . ." In clearing out a "rubbishy room" they had also dis-

* When The Mount became Government House a hundred years later, the Lieutenant Governor (Lord Sackville) scotched this story by having the staircase removed, along with the drive gates which carried another superstition that, should these ever be closed, the head of the house would die. Sentry boxes were placed on either side of the entrance and it was later rumoured that a bottle of wine was also buried to "remove the spell".

covered "five hundred bright sovereigns and £111 in doubloons" rolled up in a piece of lead foil. He estimated that altogether the Allaire father and son must have had upwards of £1,900 in loose cash about their rooms:

> ... We sent a wheelbarrow with it to the Bank. It was quite a joke for two men could not carry it a hundred yards ... You ought to have seen us rummaging out the old drawers and lockers – filled with goodies of all sorts, laces, plate, gold and silver – refreshing ourselves occasionally with a bottle of the very best champagne. It reminded me of Hogarth's picture. There we were enjoying the best of everything, bags of guineas before us, champagne, etc. – even the blacksmiths whom we took over to pick the locks, coming in for their share ...

Evidently the young Mr. Collings was also surprised by the amount of money the Allaires had invested abroad:

> ... In Russia alone the old man had £29,000 in stocks and £30,000 in a lump which had accumulated. Why, it is enough to break a House to ask for it at once, but of course they will begin with £10,000 at a time. John was worth double what was expected ... What they will do with all the estates, etc. I do not know ...

A major outcome of the winding up of the Allaire estates was that the Island of Sark passed from the Le Pelley family to that of the Reverend William Thomas Collings through his mother, Marie.

The Le Pelley family had been forced to mortgage its estates on Sark to John Allaire to raise more money for an unsuccessful silver and copper mining venture which some of its members had embarked upon on the island. When Pierre Carey Le Pelley was unable to meet the interest payments, Marie Collings, who by that time had inherited the mortgage from her father, foreclosed and in December 1852 the island, which had been owned by the Le Pelleys for over a hundred and twenty years, was hers.

Little else is known of Marie, John Allaire's elder daughter and second child, beyond the fact that she was born in 1790 and married Thomas Guerin Collings in 1810. The Collings forebears were believed to have been staunch Royalists who had escaped to Jersey from the West of England at the time of the Civil War and the branch of which Thomas Guerin was a member moved to Guernsey in 1735. Thomas died some twenty years before his wife bought the Seignory and Marie lived for only four months after the sale had been completed, so it was their son – and Sibyl's grandfather – the Reverend William Thomas Collings, who inherited the major task of putting the island into some sort of order again after the Le Pelleys' disastrous mining project.

The Reverend William loved Sark from the first. He was twenty-nine years old when he came to the island as Seigneur in April 1853, having been a curate at East Wells in Somerset since his ordination the year before.* As a boy he had lived for a time with and been much influenced by, his uncle and godfather, Frederick Corbin Lukis, an esteemed Guernsey archaeologist, whose interests in natural history, botany and geology he also shared. Frederick Lukis later became his father-in-law also, for in 1847 he married the eldest daughter of the house – his first cousin, Louisa Elizabeth. Before his marriage he was said to have been a great favourite with many of the young ladies of Guernsey and a portrait of him as a young man shows him to have been a slim, good-looking fellow with expressive hazel eyes and delicate, sensitive features – though, from all accounts, he had a stronger personality than his looks conveyed. He gained a Master of Arts degree at Trinity College, Cambridge, and held fellowships of the Society of Antiquaries, the Linnean Society, the Geological Society and FRSA of Copenhagen – clearly a man of wide interests and many parts.

In his early years he had been an enthusiastic Captain of the Royal Guernsey Light Infantry and on becoming Seigneur of Sark appointed himself Commander of the Royal Sark Militia – a position which he took very seriously, never missing an opportunity to array himself in the full uniform of a Lieutenant-Colonel, complete with sword, and insisting that his rather reluctant men should regularly go on parade and attend shooting practices.

He became immensely popular with the Sark people and brought about many improvements to the island, including the introduction of compulsory schooling for its children – the first in the British Isles to adopt such a measure. In the main he was practical and serious minded over his affairs but there were occasions when he indulged in seemingly wild flights of fancy. He had a window cut through one of the large rocks above the Port du Moulin – the bay below La Seigneurie – to provide him with a breathtaking view and made another elaborate peep-hole through his garden wall. He also saw to it that ornate arches bearing the Collings' crest were built over most of the gateways

* He was never, as the family were later led to believe, a Canon of Wells Cathedral.

around his estate. As several fine old trees had overtopped the original signalling tower in his grounds he decided, rather than fell them, to build another tower onto the roof of his house. This ugly, totally out-of-place addition nevertheless served its purpose for it commanded not only a superb view of Guernsey, for which it was intended, but of most of the surrounding islands as well as of Sark itself. He chose, however, the top of the old church tower from which to sketch a panoramic picture of his island in the late 1880s and this, with many other of his drawings and paintings give proof of his skill as an artist.

These pencil drawings from the church tower show a Sark of thatched cottages, leafy lanes, cultivated farmland and sturdily-built stone houses, many of them still owned by the descendants of Helier de Carteret's first settlers, with women working in the fields while the men fished. This was the island that was beginning to attract summer visitors, encouraged by the newly-built hotels and improved shipping service and by the natural beauties of Sark they had seen portrayed by William Toplis and other visiting artists of the day. Writers and poets, among them Swinburne, Dickens and Victor Hugo, also extolled the island's charms and were attracted back many times despite the dangers of the sea crossing, with its uncertain tides and submerged rocks that caught many a practised sailor unawares.

Numerous lives had been lost in the waters around Sark – including that of a previous Seigneur – and a Mr. Agnew Giffard, who had been engaged to supervise the building of a new harbour, was also drowned with four companions on a return journey to Guernsey on a stormy October evening in 1868. Four years later the Reverend William Collings, too, narrowly escaped drowning when the steamer *Gosforth*, which he had chartered to take his family for their regular winter sojourn in Guernsey, struck a rock off the coast of Herm and sank. After a nightmarish two hours of sailing in a small boat packed with ten people, the family reached Herm, having lost several of the much-treasured possessions which usually accompanied them on their annual journeys. Among these was the original Charter of the 1565 Grant of Sark to Helier de Carteret but, fortunately, a copy had been retained in the Public Record Office in London. That no lives were lost was largely due to the seafaring skill and quick actions of the Collings' elder son, William Frederick, then only twenty years old and who, a decade later – in 1882 – was to succeed his father as Seigneur.

William Frederick Collings appears to have inherited little of the Reverend William's temperament for he was altogether a more fiery being, who chafed against the rigid – though typically Victorian – attitudes of his father. His sudden outbursts of rage when he was thwarted were beyond his parents' comprehension and these occurred most frequently during discussions over his career.

The Collings found William's desire to join the army difficult to understand – particularly as he showed little interest in the Royal Sark Militia in which he had been forced to serve as his father's adjutant. Neither were they prepared to consider his other suggestion that, being an able sailor with no fear of the sea, he be allowed to join the Royal Navy. His father had already determined upon his son's career – he was to follow him into the Church. As William appears to have been violently anti-cleric for most of his life, the Reverend William Collings' insistence on such a course is difficult to understand. Bitter quarrels followed William's refusal of a place at his father's old college at Cambridge and in despair he was sent off on a Grand Tour, his parents accompanying him as far as Paris – where they were said to have acquired for themselves a set of beechwood and cane chairs for their Seigneurie which had been looted from the Tuileries after the fall of Napoleon III.* By a strange coincidence, it was while William was travelling through Copenhagen that a case of silver and books, bearing his father's name, happened to be washed up on the coast of Jutland and he was able to identify the crate as being part of the luggage lost from the *Gosforth* some two years earlier.

How William spent the next few years is not recorded but that he was a popular figure, particularly among the ladies, there can be little doubt for he could be a charming companion when he chose. He was certainly a fine looking man, over six feet four inches in height and with a profusion of dark curly hair, which earned him the nickname among his friends of "Mop" Collings. From his Allaire ancestor he had inherited his striking blue eyes and, sadly, a penchant for drink which, when he over-indulged, inflamed still further his uncertain temper.

It is said that William lost his heart at one time to the beautiful Lillie Langtry – then Lillie Le Breton, daughter of the Dean of Jersey – and that he kept her photograph among his private papers for the rest of his life, but it was a Canadian girl, Sophia Wallace Moffat from Montreal, whom he married.

Sophia's grandfather, the Honourable George Moffatt, had been

* As, however, a portrait of Marie Allaire, the Reverend William Collings' mother, shows her to be seated in just such a chair, it now seems more likely that these were acquired much earlier – by, perhaps, her privateering father.

a man of some eminence in Montreal, a politician of note, a prime mover in the building of the city's cathedral and one of those responsible for forming Canada's first railway company – the Champlain and St. Lawrence. Sophia was born at Weardale Lodge in Montreal, which had once belonged to her grandfather, but her family later moved to London and it was in the late 1870s, while convalescing from a bout of pleurisy in Guernsey, that she first met William. He immediately fell in love with the tall, graceful girl with the hazel eyes, whose sense of humour matched his own. As he had still not decided upon a profession and had no money to support a wife he finally agreed, reluctantly, to fall in with his father's plans for a career in the Church. With this intention he read for his Bachelor of Divinity at Durham University but – perhaps fortunately for all concerned – before he could become ordained his father died and William gave up his studies to return to Sark and become the island's twentieth Seigneur. Some seven months later, on 17th October, 1882, he married Sophia in London.

Marriage to William was not easy for the gentle-natured Canadian girl, though from all accounts he was as genuinely fond of her as she of him. Sophia's good temper and sense of humour carried her through her husband's fickle moods and even wilder moments, when all the household and the Sark people themselves lived in fear of what he might do. During the winter months he was reasonably well-behaved and drank moderately but it soon became known on the island that when the Seigneur donned his yachting cap, his trousers tucked into his socks, preparatory to a few days' sailing with an old schoolfriend from England, it was usually the prelude to another of his "sprees" – as his occasional wild drinking bouts were termed. When these moods were upon him he would set forth, either on foot or horse – a shotgun, or sometimes a rifle, over his shoulder – looking for trouble.

A particular target for him at one time was the Reverend Louis Napoleon Seichan, Vicar of Sark, whose eccentricities matched his own. According to local gossip, the long-standing feud had started over William's arguments with Seichan over the way the church services were conducted, but it is also said that he once accused the clergyman of stealing the copper stoves from the vicarage and selling them in Guernsey for their metallic weight. Whatever the origin of his dislike, he seized every opportunity to annoy the vicar, riding him into the hedges if he met him in narrow lanes or pretending he was about to pepper him with shot. He scrawled abusive slogans against him on walls and once rode his horse into the vicarage garden, a foal trotting behind, to chase his poor victim mercilessly around a clump of pampas grass. For such behaviour towards his vicar and others he was several times brought before the Seneschal, the island's magistrate and chief official, on such charges as wilfully breaking windows, assault and battery and the firing of pistols and other firearms on the public highway. Although, according to Sark practice, the Seneschal had been appointed by William, he had no alternative but to fine him in the usual manner for such offences or refer him to Guernsey for the more serious charges.

The Seigneurie servants were frequently threatened and turned out of the house in the middle of the night, but they usually returned in good heart the next morning for, like the majority of islanders, they tolerated this darker side of their Seigneur's behaviour in the knowledge that he could at other times show great kindness and compassion, particularly when rents were due and times were hard.

Throughout it all, Sophia continued in her placid way to run her household as best she could, trying to keep some semblance of order in the Seigneurie and acting as a competent hostess for her husband on official occasions. Within such an environment did their two daughters, of whom Sibyl Mary was the elder, spend their formative years.

Chapter 2

Sibyl was born on 13th January, 1884, at Hirzel House, a family home in Guernsey once owned by John Allaire. Her father's suggestion that she should therefore be named after the privateer was greeted with horror by his relatives, who thought that such an association was bound to result in disaster.

William did not as a rule winter in Guernsey – as had been the custom of his parents and several of the previous Seigneurs – but at the time of Sibyl's birth there were no proper midwives on Sark and it was thought best for Sophia to have her first child where medical help was more readily at hand. Soon after the baby's christening, at the town church in St. Peter Port, the family returned to Sark on a stormy February day when the seas were so rough that the cargo ship could not put into the harbour and Sibyl had to be carried ashore from a small boat – at the landing stage at L'Eperquerie, to the north of the island – in the arms of an old fisherman.

Having once overcome his initial disappointment that the baby was not a boy, William took a great interest in his young daughter and was as shocked as Sophia when it was discovered that their otherwise sturdy child had one leg considerably shorter than the other. This had not been noticed when she was swaddled in baby clothes but it soon became apparent when she was put into shorter garments and began to take her first uneven steps. At the time it was assumed that she had been dropped by the nurse Lizzie, who, it was later discovered, suffered from occasional fits, but medical evidence has since established that the hip deformity that caused Sibyl's lameness was almost certainly congenital. When she was five years old she was taken by Sophia to a specialist in London, but his suggestion that an operation be performed on the hip was angrily rejected by William, who feared that this might further aggravate her condition. The alternative was a heavy built-up boot which brought Sibyl much distress and there were many tearful scenes in the nursery before it was finally discarded, Sibyl having persuaded her mother that it was more of a hindrance than a help. By that time she had become quite accustomed to coping physically with her lameness – though there is little doubt that it was to affect her in other ways for the rest of her life.

When the nurse's fits were discovered, she was replaced by Nana, a kindly Sark woman whose loving care of the small, lame girl proved at times to be no easy task. Sibyl was an attractive-looking child, very like her father in appearance, with the same dark, curly hair and strong features and, much to her mother's dismay, showed at times a certain similarity of temperament, for her childish tantrums and obstinate nature caused many a rumpus in the nursery. Years later she told the story of how she had once "clouted the housemaid with her dustpan" for not getting out of her way on the stairs, and had been carried "kicking and screaming" up to her room by her father. In a fury she had thrown the water jug, basin and soap dish out of the window on to the pantry skylight, shattering the glass and frightening the kitchen staff below.

The year after Sibyl was born, Sophia had a stillborn son* and several other miscarriages followed before the arrival of the Collings' second daughter, Doris, in September, 1891. William was once again disappointed when he learned that the new baby was a girl and his thwarted desire for a son could well have accounted for his attitude towards his daughters for, from the beginning, he encouraged them to take an interest in boyish rather than feminine pursuits. He firmly believed and possibly rightly so, that the very nature of their lives on what was then a fairly primitive island, warranted a certain toughness and ability to stand up for themselves. Complaints of ailments or unhappiness were discouraged and on the rare occasions that they dared give voice to their feelings they were invariably told that they would be a "lot worse off" before they were dead and that "only the smug and self-centred" imagined that other people were interested in their troubles.

Sibyl's lameness was never mentioned and Doris, who had been a sickly, premature baby, only kept alive by spoonfuls of port and cod-liver oil, was also expected to cope uncomplainingly with her own infirmity – a speech impediment she had also had since birth. As the sisters grew up, each learnt to cope with their handicaps in their own way – according to the nature of their very different personalities.

* Sibyl never spoke of him but he was believed to have been buried in the Seigneurie grounds.

Although his erratic behaviour would sometimes frighten her, Sibyl had a great respect for her father. She would often tell of how, as soon as she could hold a revolver, he had taught her to shoot and that by the time she was an adolescent she could handle rifles and shotguns with ease.

As soon as she was old enough to ride, William bought her a donkey but, unlike her sister, Doris, whose skill with horses began at a very early age, Sibyl was never a keen rider. She was far more at home swimming in one of the lovely island bays with her father, feeling happier in the sea than she ever did upon it, although she did sometimes go out sailing and fishing with him in his boat.

From the age of eight she was always encouraged to read out to him the leading article from his weekly Conservative newspaper and comment on anything she did not understand. Later on the church services, which the family attended most Sundays, were also subjects for discussion between them – William often producing books from his student days to reinforce his own, very strong opinions. He was a fine scholar with the ability to read Hebrew and Greek and, even before the Reverend Louis Napoleon Seichan came to the island, rarely agreed with the teachings of the Sark clergymen despite his being responsible for employing them in the first place. In those days the incumbents were French and services were conducted in that language – being more likely to be understood by the majority of the islanders, who usually conversed in their own Norman-French patois. One of Sibyl's earliest churchgoing memories was of her father rising in fury from his pew at the front of the church and walking out in protest when Monsieur Vermeil, the clergyman at that time, demonstrated his anti-British feelings by neglecting to read the set prayers for Queen Victoria.

Mademoiselle Vermeil, the clergyman's sister, gave Sibyl her first lessons but her only recollections of these in later life were of being made to say the Lord's Prayer in French every morning and of the teacher's use of the ruler across her back when she stumbled through her piano pieces – which possibly accounted for her subsequent total disinterest in most music. Years later she was to recall the stories the Frenchwoman told of her own schooldays in Alsace under German occupation during the Franco-Prussian War, and of her governess's intense hatred of Germany as a result.

When her brother died and was succeeded by the colourful Reverend Louis Napoleon Seichan, Mademoiselle Vermeil left the island and Sibyl then had a succession of French and English governesses whose persecution by their young charge's father usually guaranteed their swift departure – some after only a few days. William would argue with them over the manner in which they conducted their lessons and frighten and bully them to such a degree that few could stand his behaviour for long – particularly if they had also been subjected to a nocturnal eviction from the house, during one of his sprees. One poor woman, who was engaged as governess to Doris, had to suffer carving knives being placed on her chair as she was about to sit down and another had her belongings thrown out of her bedroom window, one by one. It is hardly surprising, therefore, that there was little continuity in the education of either Sibyl or her sister.

With an age difference of nearly eight years between herself and Doris, Sibyl's childhood was, on the whole, rather lonely. Few young people visited the Seigneurie in those days and very rarely did she play with the Sark children. Because of his position as their Seigneur, William was treated with a certain amount of deference by the majority of the Sark people, despite his occasional misdemeanours, and familiarity with his family was neither expected nor encouraged on either side. What little social life the Collings had was therefore largely dependent upon visits to friends and relations outside the island and occasional, official entertaining. Sibyl particularly enjoyed meeting visitors from overseas and often recalled in later years meeting the tall, graceful Queen Liliuokalani of the Sandwich Islands, then exiled in Jersey. She dreamed of one day visiting such far-off countries, where people's life styles were so different from her own but – apart from her one London visit – most of her early years were spent in or around the Channel Islands.

Occasionally Sophia and William had official visits to make outside the island and while they were away Sibyl – and, later, Doris – usually spoke only in patois to the people who lived and worked around the Seigneurie. This ability to converse with the islanders in their own language – so difficult for an outsider to master – remained a source of pride to both in the years that followed.

Apart from Nana, her childhood favourite among the staff was the cowman, John Hamon, who had once worked in the Le Pelleys' silver mine and was something of a character. He acted as barber and dentist and she would watch him extracting teeth on Sunday mornings, his patients seated on an upturned barrel in the farmyard while he used the adjacent forge fire to sterilise his gruesome-looking instruments. These operations fascinated her and she was not in the least perturbed by the occasional cries of pain or the sight of blood as the offending molars were removed. On weekdays she would follow John as he went about his work on the farm, helping him to lead the fine herd of Guernsey cows into the fields and watching as he knocked in the tethering stakes – a traditional custom on this island of limited pasture. Another childhood pleasure was to see the rich, golden butter being churned in the dairy and she would sometimes help the dairyman as he worked, shaping the butter into pats bearing the Seigneur's stamp. Sophia often tried to interest her in household matters but she showed no interest in these – preferring to spend most of her free time away from her lessons out of doors.

William had no wish for either of his daughters to be educated away from home. One of his brothers had died while at boarding school and he had a real fear of such places. Because of this often expressed view, it must have come as a surprise to most of his relations and friends when they learned that he had given his consent to Sibyl being sent, at the age of fourteen, to a convent school in France. According to Sibyl, her parents decided to send her away to school in order to perfect her French accent which was in danger of being adulterated by the Sark patois, but this does not seem sufficient reason in itself for the strong-willed William to have so completely changed his mind and it seems far more likely that other factors were involved.

For her thirteenth birthday, Sibyl had been given a small book – *The Cloud of Witness*, described on its frontispiece as "a daily sequence of great thoughts from many minds, following the Christian seasons" – and for some years she used this to make brief, marginal notes, presumably in the absence of a diary. Many of the "great thoughts" were also underlined and these, together with the various letters and mementoes tucked inside the book provide an insight into the thoughts and feelings which, since a small child, she had been schooled by William to conceal. As shown by these jottings, the year before she went away to school had not been uneventful.

On 13th July, 1898, she wrote: "Awful row here" – and the following day: "Alone here with Dad. *Awful* night." Evidently William's summer sprees were not limited to only one period that summer for on 16th August she noted: "Row . . . All servants left" and this was followed on 17th by: "Did all work in house – no servants."

During that same year, and much to Sophia's disgust, William's capricious behaviour also left Sibyl stranded alone in a hotel in Cherbourg, after a sudden storm drove the small boat in which they were sailing to seek refuge in the harbour. Although he found rooms for them both for the night, he left Sibyl shortly after booking into the hotel and went off on his own. When after several days he had failed to return, she became truly frightened for there was no way of contacting her mother – there being no telephones at that time on the island – and she had no money with which to return home on her own. Hearing a rumour that he had been seen at Carteret some thirty miles away, she decided to borrow the fare from the kindly proprietress and set off in search of him. Failing to find him at Carteret she sought help from a shopkeeper with a Jersey name, who took pity on the small lame girl and lent her the money to board a boat to Jersey, where a family friend was able to see her safely on her way to Sark.

William's explanation is not recorded, nor how long it was before he, too, made his shame-faced return – but that Sophia was greatly upset there can be little doubt. She was a conventional woman at heart who had tried to bring up her daughters as best she could, tolerating much from William, but this latest escapade which had exposed their thirteen-year-old daughter to the unknown dangers of a strange town was something she would not have let pass. Sibyl was already a difficult child to handle, high-spirited and in some ways far too sophisticated for her age, and it is easy to suppose that Sophia was worried over the effect William's continual indiscretions might be having on their impressionable elder daughter. It seems feasible that she took the opportunity to persuade him that a change of scene, with a certain amount of discipline, would not only be desirable but of educational benefit to Sibyl. When he was sober, William always respected his wife's judgment for, despite his occasionally wild behaviour, he was still very fond of her.

Whatever the reason for his change of heart, he finally agreed to Sibyl being sent away to the Sacré Coeur Convent at Marmoutiers, on the banks of the Loire, near Tours – considered at that time to be the Order's strictest and most exclusive in France. Sibyl's memories of it and her schooldays there were always of "scrubbed refectory tables, coffee in bowls, plentiful food . . . too much praying and a rigorous accent on modesty". On the rare occasions that baths were allowed the pupils were swathed in wraps and told to remember that their guardian angel was a man, always watching over them. There were no games, except hopscotch, and entertainment consisted mainly of escorted rambles and organised visits to nearby châteaux. It is hardly surprising that for a girl of her temperament and background, adjustment to this totally foreign and restricted way of life proved difficult and inevitably she became the ringleader of much mischievous behaviour. Punishment for her misdeeds was usually to kneel, painfully on her uneven legs, on the rough-hewn stone floor of one of the abbey cells, used originally by pilgrims on their way to Rome and the Holy Land. When these penances appeared to have no appreciable effect she was summoned before the Reverend Mother who, from all accounts, seemed a trifle nonplussed by the confrontation. According to Sibyl she had pointed out to the Reverend Mother that she and the other girls would not be tempted to slide down the school banisters – her latest escapade – if ignored by the nuns usually lying in wait below, as this would take the excitement and challenge out of the exploit. Her advice was, she maintained, taken up and the nuns were "very impressed" when they found her to be right.

She was just beginning to settle down and appreciate her lessons and the companionship of her fellow pupils when, at the end of her second term, she was removed – for reasons that she herself never made clear. It is known that William feared that she might become a Roman Catholic and this may have played some part but Sophia, according to Sibyl's own account, had already taken precautions against such an eventuality. Knowing her daughter, she had given instructions that from her first term Sibyl should be made to attend every service in the convent chapel and this resulted in her becoming "saturated with prayer and in revolt of religion" even to the extent, after her return home, of refusing confirmation by the Anglican bishop when he later visited the island – something Sophia had not envisaged. Her later entries in her small *Cloud of Witness* book, however, and the fact that many years afterwards she saw to it that all three of her daughters were educated at convent schools seem to indicate that such feelings were short-lived. Far more possible was that her childish pranks had led to the convent asking for her removal, for she once hinted as much to one of her oldest friends.

On her return to Sark, Sibyl found it difficult to readjust to her old life. She missed her schoolfriends and disliked having lessons from a governess whom she now had to share with her younger sister. She had always been jealous of Doris who, like Sophia, was of a gentler and more acquiescent disposition than herself and this prompted her to tease the younger girl unmercifully, particularly when it seemed to her that Doris was receiving more of her parents' attention. Her first reaction – to what she considered to be the indignity, at the age of fourteen, of a "return to the nursery" – was to try to broaden the age gap still further by spending as much time away from the Seigneurie as possible, in the company of those much older than herself.

During the family's frequent visits to relations in Guernsey she had gradually been drawn into the social life of that island and was by this time allowed to attend some of the well-chaperoned parties or private dances at St. Peter Port. As these often included a sprinkling of young officers stationed at the Fort or on shore leave from visiting ships, mixing with this new circle of friends made her feel very grown up and sophisticated.

Not all of Sibyl's Guernsey relations approved of her activities – particularly her great-aunt Mary Ann Lukis with whom the Collings family usually stayed. This stern and formidable maiden lady lived with her brother, Francis, in the old house that had once belonged to their archaeologist father Frederick, and Sibyl's memories of her visits to their home – part of which had been turned into a museum – were always vivid. Sherry and biscuits were taken at noon, dinner at four o'clock and once-a-week baths were from an ornate tin tub "raised from the ground like a soup plate". She usually slept in a large four-poster bed hung with heavy red curtains and, even on the warmest of nights, was forbidden to open her windows for fear the air would make her deaf. Great-uncle Francis had served in the army at the time of the Indian Mutiny and claimed to have been the first man to enter the powder store which had been the scene of the horrific massacre at Cawnpore. There he had picked up various articles for relatives to identify and Sibyl never forgot how she had once opened a drawer at Lukis House and discovered two blood-stained children's dresses and some locks of hair stuffed inside.

Great-aunt Mary Ann held very firm views on how young women should behave and when she first heard that Sibyl intended to go bicycling with her Guernsey friends she was appalled, saying that not only was such a pastime "unladylike" but that it would almost certainly lead to her great-niece becoming "bow-legged". But Sibyl was not in the least deterred by such grim warnings and soon learned how to master the machine, once she had become accustomed to pedalling with her uneven legs. This new means of conveyance broadened the scope of her activities considerably and she particularly enjoyed the bicycling expeditions to one or another of the Guernsey bays for an evening picnic, catching sand eels and cooking them afterwards over a fire on the beach. Pedalling home later in the moonlight and pretending to "lose" the chaperons, travelling sedately behind in carriages, was all part of the fun which Sibyl entered into with gusto.

During the summer following her return from school, she met

several young men who seemed to find her dark good looks and ebullient personality attractive but it was through encounters such as these that for the first time she became really conscious of her lameness. On Sark her condition was accepted because the islanders had never known her otherwise and there were no averted eyes when she limped by, or embarrassed moments at parties when she got up to dance. The realisation now that some strangers seemed to regard her as a cripple came as a great shock to her and for a while made her life miserable.

Sibyl's feelings are, perhaps, understandable in an age when both upbringing and literature did much to propagate the idea that handicapped children, particularly cripples, were sad, pathetic creatures incapable of leading normal lives. Doubtless this was meant to stress the good fortune of Victorian children not similarly afflicted but for young people like Sibyl, whose conditions had only spurred them into making greater efforts, such attitudes only served at times to accentuate any feelings of inadequacy.

During the long, bleak winter months that followed she was desperately unhappy. She once said of this time that night after night she would bury her face in the pillow and sob with despair and indignation that fate had treated her so unfairly. Restless and bored, with no one of her own age in whom to confide and with few boats or visitors to Sark at that time of year, she let herself brood on the events of the summer and imagined herself living alone for the rest of her life, unmarried and unloved because, she was convinced, nobody would want a cripple for a wife. Sophia and William were concerned to see their normally bright young daughter unhappy, but having always been taught by her father never to burden other people with her worries, her parents were the very ones she felt she could not approach.

According to her own account, she finally emerged from this "miserable condition" by deciding that, "as romance and marriage were out of the question", she would devote herself to being indispensable to her father – helping him as much as she could with his island affairs, writing his letters and checking his farm accounts – and once her mind became occupied with these tasks her handicap was forgotten. But was this the complete story?

It is no doubt true that her first glimpse into the adult world brought with it the fear that she might not measure up in some way to other women's physical attractions and that this prompted her to seek compensations in other directions. But was it not, perhaps, at this moment that she also began directing her energies and thoughts towards one day becoming her father's successor and that it was this that provided her with the main compensatory objective she needed?

By the spring her confidence had already begun to return and her morale received a further boost in the shape of a young man from Tasmania, who was staying on Sark with his family and tutor before going to Cambridge. Sibyl was delighted to have such a personable companion during the summer months and together they climbed, swam and explored the caves of the island. He was full of admiration for the fearless and skilful way in which she tackled even the most difficult of climbs or formidable of seas and did not hesitate to tell her so, which pleased her immensely. Their friendship, according to Sibyl, "developed in a very youthful and romantic way" and she always described him afterwards as being her "first real beau".

It was shortly after this young man's departure for England that another visitor, who was to play a far more important part in her life, caught his first glimpse of her as the boat bringing him to the island put into Creux Harbour.

Dudley John Beaumont had been persuaded to make the journey over to Sark by an artist friend, Cecil Hayter, who knew it well. Hayter had extolled the island's beauties so often that this time Dudley, on an impulse, had decided to join him for a painting holiday. Dudley Beaumont was a quiet, shy young man of twenty-two, not given to making sudden decisions, so his action had come as a surprise to his friend, as did his later announcement that he intended to paint the girl in the white dress standing at the end of the harbour wall, the October breeze ruffling her dark curls. Although Cecil knew Dudley to be a talented artist, his first reaction had been to laugh at the very idea of such a proposal, for he knew the girl's identity and had visited the island enough times to realise how the Seigneur and his wife would receive an approach of this nature from a total stranger. Dudley would not, however, be dissuaded. Through Cecil he was introduced to Mrs. Judkins, a kind, much-respected amateur painter, who was one of Sophia's greatest friends and the only person on the island that Cecil thought would be in a position to help. Mrs. Judkins invited Sophia and the two friends to tea at her home, Rose Cottage, and within a month of his arrival on the island Dudley was invited to the Seigneurie and permission was given for Sibyl to sit for him.

The miniature Dudley painted took several weeks to complete and she found the whole procedure immensely boring. Her first impression of the young man was that he was singularly unattractive and altogether too delicate-looking for her taste. He had a stammer which became more pronounced when he was nervous and she was irritated by his efforts to enunciate her name, teasing him when he finally had to settle for "Ibble". But her opinion of him improved considerably when she found that he took all this teasing in good part – and even more so after she had taken him out climbing to "test his nerve" on some of the more precipitous island cliffs. To her astonishment – and chagrin – she discovered that his fearless skill more than matched her own and that his quiet, restrained exterior shielded a much stronger personality than she had at first supposed. When he returned to England a few weeks later she was quite sorry to see him go but he promised to write and send her books during the winter. This he remembered to do and she noted with pleasure, on their arrival, that he had chosen these with great care and an obvious appreciation of her taste.

By her sixteenth birthday in January, 1900, she was beginning to feel that her future was looking considerably more rosy. Dudley was writing regularly and with her newly-restored confidence she was enjoying the occasional winter parties and dances in Guernsey which, providing the weather was suitable for the crossing, her parents allowed her to attend. Her refusal to accept their decision on one such occasion, however, was to result in an experience she was never to forget.

Sophia and William had both forbidden her to go over to Guernsey on that particular day, for they could see that a storm was blowing up but Sibyl – determined, as always, to have her own way – chose to ignore their warnings and take a chance. She had never been a particularly good sailor but she had a new dress to wear for the dance and this time vanity won the day. All was well at first but when the small steamer approached Jethou it met a sudden squall, the engines stopped and the vessel began to roll helplessly. As it drifted closer to the treacherous rocks around the grim island that had once belonged to John Allaire, she thought fearfully of all the tales she had heard of the wrecks in those waters – including that of the *Gosforth* on which her father and grandparents had so nearly lost their lives – and this made her more terrified than ever. She clung helplessly to the deck rail as the small boat was tossed like a cork by the giant waves and wondered if drowning was her punishment for disobeying her parents. She had all but given up hope of ever setting eyes on them again when a small tug, which somehow managed to put out from Guernsey, succeeded in reaching the floundering vessel and towed it safely into port. Still very shaken and feeling sick with fright, she arrived at Lukis House to find her great-aunt ill in bed and her great-uncle out at his club. Their old servants gave her supper and she sat for the rest of the evening curled up alone by the fire, brooding on her nightmare crossing with no one around to whom she could tell her story. After a troubled night in which she relived the crossing, feeling the motion of the waves from within the four-poster bed, she could hardly bear to think of the return journey and when she did manage to summon enough courage to make it a few days later, the memory of that earlier stormy passage made her so ill that she was never again to travel on that narrow strip of sea between the two islands without being overtaken by the same sickening fear. Events in later years by no means helped to diminish these feelings and those close to her knew just how much she always had to steel herself to make that short crossing each time she had to leave or return to Sark. Tides and weather prospects were carefully checked beforehand and if either were unfavourable she usually postponed the journey.

It is nevertheless a measure of Sibyl's strength of character that, despite this, she refused to allow her gruelling experience to deter her from travelling on her own to England only a few months later, to visit friends at St. Neots in Huntingdonshire. This proved to be a summer holiday she always remembered. She revelled in the change of scene and being treated as an adult rather than as a child member of the household and was particularly flattered by the attentions paid to her by the son of the house, who was older and – in her opinion – considerably more sophisticated and attractive than any of the young men she had previously met. Dudley and the rigours of her life on Sark were temporarily forgotten and it was with mixed feelings that she received a letter from her mother shortly before she was due to leave, saying that the young artist had been invited to stay at the Seigneurie and suggesting that Sibyl should meet him at Waterloo so that they might travel back to the island together. A few days later Dudley himself wrote to tell her of Sophia's invitation and – much to Sibyl's surprise – to let her know, before accepting, that it was his intention to ask her to be his wife. Although his proposal did much for Sibyl's ego, she was not quite as sophisticated for her sixteen years as she would have liked others to suppose and she admitted later to feeling "trapped" by a situation she thought she would be unable to handle on her own. She dodged the immediate issue by writing what she considered to be a tactful reply, saying that she would like to see him again so that they might "get to know each other better" – but at the same time took care to miss both Dudley and the train at Waterloo in order to defer the moment when they would be alone together.

She was agreeably surprised however to find on her return that he was altogether more attractive than she had remembered him from the previous year and that their correspondence over the intervening months had helped to strengthen their original friendship. They shared several interests and, having just had her first taste of the pleasurable English social scene, the prospect of an exciting new life as Dudley's wife – away from the occasional hardships and traumas at the Seigneurie with her father – became increasingly more appealing. Dudley was overjoyed when she told him of her feelings and the pair decided to approach Sophia first with their plans.

Although she considered that Sibyl, at sixteen, was too young for marriage, Sophia had taken a liking to Dudley from the beginning. He came from a family of some wealth and position and appeared well able to cope with her high-spirited and strong-willed daughter. She nevertheless urged them both to make no public mention of their intentions until Sibyl's seventeenth birthday the following January, by which time she would have had an opportunity to break the news to William and accustom him to the idea of an engagement, for she felt sure he would not take kindly to such a proposition. As it was, he tolerated rather than liked Dudley – and then only because Sophia thought him to be a sensible and pleasant companion for their elder daughter. William considered the young man to be a "weakling" and certainly Dudley did not look particularly robust beside the hardy Channel Islanders with whom the Collings family normally mixed. To make matters worse, when he was nervous his stammer became more apparent and this was invariably the case when William was present.

Although the young pair agreed to Sophia's suggestion that no public announcement should be made, Dudley gave Sibyl a small diamond ring during a romantic walk by the old monks' ponds in the Seigneurie grounds and the day – 3rd September, 1900 – was recorded in her *Cloud of Witness* book as that on which she became "engaged". Two days later the Collings family left the island for a month's stay with relations in Guernsey, and Sibyl could not resist showing off her new ring – worn on a chain around her neck – to all her friends, pledging them to secrecy over her "engagement". Dudley meanwhile went home to England but was back in Sark by the time the Collings returned from their Guernsey visit.

On 21st October Sophia decided to broach the subject of the proposed marriage to William, who immediately summoned Sibyl to his study and told her that he had no intention of considering such an "idiotic" proposal until she was at least eighteen and refused to listen to any of her protestations. Thanks, however, to Sophia's persuasion he did agree to see Dudley now and then and even allowed his family to accept the young man's occasional invitations to dinner at Sark's Bel Air Hotel – for the persistent young suitor had decided to stay on the island for the winter. Although William was forced to admit that Dudley was not easily dissuaded and had more strength of character than he had first supposed, he remained adamant that Sibyl was far too young to consider marriage and repeatedly told her so in the months that followed.

Sibyl later confessed that such opposition only served to strengthen her resolve to marry Dudley and the underlining of various quotations and her marginal notes in *Cloud of Witness* during this period give an insight into her feelings towards her young lover and how much his unswerving devotion meant to her. She told one of her Guernsey friends that if her father would not consent to the marriage she and Dudley would "probably run away together" and no doubt she would have persuaded her fiancé to do this if other events had not precipitated her plans. At about this time her sister Doris wrote an essay for her governess about Sibyl which gives a very clear picture of her sister and seems to establish that, despite William's opposition, the rest of the family considered her to be "engaged", albeit unofficially.

> Sibyl Collings was born on 13 of January 1884. She was named Sibyl Mary Collings on the 10 of February at the town church of Guernsey. She broke her leg at the age of 3 weeks and her arm at the age of six years. She went to England for the first time in her life at the age of 5 years. She began her lessons at the age of 3 years old. At the age of 16 she began to make her fortune out of beekeeping. At 16 years old she put her hair up. She got engaged at the same age as mentioned above to a very nice gentleman, Mr. Beaumont. She often goes to England and Jersey and Guernsey to stay with her friends, her home where she always lives at with her Mother and Father and sister is at La Seigneurie, Sark, Channel Islands. Her age is *sweet* 17, her height is 5 foot 9. She is sometimes naughty but she is *generally good.* She is not ill very often which I hope you are *glad* to hear, her chief illness is toothake (she told me that she thinks she won't be long before she has false teeth) the toothake is generally in the winter. She is dark, her hair is black, her eyes are dark green her skin brownish and all over her body she

has rather long hair for a human being. She dresses very very prettily. She changes every day nearly for supper. Her hair is done up very low down. She never eats fat because it makes her ill, she also doesn't take a very big breakfast. She smokes cigarettes, but not cigars. The cigarettes she smokes are called the Three Castles. She writes rather a bad hand. But she writes a lot, lot of letters. Her room is adorned with photos. I will tell you the names of some of the people she has – Mr. Beaumont, her Father, her Mother, her sister and a lot more people, heaps of them. She sometimes but very seldom, crys. She is always laughing and jokeing. She can bring smoke down her nose. She flirts with Mr. Beaumont very much.

Perhaps it was her very obvious flirtations with Dudley that antagonised William still further and brought father and daughter into a state of constant conflict. According to her notes in *Cloud of Witness* she slipped out of the Seigneurie to meet her young lover on many occasions during the early months of 1901 – and generally at an hour that her parents would certainly have considered unsuitable for one of such tender years, creeping up the back stairs on her return. Not surprisingly the arguments with her father became more heated as time passed and after one particularly acrimonious session with William in his study, during which he forecast – according to Sibyl's account – all the "awful things" that would happen to her if she continued to be "infatuated" with Dudley, throwing a book at her as she was about to leave, she rounded on him in such a way that he was temporarily stunned into silence. She told him what she thought of his outrageous behaviour towards her mother and the rest of the household, cataloguing many of his past misdeeds in such a violent torrent of words that she surprised even herself. After he had recovered from the shock of her outburst and the sight of her standing shaking with rage before him, his manner changed and although he called her "a damned virago" he added, affectionately, "but all the same, you're a chip off the old block".

By early June he had commenced yet another of his sprees and on the 15th Sibyl noted in her book: "Row. Rose Cottage 3 a.m." – such a brief entry to record one of the most important, if traumatic, events of her life. William had been drinking alone in his study after yet another verbal battle with his daughter during which, emboldened by her previous encounter, she had told him that she did not intend to put up with his bullying and gibes against Dudley much longer and that if he did not stop, she herself would announce the engagement. The more he drank, the more enraged he became at what he considered to be the impudence of her remarks until – according to her account – just as she was dropping off to sleep, he burst into her bedroom. Pulling her from her bed and dragging her down the stairs he pushed her, clad only in her nightgown, out onto the gravel drive threatening to shoot her or throw her over a cliff.*

Sibyl always maintained that this was the one and only time in her life that she had felt truly afraid of what her father might do to her, for his eyes had been so wild and his manner so unpredictable. She ran in her bare feet, not sure which way to go to escape, and finally huddled down to rest under a hedge at the edge of a field, shivering with cold and fright, her nightgown torn by brambles and her feet bleeding. In the early hours of the morning when all seemed quiet, she ran to the house of her mother's friend Mrs. Judkins, who had also befriended Dudley, and she sympathetically took her in, put her to bed and sent word to Sophia that her daughter was safe. While William, with a gun over his shoulder, was searching the island on his mare, Sophia managed to bring a case of clothes for Sibyl and suggested that she should stay for a second day with Mrs. Judkins and then board the boat bound for Guernsey and get away to England and her cousins in Somerset who would look after her. The captain of the boat, well accustomed to William's ways, would see that she came to no harm.

Everything went as planned. William even came aboard the small steamer looking for Sibyl but the captain managed to head him off with a drink in the bar while she hid in his cabin and prayed that her father would be persuaded not to search the boat before it sailed. She eventually arrived safely in England and stayed with her Grandfather Moffatt in London before travelling to the relatives in Somerset. Dudley, meanwhile, remained quietly in Sark, for Sophia had persuaded him that to travel back to England with Sibyl would seem too much like an elopement and would almost certainly cause further trouble for them both. She did, however, agree to her daughter's marriage two months later and gave her written consent for the special licence, Sibyl being only seventeen years of age.

The wedding took place in London – at St. James's Church, Piccadilly – on 20th August, 1901, the Reverend Eaton McCormick officiating. Her Grandfather Moffatt gave her away and she wore,

* Even for William, such violent unprovoked behaviour towards his daughter, seems unlikely and it is easy to suppose that another version of the story – that he had actually caught her with Dudley at the Seigneurie – might well be nearer the truth.

according to the newspaper reports of the time, "a going-away dress of white-faced cloth, trimmed with Russian lace" and "a large white hat trimmed with ostrich feathers". She carried "an exquisite bouquet of lilies of the valley, white carnations and orange blossoms". Two of Dudley's sisters, Nora and Rachel, were bridesmaids and Ernest Platt, a Coldstream Guards officer, was Dudley's best man. There were some fifty guests and, again, according to the reports "the wedding presents were numerous and costly". Sibyl would often tell in later years how she had the uncomfortable feeling throughout the ceremony that her father would burst into the church with a gun and prevent the marriage taking place. She had sent him a telegram beforehand, hoping, perhaps, for some reconciliation so that at least her mother might attend but, although both her parents were in England at the time, Sophia decided that it would be wiser not to go to the wedding on her own for fear of exacerbating the situation.

After a brief honeymoon at Oxford and in the Wye Valley, the couple returned to London and stayed for a time with friends and relations while they searched for a suitable home. During this period Sibyl had another occasion to wear her wedding dress – and at the same church. Shortly after their marriage, Dudley discovered that she had never been confirmed and was so shocked by the revelation that Sibyl, more to please him than for any deep religious feelings of her own, agreed, and the service was conducted by Bishop Barry before the same altar at St. James's, where seven months previously she had stood as a bride. By that time she was already four months pregnant with her first child.

Chapter 3

At first Sibyl found difficulty in adjusting to her new life – so very different from the one she had known on Sark. She missed her mother and felt overwhelmed by Dudley's numerous relations.

His father, William Spencer Beaumont, was a retired officer of the 14th Hussars who had inherited a certain amount of wealth and property from his grandfather – John Thomas "Barber" Beaumont. During his early years, Barber Beaumont was best known for his historical and miniature paintings which had secured him recognition from both the Royal Academy and Society of Arts but in 1807 he founded, in buildings designed by himself, the County Fire and Provident Life Insurance offices in London's Regent Street which proved a profitable undertaking. A man of many interests, Barber Beaumont also wrote pamphlets and books, established the Philosophical Institute and left money in his will to provide for the "intellectual improvement and rational recreation and amusement of people living at the East End of London". Dudley had inherited his great-grandfather's artistic talents and, along with other male members of his family, an interest in military affairs and national defence – another of Barber Beaumont's achievements being to raise the first independent rifle corps, the Duke of Cumberland's Sharp Shooters, during the period of Bonaparte's threatened invasion. Few of the Beaumont family, however, seemed to have acquired their illustrious forebear's keen business acumen and, despite the great wealth Barber handed down to them, many lived most of their lives extravagantly beyond their incomes. In this Dudley's father was no exception for with Honoria, his beautiful wife, William Spencer continually overspent his share of the inheritance and, as he had little understanding of financial affairs, his several ventures into the world of commerce generally proved disastrous.

Honoria Beaumont was one of the nine daughters of Joseph Cooper of Limerick, all famed throughout Ireland for their beauty. She had been married at eighteen and widowed a few years later, shortly before the birth of her second child. William Spencer

Beaumont had been one of her husband's fellow officers and her subsequent marriage to him had produced another son, Dudley, and two more daughters. Honoria was a capricious woman, whose frequent changes of mood made life difficult for all those with whom she came in contact. Although she doted on her two sons, she had little time for any of her daughters or, indeed, for any woman and it was therefore not surprising that when an equally strong-minded, intelligent and attractive daughter-in-law appeared on the scene, the situation was by no means to her liking. At first she treated the young bride with kindness but when she realised that seventeen-year-old Sibyl was far from being the pliable young woman she had first supposed, and had no intention of being moulded into the kind of wife Honoria considered suitable for her beloved younger son, relations between the two became strained and Honoria invariably referred to her daughter-in-law as "that Channel Island termagant".

Dudley had no desire for an ostentatious life. After an education at Eton he had lived quietly on his small allowance, travelling occasionally, when the mood took him, in search of fresh subjects for his paintings – his major interest. His allowance was not increased on his marriage to Sibyl and she had no money of her own since William steadfastly refused to give her any form of marriage settlement. When Sibyl became pregnant it was therefore with some relief that the couple heard through friends of a clergyman in Suffolk who was prepared to let them have his house for a limited period at a modest rent. They moved into the rambling, four-hundred-year-old Rectory in the small hamlet of Lawshall, neary Bury St. Edmunds, on a spring day in 1902 and some three months later, on 6th August, Bridget Amice was born – the daughter whom Sibyl once described as being her "delight" from the moment she had first held her in her arms. She was interested at that time in astrology and marked the occasion by writing out a horoscope for the child, noting carefully the positions of the stars at the time of birth and by all accounts it proved to be an uncannily accurate portrayal of the woman she was to become. Exactly one year to the very day after Amice's birth, a son was born, Francis William Lionel – or "Buster" as he became known to the family.

With such a short period between the births of these two children, Sibyl found her new life of domesticity more than a little trying. She hated the restrictions imposed upon her, particularly as, before Amice's birth, she had just begun to appreciate the bright new Edwardian social life of London. She had always enjoyed wearing pretty dresses and fine jewellery and this had given her an opportunity to do both. But there was little chance for either at Lawshall. The village was set in the middle of a flat agricultural plain with few houses and, compared to the excitement of the London social scene, life was altogether too quiet for her taste. There seemed little for her to do during those two years but prepare for the births of her children, help the nurse tend them when they arrived and manage her household affairs – all of which she found irksome and boring. Dudley did what he could to alleviate the monotony by taking her on occasional visits to London or to stay with one or another of his numerous relations. She particularly enjoyed visiting Dudley's Aunt Augusta and her husband Sir Ronald Lane – an equerry to HRH the Duke of Connaught – who entertained many interesting people of the day. The Lanes' son, George, had been a page to Queen Victoria – a position in which Dudley, as a boy, had occasionally deputised for him. When Sir Ronald was appointed Military Secretary at the War Office in 1903, he and his two great friends, Lord Roberts and Sir Charles Dilke, became involved in the promotion of National Service. Several years later Sir Charles persuaded Sibyl to speak on behalf of the recently formed National Service League, and to act in some of the recruiting playlets touring the country. Although she had never before spoken at public meetings, nor acted on a stage, she enjoyed both experiences immensely.

Dudley was obviously very much in love with his lively, often impetuous young wife and in his quiet manner guided her around many social pitfalls in their early married years, not hesitating to rebuke her gently but firmly when he thought the occasion merited it. Though she would not have accepted this from other quarters, surprisingly she seemed to respect him the more for it – sensing, perhaps, that his criticism was born only from his love and concern. She, in turn, was, from all accounts, equally understanding and patient over his speech impediment, which was often of great embarrassment not only to himself but to those around him. This was particularly so at dinner parties and other social gatherings when he would hesitate or stumble over a word to such a degree that those assembled would often wait upon him in painful silence. It was then that Sibyl would quickly come to his aid, tactfully drawing the conversation away from him to herself with her bright chatter and compelling personality and it was very evident that their relationship at this time was of a loving and caring nature. Certainly Dudley was as pleased as Sibyl when Amice's birth brought about a reconciliation with William, for despite her father's behaviour he knew how upset Sibyl had been over the rift between them.

Sophia had corresponded regularly with her daughter since she had left home but William had refused to communicate in any way. After Amice was born, however, he did relent enough to send a telegram bearing the words, "Sorry it is a vixen" – a comment which Sibyl greeted with wry amusement, so typical was it of her father. But contact had been renewed and William seemed genuinely pleased to see his first grandchild when Sibyl and Dudley took her over to Sark the following Christmas, and even agreed to accompany Sophia and Doris on a visit to Lawshall after Buster's birth. By that time William was so delighted that his daughter had produced the boy for which he had always craved, he appeared to be quite prepared to forget all that had gone before.

When the time came for them to leave the house in Lawshall, the small family moved to a large Queen Anne house at English Bicknor, on the edge of the Forest of Dean, near the Welsh border – an area of scenic beauty which Dudley had known since boyhood and in which he and Sibyl had spent part of their honeymoon. Before the move they had time to enjoy something of the London season and on 20th May, 1904, Sibyl was presented at Court – an occasion she was never to forget. She later wrote her impressions of the "glittering splendours" of that Edward VII Evening Court:

> . . . the hundreds of young girls and older women wearing lovely gowns and family jewels, the trains of regulation length, the long, white gloves, each head surmounted by a cluster of white feather plumes. The scarlet uniforms glittering with gold thread worn by officers attached to the Household and the uniforms and decorations worn by the Diplomatic Corps all added to the grandeur. After the presentations the Royal Party walked through a lane formed by debutantes and their mothers. As they curtseyed, the dipping feathers were like a wave of white surf at the edge of a shore.

This was one of the many occasions during her lifetime when Sibyl must have been very much aware of her lameness but she held herself erect and carried off the whole affair with her usual equanimity – walking, as she had now taught herself to do, with only the toes of her shortened leg on the ground to camouflage the discrepancy. She and Dudley were summoned to Court several times during the next few years and in 1909 she presented her sister, Doris, to Edward VII and Queen Alexandra.

By Christmas the Beaumonts were well settled into Bicknor

House, their new home, and were very quickly drawn into the social life of the area which was centred on Ross-on-Wye, some six miles from Bicknor. The couple sometimes made the journey by car and very occasionally Sibyl herself was allowed to drive. She had been driving since her marriage when the couple had been given a Benz car – "belt-driven and like a dog cart with a tiller and two gear levers", as she once described it. The belt had a habit of slipping and Sibyl invariably seemed to finish her solo journeys by being towed back by a horse. The sight of a car on the roads at all in those days was rare enough, but to see a woman at the wheel was even more so and Sibyl, as was her nature, revelled in the interest she aroused. After the Benz the Beaumonts drove a 6 h.p. De Dion and in 1908 when Dudley bought a "Gladiator" it was necessary for her to have a driving licence, which also gave her the distinction of being, in those days, one of the only two women in the county of Herefordshire to possess such a document.

Dudley soon became involved in a detachment of the Territorial Army at nearby Coleford and set about organising various activities to raise money for a drill hall. Sibyl enthusiastically gave her help and, despite giving birth to another son, Cyril John Astley, in October, 1905, took one of the leading parts in an amateur production of a three-act comedy *A Lesson in Love* the following January. The play, part of another fund-raising entertainment for the hall, ran for two nights and the local newspapers gave a glowing account of both Dudley's production and Sibyl's acting prowess as "Miss Winterberry". One report even went so far as to comment that ". . . this lady could not have been making her first appearance on the stage judging by the abilities she displayed in this piece" – which pleased her considerably.

This was the first of many such amateur productions, usually organised by Dudley, in which she took part. There was no denying her skill as an actress, for her personality on stage drew the audience to her and few noticed that she was in any way handicapped. Many of her acquaintances who remember her during those years, recall how she was usually at the forefront of most groups, interested in everyone and everything, her vibrant personality attracting people towards her from the start – though some dowager ladies thought her too flighty and forward for their tastes, one even cautioning her sixteen-year-old daughter to "keep away from that *fast* Mrs. Beaumont". Certainly Sibyl often flirted outrageously – carried away by the excitement of the theatrical atmosphere – but she was always under the watchful eye of Dudley and there is no evidence to suggest that her admirers' attentions were welcomed in any way other than as further boosts to her ego. Her critics' assertion that she was inclined to push herself too much to the fore on occasions appears to be justified, for her friends also remember her constant craving for attention and acclamation and her annoyance when this was directed elsewhere – especially towards other women. Generally speaking she seemed to get on better with the men than the women – a trait which was apparent throughout her life for at no time did she enjoy "domestic" talk of babies or household affairs.

In the main, Sibyl was happy at Bicknor and only one event clouded those years. Early in 1905 Sophia became ill and soon afterwards underwent an operation for breast cancer in Guernsey. When she showed no signs of improvement Sibyl urged her to visit a London specialist for further advice and on the evening of Monday, 1st May, 1906, looking the sick woman she undoubtedly was, her arm in a sling and with a worried William beside her, she left Sark for Guernsey on the small steamer, *Courier*. Although windy it had been a fine, clear spring day and the crossing should have been uneventful but just off the island of Jethou the steamer struck one of the Annons rocks and before the thirty-nine passengers and crew were fully aware of what was happening, the vessel began to sink rapidly in ten fathoms of water. The crew quickly set about lowering two lifeboats on the upper deck but before they could do so, or lifebelts could be distributed, the ship took her final plunge and those aboard were thrown into the sea. Fortunately the "jolly boat" on the main deck had been successfully launched and Sophia and two other women had been helped into it, followed by William and several others, only seconds before the steamer sank. The captain and another passenger were also picked up from the water and the small boat was then rowed to a nearby rock where its pitiful load was deposited. The tug *Alert* arrived from Guernsey just in time to rescue more survivors from the sea and to take Sophia and the others – wet, cold and shivering with fright – from the rock which by that time was nearly submerged. Ten lost their lives in the disaster, which was widely reported, and questions were asked in Parliament. At the subsequent enquiry the captain was found guilty of negligence.

When Sophia and William finally reached England, Sibyl was greatly shocked by her mother's appearance and she accompanied her to the specialist who only confirmed what Sophia already knew – that she was a dying woman. A photograph of Buster and Amice with their grandparents in the garden at Bicknor in May, 1906, was the last Sibyl was to take of her mother, for two months later Sophia died in Sark, having returned home with Sibyl some weeks beforehand.

Her death upset Sibyl greatly and she always kept a photograph of her mother's grave tucked inside her copy of *Cloud of Witness* – along with a printed tract of comfort and reassurance that Sophia had given her just after the visit to the specialist. It was the first time she had experienced the death of someone close to her and it had obviously come as a shock, for her mother meant a great deal to her. For many years afterwards she kept Sophia's photograph in a prominent position on her desk though she once confessed to her youngest daughter, with unaccustomed candour, that she never really liked it because it was taken shortly before Sophia's death and "she looks so sad".

During the final months of her life, William had tenderly nursed his wife as best he could – by no means an easy task, for her pain made her a trying patient. For someone who could on occasions show such violence he was surprisingly gentle, and it was during those last weeks together that Sibyl realised for the first time just how much Sophia had meant to him. He was greatly stricken by her death and, when Sibyl returned to England, it was to his youngest daughter – fourteen-year-old Doris – that he turned for comfort and care, for she had many of the qualities he had loved and admired in his wife. Although she, too, was grieving for the one person who had provided her only stability in an otherwise stormy home life, she did not fail him. She at once took command of the situation, putting up her long, black hair as a gesture of her adult status and taking on all the household arrangements, acting as her father's hostess for his official guests and even collecting his long-neglected tithes, including the "poulage" (the house tax, payable in fowls) and starting up her own chicken farm at the Seigneurie with the proceeds. For the next six years she continued to care, single-handed, for him – coping with his taunts, drunken rages and other wilder moments with the same courage and sense of humour Sophia had always shown.

Sibyl rarely visited the island during those years for she was too occupied with her own affairs, but she did occasionally invite her sister over to England for a much-needed change – though she spent little time with Doris when she came. To her, Doris was always very much the younger sister and she, good-natured as she was, would usually allow Sibyl to call the tune – often to her own detriment. An example of this was the removal "for safe keeping" by Sibyl, after her mother's death, of many of Sophia's personal effects, including various items of jewellery which by rights should – according to island laws – have remained with

John Allaire, Sibyl's privateering great-great-grandfather, above left; and right, Marie Collings, née Allaire, her great-grand-mother. Below left, the Rev. William Thomas Collings and, right, the young Sibyl.

The Collings family: Sibyl with her parents and baby sister, Doris.

Sibyl's father, centre, dressed for a "spree" with some of his staff at the Seigneurie. John Hamon is holding the Militia drum. The bronze cannon was that presented by Queen Elizabeth I.

William until his death and then have been equally divided between the sisters. When William protested, Sibyl made the excuse that Doris would lose them – but her sister was never to see them again. This acquisitiveness was, sadly, yet another facet of Sibyl's character which was often to reappear in later life.

Early in 1907 the Beaumonts again moved house – to the nearby market town of Ross-on-Wye, which had for some time been the centre of so much of their social life and was more to Sibyl's liking than Bicknor, which she now considered too remote from most of their activities. She was later to look back with affection on the busy, eventful years spent with her young family at Edde Cross House – the old summer palace of the Bishops of Hereford, which stood high in the centre of the town, its garden stretching down to the banks of the Wye.

Two more children were born to her during this period, though the elder – Basil Ian – was barely nine months old when he died of whooping cough. Sibyl rarely, if ever, spoke of him in later years, yet her *Cloud of Witness* book again provides evidence of her true feelings about his death. The date – 19th August, 1909 – is alongside a heavily scored passage from Browning beginning: "God lent him and takes him . . ." and tucked inside the book, on the same page, she kept a folded piece of paper – inscribed "Baby Ian, October, 1919". This contains a small, pressed flower, evidently taken from his grave in Ross churchyard, ten years after his death – a token that he was not forgotten and an action that would have surprised the many who considered Sibyl to be unsentimental.

A year after Ian's death, on 27th August, 1910, Douce Alianore Daphne was born – whose looks, even as an infant, hinted at the beautiful woman she was later to become. When Douce was two, Sibyl engaged a new Nanny to look after her growing family – a local girl, Gertrude Bishop, destined to become a very important member of the Beaumont household and to see the family through many years of changing fortunes.

Now that they were living in the town itself, Sibyl and Dudley found themselves drawn even more into the social activities of Ross-on-Wye. They continued with their amateur theatricals and helped to organise several productions in aid of such varied causes as the Ross Cottage Hospital, the Rowing and Cricket clubs, National Service League and the Hereford Boy Scouts – Sibyl recruiting many a reluctant amateur actor or actress with her persuasive charms. Dudley was usually more content handling the business side and at this, according to press reports of the time, he proved highly successful for due to his efforts "considerable sums" were raised for the charities concerned.

Tennis was another interest they shared and Sibyl won a small silver trinket case for her prowess in a tournament at Ross in the summer of 1912 – the year Dudley formed the South Herefordshire Tennis and Croquet Club. He was interested in most of the local sporting activities and often played in charity cricket matches. He also kept up his interest in the Territorials and Sibyl enjoyed arranging dances and tennis parties for the battalion when they were at training camp in the vicinity. Her own form of "National Service" was to train as a Red Cross nurse and towards this end she helped for a few weeks on the wards of a London hospital. According to the medical officer, who was also the British Red Cross Commandant of the "Hereford 8 (Ross) Women's Voluntary Detachment", she was a "very proficient" nurse, holding certificates in both First Aid and Home Nursing from the St. John Ambulance Association – useful acquisitions which Sibyl was within a short time to put to good use.

She was always seeking to broaden her activities and revelled in each new experience as it came along. Meeting fresh people was a particular delight to her – whether in Ross, London or on one of their several trips to Europe during those years. Dudley took her skiing for the first time at Mürren in Switzerland in 1912 and she enjoyed the combination of sun, snow and the bright social scene of the winter-sports resort. She had learned how to roller-skate many years before in Guernsey and although this had proved difficult enough she refused to let her uneven legs prevent her from at least attempting to ski, if only on the nursery slopes. Two years later she repeated the experience when she again joined a winter-sports party in Wengen and this proved to be the forerunner of many other similar holidays.

Although Sark seemed far removed from her life in England, most of her acquaintances were well aware of her connection with the small Channel Island and knew that she would one day inherit the Seignory from her father. She had very quickly discovered that her unique position created interest wherever she went and she frequently entertained her dinner guests with much-embroidered stories of the island and of her father, enjoying her friends' joking references to her as the future "Queen of Sark". It was therefore with considerable embarrassment and consternation that in the summer of 1912 she learned that William's antics had landed him in prison in Guernsey, awaiting trial. The circumstances of his arrest received great attention from the national press and such headlines as "Seigneur of Sark in handcuffs" and

"Island's overlord alleged to have shot at guest", were spread over most of the daily journals. Even such an august publication as *The Times* carried the story and the *Daily Mirror* gave a detailed account of how he had threatened the life of George Lovibond, a journalist, and of how Lovibond and Doris had both sought the protection of the Guernsey police. It appears that the journalist had been staying at the Seigneurie during one of William's sprees, and had gone to Doris's aid after a particularly brutal attack upon her by her father. There was a scuffle and William had gone off in search of his gun. Lovibond and Doris had then made a dramatic escape from the Seigneurie and over to Guernsey but there William had caught up with them, and, according to the press reports, had again threatened to shoot Lovibond. He was later arrested as he boarded the Sark boat and was held for a fortnight pending medical reports. It was at this stage that Sibyl and Dudley were summoned to Guernsey and their own and William's futures were discussed.

Once he had recovered from the initial shock of Sophia's death, William had soon taken up his old ways. His drinking bouts recommenced and Sark gossiped about his inamoratas in Jersey and other places outside the island. Only a few years before this Guernsey court case, he had been found wandering in a drunken condition around St. Helier dressed only in a woman's red-flannel petticoat, and other stories of his eccentric behaviour abounded around the Channel Islands, but the affair with Lovibond and Doris had been the first of his misdeeds to receive attention from the world outside.

At his trial the two doctors who had examined William while he was in custody pronounced him perfectly sane, though subject to occasional "lapses" and he was bound over in his personal recognisances to keep the peace for a period of twelve months, "the alternative to finding the bail being further imprisonment". On the same day in the ordinary court at St. Peter Port, Dudley – on behalf of Sibyl and Doris – actioned William "to see his relatives appoint him a guardian". The action alleged that the defendant was unable to control his affairs "owing to his intemperance, prodigality, disordered conduct and feeble-mindedness". Strong words to use about his father-in-law but perhaps Dudley thought such firm action would jolt William into more reasonable behaviour. The matter was placed on the pleading list but was not pursued for, after further talks with William, Dudley and Sibyl came to a decision.

Doris, fond though she was of her father when he was his sober, benevolent self, had by now had enough. She had stayed with him until she was of age but now thought it time she had an opportunity to enjoy a more peaceful life of her own. When she had managed to escape from her father – down knotted linen sheets, from her bedroom – she had realised that the gun William had been flourishing was loaded. He had many times threatened to shoot her during his sprees but this had been the first time that he had used real bullets with actual intent – firing two into her bedroom ceiling* and more into the grounds on catching a glimpse of the escaping pair. Not unnaturally she now felt she could no longer cope with him on her own and after the trial accepted an invitation to live with relations in England. Some months later she married in Gibraltar Captain Henry Verschoyle, whom she had first met during one of her holidays with Sibyl at Ross-on-Wye.

There is no record of what transpired during the family's discussions but it was evidently agreed that Dudley and Sibyl should give up their house and pleasant life in Ross and settle on Sark – presumably in order to prevent William from getting into further trouble. Sibyl was also concerned over an attachment he had formed with – in her eyes – a most "unsuitable" woman in Jersey. With Doris away she feared that loneliness might well precipitate him into remarrying and any male child born of such a union would inherit Sark instead of herself on her father's death – a situation she was determined should not arise. With his grandchildren on the island she felt confident that she could avert such a threat. Commenting on their decision years later she wrote:

> He [William] had never provided me with a settlement, nor given me a penny; but I was his heir and I loved the island passionately, more than anything or anyone in the world. When the time came I intended to do as much for Sark as my grandfather had done. This was my future and I had no intention of allowing Father to take it away from me.

Dudley accepted the move with some reluctance for he felt well settled in the Wye Valley, but, as always, he put his wife's happiness first and early in 1913 took up the lease on La Valette de bas, a charming stone farmhouse close to Maseline Bay on the east side of the island. The house was one of the original forty "tenements" and the land included a small, wooded valley which led down to a sheltered cove, ideal for bathing, as the

* These bullets remained in the ceiling for some forty years as Sibyl thought they made an amusing topic of conversation.

Beaumonts were soon to discover. There was also enough arable land to grow vegetables and to keep one or two cows in pasture.

As Dudley knew little about dairying, Sibyl took it upon herself to further the knowledge she had acquired as a child by taking a short course in butter and cheese-making at the British Dairy Institute at Reading. In those days the Institute was part of the University and Sibyl enjoyed meeting the other students, many of whom came from overseas. She was then twenty-nine years old, one of the few women attending the course and a more mature student than the average, all of which, together with her Sark background, made her the object of some interest – a situation which, as usual, she found enjoyable. She returned to Sark in the spring of 1914 but had little time to put her brief training into practice for she had a busy summer acting as hostess to many friends visiting her for the first time in her new home and, by the end of that pleasantly hot season, England was at war and both Dudley and she were occupied elsewhere.

Chapter 4

SOON AFTER WAR was declared, Dudley joined his Territorial detachment, the 2nd Volunteer Battalion, Gloucester Regiment, and Sibyl – anxious as always to be actively involved – donned her Red Cross nurse's uniform and joined her sister-in-law, Mrs. Harold St. Maur, who had converted her home at Stover Park in Devon into a small surgical unit.

Betty St. Maur, an attractive woman of strong character, several years older than Sibyl, had first interested the younger woman in becoming a member of the Voluntary Aid Detachment of the Red Cross and together they had taken courses in home nursing and first aid. Her staff at the small, twenty-bed, "hospital" included only one fully-qualified nurse, the rest being friends and relations who with Sibyl and herself, nursed as VADs. The family butler acted as orderly and an elderly Red Cross worker performed the duties of quartermaster, while the local doctors from Newton Abbot and Bovey Tracey attended to the general medical care and occasional minor operations.

After the Battle of Mons the casualties were so heavy that the main hospital at Plymouth sent some of the men straight on to Stover Park and after the long train and sea journey from France, these patients frequently had wounds which had not been dressed for days and in many cases were not only suppurating but maggot-infested. Sibyl took it all in her stride, helping at some of the operations and busying herself about the wards, sometimes reorganising them according to her own ideas – much to the annoyance of Betty St. Maur who, having given herself the position of matron, greatly objected to such interference with the running of her hospital. There were several clashes of personality between the two and it was, perhaps, fortunate for them both that Sibyl's service as a VAD should be brought to an end early the following year when she discovered that she was again pregnant. The hospital continued functioning for another year but was eventually obliged to close owing to lack of sufficient financial support.

With the exception of Douce, the children were by this time

all at school but they did have a chance to be together again as a family during the summer of 1915, for Dudley was on embarkation leave, en route for the Cameroons, and they spent the time at a rented cottage near Mortimer in Berkshire. He sailed for Duala on 25th August and Sibyl stayed on at the cottage for a further two months to give birth to her third son – Richard Vyvyan Dudley – on 13th September.

Although they wrote tender, affectionate letters to each other regularly, Sibyl missed her husband greatly and felt she must do something to occupy her days other than caring for her children – which she felt Nanny Bishop did more than adequately. For a short while she helped a younger friend, whom she had first met at Ross, run a small cosmetics shop off Bond Street for a relative, and they both looked back on this period afterwards as being "hilarious". The shop soon became the meeting place for most of their acquaintances in London and some of the customers they served were as eccentric as the mysterious people who inhabited the apartment above the shop, who kept strange hours and drank quantities of champagne, judging by the number of empty bottles regularly awaiting collection by the dust cart. The solicitor who was handling the family's affairs in Dudley's absence asked Sibyl one day – with some amusement – if she had any idea of what went on over the shop for he thought Dudley would not approve of her being seen going in and out of the same building. She was by no means a naïve young woman but always maintained that until that moment the implication had not registered. When it did, she lost no time in telling her friend and it was with much relief that they were able to get out of the shop before the premises upstairs were raided by the police for being used for "immoral and gambling purposes".

The climate of West Africa did not suit Dudley whose constitution had never been strong and, although he stuck it until the campaign there was almost at an end, several bouts of malaria and other health problems sent him home on sick leave in February, 1916. In late June, however, conscientious as always and anxious to get back into action, he joined the 7th Service Battalion of the Gloucester Regiment and was posted to France – but less than a year later he was again invalided home and finally obliged to relinquish his commission on 19th July, 1917, on health grounds. While he convalesced at Leamington, Sibyl took the children to La Valette de bas, and later in the year Dudley was able to join them in Sark for a family Christmas.

During his absence in France, Sibyl had taken a job at the War Office in the Postal Censorship Department and from there had gone on to the Foreign Office where she worked in the library. She greatly enjoyed both situations and while at the Foreign Office had an opportunity to put her Red Cross training into practice once again, for she helped to man one of the ambulance stations during the occasional air raids. A letter, written soon after her return to Sark, from an Edward Parkes and dated 7th August, 1917, gives some indication of her duties and the calibre of her work at that time:

> ... We were so glad to hear that you had crossed safely and that you were happily installed in your island home. I daresay that you will be reluctant to leave it again, for some time at all events. Certainly after the hard work done at the FO you deserve a long holiday. We are very appreciative of your courage and success in grappling with the many duties thrust upon you here. I am afraid that we took advantage of your quickness, grip and industry to put a greater burden on your shoulders than perhaps was quite fair. Personally it was a great comfort and convenience to me to have someone at hand capable of undertaking any task however intricate, and of carrying it through without semblance of fuss or seeming exertion. We shall always be ready to welcome you back to the Library if you care at any time to join us again. I have already taken soundings and do not think there will be any difficulty in getting you specially appointed as a supernumerary, probably with "higher grade" rank ...

However the thought of a return to such work was far from Sibyl's mind at that time for she had become reconciled to settling down once more to a quiet farming life on Sark and to seeing that Dudley was nursed back to health.

For the older children it seems this period was always regarded, in retrospect, as being one of the happiest of their young lives for this was one of the few times that they had all been together as a family during the school holidays, with both their mother and father. Amice loved to help Dudley in the garden, planting trees and shrubs and sowing flower and vegetable seeds. Her mother meanwhile showed her how to make butter and cheese. They all enjoyed bathing together in the little cove below the house and taking boat trips to nearby islets for picnics. Sometimes they would join up with other families for these excursions and in his writings an English poet, Trevor Blakemore, at that time living on the island, recalled these days with pleasure. He saw Sibyl then as "a brilliant and versatile woman ... a magnificent climber and swimmer, fearless, enterprising and as agile as a gazelle". Together they attempted to climb or swim their way around the entire coastline, taking it section by section when the tides were right and by the summer of 1918 had almost achieved their goal. Two schoolboys of that time remember Sibyl as a "kind and fun-loving person" who was also a "very intrepid cliff climber", on one occasion taking them down what she considered to be a short cut to Derrible Bay. This turned out to be a hair-raising experience, the path steeply zig-zagging so that the boys were forced to slide down much of it on their tails but Sibyl appeared to be quite unruffled and oblivious to her lameness which spurred the others into carrying on, despite their fears.

In the early autumn of 1918 Sibyl and Dudley set out from Sark in a chartered motor-boat bound for Guernsey on the first stage of a journey to England, where Dudley was due to appear at one of his periodic medical boards for his army pension. The day was stormy, and on reaching the Bec du Nez at the northernmost tip of the island, the seas became so rough that the boat was forced to turn back and make another attempt the following day. On seeing the vessel return to harbour, one old Sark fisherman is said to have shaken his head sadly and proclaimed that no good would come of it for it was an old belief, held by some in the island, that bad luck would attend those aboard any vessel that turned back – a comment which many were later to remember.

After a few days together in London, Dudley travelled on to Droitwich Spa where he planned to take the waters at the Worcestershire Brine Baths Hotel while awaiting his medical board at Birmingham. Sibyl, meanwhile, stayed behind in a service flat they sometimes used at 2, Whitehall Court – taking the opportunity to visit friends in London. While there she received a letter from Dudley which she was later to keep with other special mementoes tucked inside her *Cloud of Witness* book. It was dated the day after the Armistice was signed – 12th November, 1918 – and written from the hotel:

My own dearest one,

I do hope you have not got flue [*sic*]. Let me know at once if you have. It's so cold here you can hardly move. I did not write yesterday as I was rather done after my bath and then the Dr. came round and took me out in his car while he saw patients and we did not get back till after post time. Things here were pretty quiet, no excitement at all, but at Brumm I hear they went half mad . . . I have written to the SMO at Bir-

mingham asking him to arrange my board by wire if he gets notice of it by Friday after that I have told him I shall not be here – I shall in any case come up to you then . . . Well, dearest, there is no news here at all. God bless you, dearest, and all my love.
Ever your devoted husband.

The influenza to which Dudley refers was later to be known as "The Plague of the Spanish Lady" – Spanish Flu – which raged throughout the world from October, 1918, to January, 1919, killing more than twenty-one million people, of which almost 230,000 were from the United Kingdom. London, as with so many other capitals of the world, was to suffer heavy casualties. Although on Armistice Day Sibyl had been to a theatre and dined out with some women friends she was not feeling too well and by the time Dudley's letter arrived she had caught a mild dose of the disease herself – aggravated by the fact that she was once again pregnant, a condition which the medical authorities considered to be particularly risky during the epidemic. After he arrived in London Dudley did his best to look after her but within a few days he, too, became extremely ill – his already weak lungs and poor constitution putting him at a disadvantage from the start. His influenza developed into pneumonia and on 24th November he died. He was forty-one years old. Sibyl's own description of his death was as follows:

For me, time and events telescoped and jumbled together as in a nightmare. The entire block of flats was without staff and it was impossible to get a nurse until the last hour. Then there was no possibility of arranging for a funeral on a fixed day: the number of deaths in London was so great that it was necessary to wait for a date. Had it not been for my wonderful Cockney daily I would have broken down completely . . .

Though she rarely spoke of those horrifying days, many years later she revealed to one of her daughters just how traumatic the experience had been, for Dudley had died on a Sunday evening and due to the already overstretched undertakers' services, she had been forced to remain with his body in the one-roomed flat for some days. She had also been brought up with the Sark tradition that a body must never be left alone in a house and she also believed, with many other Channel Islanders, that if someone lies dead over a Sunday there would be news of another death within three weeks.

The funeral service was at the same church in which they had been married some seventeen years before – St. James's, Piccadilly – followed by burial at Brookwood in Surrey. Friends who attended the funeral or saw her in the weeks following, all recall that Sibyl appeared to be so beside herself with grief that they could never visualise her marrying again and, from all accounts, this was one of the few occasions in her life when her real feelings were only too apparent to all. Once again her *Cloud of Witness* book with the date of his death beside heavily underlined passages leaves no doubt as to the depth of her sorrow. Until the war they had never been separated for more than a few weeks at a time and, as Sibyl herself once wrote: "Every detail of our life had been planned together and he was more to me than all my children, fond though I was of them."

At the time of Dudley's death she was thirty-four years of age, the mother of five children, whose ages ranged from three to sixteen, and another child was expected in seven months time. The prospect of having sole responsibility for them all until they became of age must have been worrying enough, but far more so was the financial situation that now confronted her. Owing to mismanagement during the war years, Beaumont property in the East End of London had been allowed to fall into disrepair and this had consequently affected Sibyl's income on Dudley's death. When his affairs were settled she realised that there was little in addition to her widow's pension on which to bring up and educate six children – let alone have much over for herself if the family were to continue to live in anything like their accustomed style. Even her pension from the army did not stretch to include her unborn child, for the Pensions Department made it clear that as the baby would be born more than nine months after Dudley had relinquished his commission, according to their regulations, no provision could be made. Sick with worry and grief she returned to Sark in early December and the family spent a sad Christmas together at La Valette de bas, mourning a much-beloved father. But the courage instilled in her by her own father's stern upbringing won through. Early in the new year in her *Cloud of Witness* book Sibyl heavily underscored the following quotation:

> The man who consecrates his hours
> By vigorous effort, and an honest aim
> At once he draws the sting of life and death.

The significance of the date she wrote beside it – 8th January,

1919 – is nowhere revealed but it seems likely that for reasons that are not explained, this marked the beginning of Sibyl's coming to terms with her new situation. Certainly by the time her third daughter, Jehanne Rosemary Ernestine, was born on 18th June, she had a clear plan of action. A friend who went to visit her soon after the birth remembered seeing her sitting up in bed at La Valette de bas – "wearing the most glamorous black crêpe-de-chine nightdress, then considered to be the height of sophistication" – and talking of a proposed move to Guernsey and her children's future education.

According to Sibyl, neither her father nor her father-in-law was prepared to give her any help at this time. Spencer Beaumont had brushed aside her plea for a contribution towards Buster's education by saying, "My good soul, I shall soon be dead and then you can dance on my grave" – a comment which she felt was singularly unhelpful. For some years Spencer and his wife had tolerated rather than liked their forthright, often unconventional, daughter-in-law and saw no reason why she should not endeavour to manage on what Dudley had left her – at least until such time as Spencer should die and she and her children would obtain their share of the Beaumont inheritance. William had been equally unforthcoming. He had told Sibyl that, as he had always brought her up to be independent, she was now quite capable of taking care of herself and her children – which she later thought was probably his way of encouraging her to get out into the world again and make a new life for herself. But she had first to consider the welfare and education of her children.

Amice was by this time seventeen – an attractive girl with a pleasant personality and capable manner. She readily agreed to her mother's suggestion that she should leave school so that more money could be made available for a private tutor for Buster, who was hoping to enter Cranwell as a cadet, prior to a flying career in the RAF. Astley's school fees were already being taken care of by his godmother – Dudley's aunt, Lady Augusta Lane – and Sibyl thought that the education of the other children would be easier and the living cheaper if she moved with them to Guernsey and gave up the smallholding on Sark. By November this had been accomplished and the family were happily installed at La Pierre Percee, a comfortable old house above the town of St. Peter Port.

With several of her relations and many old friends living in Guernsey it was not long before Sibyl found herself drawn into the social life of the island, which was enhanced – as it had been in her youth – by a number of young service officers from Fort George or visiting ships.

Amice was now of an age to accompany her to some of the functions and Sibyl enjoyed her companionship. With barely eighteen years between them and Sibyl's youthful appearance, they were occasionally taken for sisters and this and the attention she received from many of the visiting officers did much to restore Sibyl to her old self. Amice was also proving a useful and responsible person to leave with Nanny Bishop when she wanted to get away and this period marked the beginning of a new pattern of life for them both which was to continue for some years.

In the early months of 1921 Sibyl heard through friends that the YMCA were asking for volunteers to help man canteens for the British Army of Occupation on the Rhine. The work was unpaid but free accommodation was provided and the whole scheme appeared to offer just the sort of interesting outlet her restless spirit needed to take her away – if only temporarily – from what she felt had by that time become a rather monotonous and restrictive life with her young family in the confines of a small island. Nanny Bishop and Amice were, she considered, quite capable of tending to the younger children and there were many friends and relations upon whom they could call in an emergency. Fortified by the thought that she had made adequate provision for their welfare, she left for Germany and by the late spring was happily installed at the Signals' Canteen in Cologne, serving food, washing dishes – and getting accustomed to being referred to only by her surname. After a while she found the actual canteen work irksome but her enjoyable social life provided ample compensation.

The past year in Guernsey had helped Sibyl to regain much of her old sparkle and in Cologne she was never short of admiring escorts from among the serving officers whose club was also open to the YMCA volunteers and her diary for the first three months shows something of her popularity. Every day has mention of one or another of these young men taking her dining, dancing or motoring into the surrounding countryside. She played innumerable games of bridge, badminton and tennis and enjoyed visits to the opera and the races in what appeared to be some of the happiest and carefree months since Dudley's death.

With the inflation of the mark, the cost of living was cheap and this prompted her – during a short visit to England in June to see Buster after his examination for Cranwell – to make arrangements for Nanny, Amice and the three younger children to join her in Germany. She had found what she considered to be an excellent apartment in Cologne and saw no reason why she should not let the house in Guernsey and use the money she was saving on rent more profitably out on the Rhine. According to her own account, she did in fact manage to let the house at three times the rental she herself had paid and this went a long way towards alleviating her financial situation.

By the time the children joined her later that summer she had become involved with the Rhine Army Dramatic Company, under the direction of Saville (Esme) Percy, and at the beginning of August took the part of Lady Markby in a performance of Oscar Wilde's *An Ideal Husband.* The army newspaper's account of her performance made the comment that "as the garrulous Lady Markby she did well and with greater experience should be very successful in this type of part..." This caused some wry smiles among her fellow helpers who thought her "garrulousness" was not only confined to her acting rôles. She was invariably to be found in animated conversation at the centre of a group of young officers at the club or the theatre, drawing others around her by her vivacious personality, as she had done so often in the past – though nowadays there was no watchful Dudley at her side to curb her exuberance or prevent some of her flirtations from getting out of hand.

Just how serious some of these encounters became is difficult to gauge. Men obviously found her physically attractive and she made no effort to disguise the fact that she found men equally so, but once her family had joined her, Amice was invariably at her side and she had little opportunity, even if she had the inclination, of carrying any love affair into the bedroom of her small Cologne apartment. There is no doubt that she and Amice together attracted a great deal of attention wherever they went, but there is no evidence to suggest that either formed more than mild romantic attachments to any of their numerous escorts. Not unnaturally, though she was of a quieter disposition than her mother, it was usually Amice's youthful good looks that at first attracted the young men but Sibyl would never allow any competition, even from her own daughter, for long and on at least one occasion managed successfully to divert one of Amice's chief admirers to herself – much, in this case, to her daughter's chagrin for she had been very fond of this particular RAF officer.

Sibyl's personal photograph album, with its slightly bawdy captions, show how uninhibited, in some respects, she eventually became during those years in Cologne and it is easy to see how she earned the title among her friends of "The Merry Widow of the Rhine". There are photographs of skiing holidays, picnics and motoring excursions and of her and Amice bathing in a lake in the company of a party of Royal Air Force officers, whose shirts they had obviously borrowed for the swim. In most of these, Sibyl's shapely legs are very much in evidence at a time when hems were only just being raised above the calf in England – and in another she is – daringly for those days – wrapped only in a towel with bare shoulders exposed as well. Included with the photographs is some verse, written by one of her officer companions which, unsophisticated though it is, captures something of that carefree period. He was evidently one of a party on a visit to Luna Amusement Park "on pleasure bent" where:

> ... A certain lady, Syb by name
> Increased still more her noted fame
> (Or rather notoriety
> She not a one for piety).
>
> We all went in the Haunted House
> And started on a mad carouse,
> Pitched up and down the moving stairs
> Where Ma Superior said her prayers
> And Mrs. B. it came to pass
> When on the belt sat on her *back* ...

After visits to other side-shows where "poor, pure Clark" became "quite red, to see a lady get in bed", they found themselves in the Maze:

> ... Wandering around in various ways
> Leaving together in our haste
> Syb and the Pure one – oh, what waste
> Oh, longed for opportunity!
> Alone with charming Mrs. B.

Sibyl took part in several more theatrical productions during her two years on the Rhine – her experience with amateur dramatics at Ross, her good memory and quick brain making her a useful member of the company. She found also that the German she had first learnt as a child soon returned and this proved to be another valuable asset – particularly during a trip she made with Amice in 1922 to see the first Passion Play held at Oberammergau since the war which, but for her command of the language, could have had serious consequences.

Sibyl had often travelled into the Unoccupied Zone before – despite warnings that this could prove unsafe – and until this particular visit to Oberammergau these journeys had been trouble-free. At first all went well. Their passports with their Military Zone stamps were visaed for Bavaria and their rooms in Oberammergau were booked in the house of the man playing the part of Pontius Pilate. After three exciting days, during which they saw the play and met and talked with Anton Lang, who took the part of Christ, they started back for Cologne. On an impulse, Sibyl decided to break the journey at Munich, but a French officer they met on the train advised against staying in the city itself so she and Amice spent a couple of days by the Starnberger See instead. It was when they boarded the train at Munich for the return journey to Cologne that trouble started. The conductor who examined their passports told them that their visas did not take them out of Bavaria, only into it, and that they needed to get fresh ones from Munich. Sibyl chose to ignore this and she and Amice remained on the train until it reached Aschaffenburg where, along with a young English cyclist and two American women, they were taken to the local police station and locked into the cells for the night. When a young policeman came in the morning to ask if they would like some coffee Sibyl, according to her own account of the affair, "decided it was no time to be haughty" and made herself "as pleasant as possible to him". He obviously succumbed to her charms for he escorted her and Amice to a nearby café for breakfast, where she told him that she had "a houseful of children and a husband" waiting for her in Cologne who would be "heartbroken" if she did not get back soon. So convinced was he of her story that he managed to get their visas and passports from the permit office and they were able to resume their journey. Sibyl had left her young children behind in Cologne with Nanny Bishop and, while she had been away, rioting by Communist workers had broken out in the city. On the morning that she and Amice returned a German policeman was killed, trams were overturned and the city was in a ferment. Fortunately the British transport officer and his two Alsatian dogs were at the station and were able to escort the two women safely back to their billet.

Another incident of those days that she often recounted was her first flight in a light, fragile aircraft belonging to Instone Airways. Due to fog it never made its London destination but had to turn back before it reached the Ardennes. On a later occasion she flew with Dr. Weldon, then Dean of Durham, whom she described afterwards as "a really outsize cleric". As there

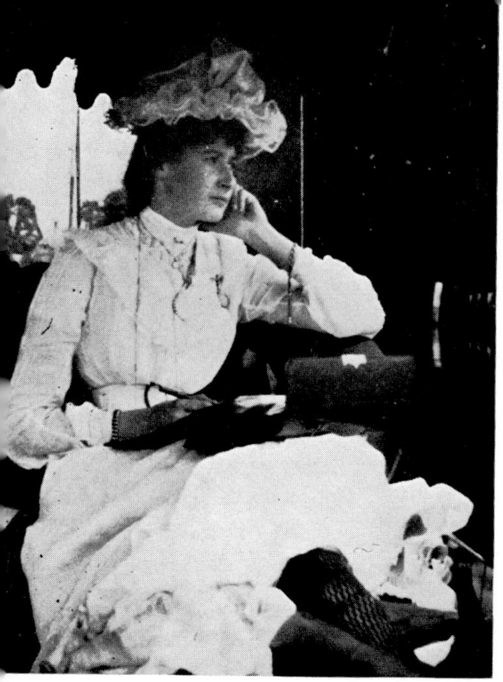

Sibyl on her honeymoon.

udley Beaumont in his Territorial
ays at Coleford. Caricature by
. Allen ("Pip") 1907.

A skiing holiday at
Mürren in 1912.

At rest and work in Cologne in 1921.

Family group, 1923: behind, Buster, Sibyl, Amice, Astley; in front, Richard, Douce and Jehanne.

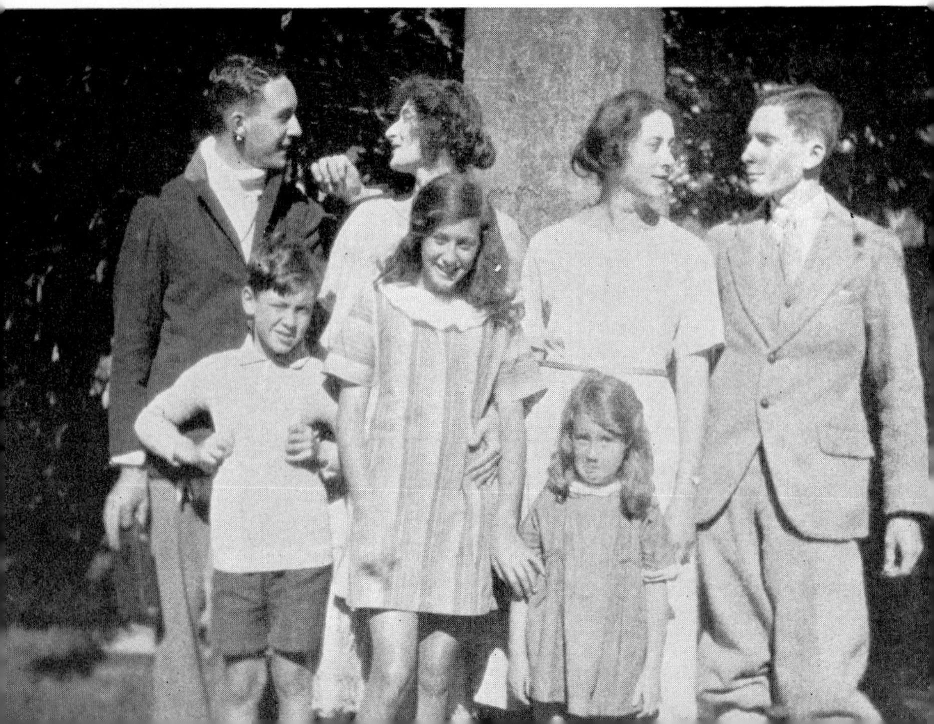

was only one escape hatch in the roof, through which passengers were expected to scramble, lifebelt and all, she had, she used to recall, spent the journey eyeing the small window thinking that should an emergency occur she would make sure that she, rather than the dean, would be the first to get through, lest he get stuck in transit.

By this time the Beaumont family's finances were beginning to improve and Sibyl decided to return later in the year to Guernsey. In July Nanny Bishop took the younger children to stay with her parents in Herefordshire and Sibyl prepared for a late summer cruise with friends to Norway, after which she planned to move into Cambria Villas, Brock Road – the new home she had found for her family, which was closer to the centre of St. Peter Port than La Pierre Percée, the Guernsey house she had previously rented.

Her life on the Rhine had given her more of a taste for travel than ever and, now that the children were older, she saw no reason why she should not travel further afield and continue to enjoy her new-found freedom, with its bright social life and attentive male admirers, without what she considered to be the "encumbrance" of her family.

E

Chapter 5

Although she was fond of her high-spirited, attractive-looking children and they had a great respect for her, Sibyl was not a maternal woman by nature and, possibly due to her own upbringing, always found it difficult to demonstrate any feelings of affection towards them. Like many other women of a similar social position at that time, she had been content to leave most of their care and early training first to a nanny in the nursery and later to the staff of their public boarding schools. Her own childhood with her father had also schooled her to the view that children benefited from tending more for themselves and, providing they were adequately educated, clothed and fed, she saw no reason why her duties toward them need be extended further – nor why she should not leave them occasionally to pursue her own interests. She was, after all, an attractive woman who had married and had several children at a very early age, been widowed while still young, before she had really had an opportunity to explore fully all that she felt the world had to offer. But in the light of what was to follow, perhaps it is understandable that many who knew her in those years claimed that her apparent lack of interest in her children and her attitudes generally – together with certain hereditary traits – had some bearing on their futures, particularly in the case of her sons, with no father to guide them during their most formative years.

By 1922 warning signals were already apparent. Even before the death of his father, Buster's behaviour at Elizabeth College in Guernsey had prompted several stern letters from his headmaster. On 26th May, 1918, he wrote: "... My instinct as a schoolmaster makes me feel a wee bit anxious about him ... the world has pitfalls for an attractive young person who is also a goose." Buster was, apparently, popular with his fellow pupils and good at sports but lazy, disobedient and easily led. A series of schoolboy pranks had culminated in the "borrowing" of a sailing boat from the harbour which, according to the headmaster, "he had mistakenly thought was Sark owned and, as such, that he had ancestral rights over it" – an escapade which had finished with Buster being ignominiously towed in by a passing motor-boat after succumbing to sea-sickness. He constantly overspent his allowance and although he was now doing well at Cranwell with the prospect of qualifying as an excellent pilot, he continued to live beyond his means, despite constant warnings from the solicitor who handled the family's affairs. Astley did the same and – for reasons that are not recorded, but are thought to have been due, also, to the "borrowing" without permission of other people's property – had been expelled from his previous school early in the year. By the end of 1922 Douce, too, had been sent home from her convent school for similar reasons and for what was described at the time as being "general naughtiness" – though Sibyl could see likeness in some of her pranks to those of her own at school. She often recounted in later years, with some amusement, how Douce had placed blotting paper underneath the keys of the school piano to prevent it being played. A pretty, affectionate little girl, Douce, perhaps more than most of Sibyl's children, seemed to miss the demonstrative warmth of her father's love and appeared to crave more and more for the attention from her mother that she so rarely received. Although only seven, Richard – "Tuppenny" to the family – was also showing a wilful, mischievous nature which Nanny Bishop was finding difficult to curb. It did not help that Sibyl seemed to go out of her way to spoil her beguiling youngest son. During the summer holiday in Herefordshire with Nanny Bishop's family he had, despite several warnings, continued to play with a sharp axe and a broken tin and, much to everyone's horror, had chopped off the tips of three of his fingers. Despite immediate medical attention it was too late to save this left hand from permanent damage and as the bone grew over the years it necessitated further operations, over which – possibly due to their disabling nature – Sibyl always showed great sympathy.

Only Amice and Jehanne – her eldest and youngest daughters – appeared more equable in temperament and gave her little cause for concern. But so taken up was Sibyl by this time with her busy social life, that she generally paid little attention to what was happening at home.

The whole family spent Christmas together winter-sporting in Austria and Sibyl stayed on at Igls with Nanny, Jehanne and Tuppenny until after Easter, renewing old friendships from her days in Cologne. On returning to Guernsey, in the spring of 1923, she soon became involved once more in the activities of St. Peter Port and as the year progressed began to figure prominently in all the local society columns. There was scarcely a function of note which she did not attend and although she was officially "bringing out" Amice, before her presentation at Court in June, it was Sibyl's clothes and presence at the various Channel Island dances and official balls that were usually commented upon – generally in glowing terms – rather than those of her daughter. Even the paragraph relating to Amice's presentation at Court described Sibyl's dress for the occasion in detail: "... a gown of silver tissue and silver lace embroidered with pearls, the train grey charmeuse, fastened on each shoulder with handsome pearl ornaments" – whereas Amice's dress was dismissed in a few words: "gold tissue, brocaded with pale pink".

While she was in England for Amice's presentation, she attended the Aerial Pageant at Hendon and sat in the Royal Air Force Club enclosure to watch Buster flying with other Cranwell cadets. Several of the officers she had first met in Germany were also taking part and she again found herself at the centre of a bunch of admiring young men who seemed only too happy for her to join their party for dinner and dancing afterwards.

She was back in Guernsey in time for the island's annual race meeting the following month and this year had a special interest because she had entered a horse herself. On an impulse, she had bought Fiona and Father Collins soon after moving into Brock Road and kept the pair in a stable at the back of the house, helping to tend them herself and often exercising them, with Amice, before breakfast. When Fiona won the Channel Islands' Racing and Hunt Cup Plate at this 1923 meeting, the local papers reported it as being "a very popular win" and Sibyl looked forward to further successes but other interests soon took precedence and the horses were eventually sold.

In August she took her family over to Sark for a few days and, as daughter of the Seigneur, was called upon to present the prizes at the island regatta which had been started up by Captain Ernest Platt, Dudley's best man, who with his wife had now come to live on the island. William by this time had changed into a benevolent, placid old man, who walked with a stick and was no longer a worry to his family. His annual spree was now a thing of the past and there were only occasional glimpses of his former eccentricities – one example being his refusal to accept the introduction of summer time and the Seigneurie clocks and his appointment times were consequently kept at an hour earlier than everyone else's. He enjoyed Sibyl's visits and hearing news of his grandchildren and was particularly interested in Buster's progress at Cranwell. It is doubtful, however, whether she told her father later that same year that both Buster and Astley were, once again, in trouble.

When she returned from a short cruise with friends to the Canary Islands in the autumn, it was to discover that Astley, who was barely eighteen, had been running up bills with various Guernsey shopkeepers and had written cheques which he knew could not be honoured. Like Buster he had always been led to believe that he would one day inherit a share of the vast Beaumont estate, through either his grandfather or great-aunt Augusta Lane, his godmother, and he had conducted his affairs as if the money were already at his disposal. After discussions with the family solicitor, Sibyl arranged for the debts to be settled and for Astley to be sent away from the Channel Islands for a time, to follow a two-year agricultural course in New Zealand at the Ruakura Farm of Instruction in Hamilton East – the hope being that this might provide him with a fresh start and a useful training for the future. While in London making the necessary arrangements for his journey, she took the opportunity of helping an old friend – Colonel Hilder, Conservative parliamentary candidate for South-East Essex – with his election campaign but was back in Guernsey in time to spend what was to be the last Christmas with all her family together, for by the end of the year Astley had sailed for New Zealand, never to return.

Buster, meanwhile, was also in similar financial straits and Sibyl was shocked to receive a letter from his Commanding Officer informing her that unless his debts were settled her son would be cashiered from the RAF. Once again she was obliged to make arrangements for the bills to be paid and then took it upon herself to seek out a high-ranking air force officer she had met only once before, at an RAF ball in Uxbridge. According to her account of the affair, she pleaded with him to use his influence to get the young flying officer, as Buster had by this time become, posted overseas, "away from the crowd of young irresponsibles" he was running around with. The officer was sympathetic but pointed out that Buster was under age for foreign service. Although he made no promises, Sibyl's persuasive powers evidently had some effect for within the year her eldest son had been posted to Iraq – by which time she herself was even further away from home.

After spending the first three months of 1924 with Amice and friends on the French Riviera, she returned to London to make plans for what was to prove the most memorable journey of her life. Since the age of eleven, when she had read *Where Three Empires Meet*, she had dreamed of visiting Kashmir and now friends who were living there suggested she join them for a holiday, and take in visits to other acquaintances in India and Ceylon at the same time. It was consequently with some excitement that on 8th August she sailed from Tilbury in the SS *Macedonia* but, according to her diary, her first impressions of her fellow passengers were not particularly favourable:

> Cdr, quite cheery. Dull crowd, mostly getting off at Gib. – Thank heavens.

Nevertheless, being Sibyl, she was soon on Christian name terms and dining and dancing with most of the male passengers and by the time she had reached the "seething heat" in the Red Sea, was learning how to play mahjong with one particular man in whose company she had been for most of the voyage. When the ship arrived at Bombay he made it his business to look after her and put her aboard the train for Rawalpindi the following day.

The friend who should have met her at Rawalpindi was delayed by the rains so, nothing daunted, Sibyl bravely sought to make her own way to Srinagar but was forced to abandon this attempt and spend the night at Murree when the rains made the roads quite impassable. This was the exciting beginning to nine months during which, among other things, she visited the Shalimar Gardens, camped in the Sind Valley, went hunting for bears and shot *chikor*, saw the Taj Mahal by moonlight, watched a Hindu wedding and toured a tea factory in Ceylon. Her crowded diary throughout shows that she gave herself little time for relaxation or sleep and appeared to have a stamina, even in extreme heat, that her friends found remarkable. But she did have her moments of quiet. While camping in Kangan in Kashmir, she went out walking alone one early evening and later noted in her diary some lines by Browning that she evidently thought appropriate:

> Silent silver lights and darks undreamed of,
> Where I hush and bless myself with silence...

As usual, throughout her holiday, she was mainly in the company of men rather than women and some of these escorts obviously provided her with more than just a platonic relationship, though Sibyl gives no indication in her diary notes as to how seriously she herself treated these affairs. She revelled in being at the centre of any social gathering, brooking no competition, and in the case of at least one young man in Ceylon, whose sister she had known in England, there is little doubt that she played a part in the breaking of his engagement. She took many photographs of the fascinating countryside through which she travelled and collected many souvenirs, which she always maintained afterwards provided her with "enough enchanting memories to last a lifetime".

She journeyed home on the SS *Leicestershire* and arrived at Marseilles on 16th May. After a few days in Paris she went on to London where she was lunched, dined and taken out dancing and to the theatre by a variety of escorts, several of whom she had first met in Cologne. Early in June, having ordered a new car in London, she flew back to Guernsey for a reunion with her family and a summer season which included the arrival of a new Lieutenant Governor, Major-General Sir Charles Sackville-West (later Lord Sackville). Although she wrote later that "England seemed very humdrum and unromantic after the glamour of India" her family's life could scarcely have been described as having been uneventful, while she had been away.

Four months after leaving home, her solicitors in London, who had been acting for her while she was away, received a letter from the High Commissioner for New Zealand asking for Astley to be removed from the training college as he "took no interest in his studies". Several cables had also been received from Astley himself asking for money to be sent out to him as he was once more in financial difficulties – this time involving him in police enquiries. In the February Sibyl, who had been kept informed of the situation, cabled instructions from Colombo for money to be sent to Astley for his fare to join her in Ceylon, where she had managed to find him a job. He duly collected this and left for Australia, en route for Colombo, but on reaching Sydney disappeared. Police efforts to find him so far had met with no success.

Buster meanwhile had met and become engaged to a charming young woman, Enid Ripley, whom he had first met during the winter of 1924 shortly before receiving news of his posting to Iraq. In her mother's absence, Amice made a hurried journey over to England to meet the girl her unpredictable brother was proposing to make his wife and was greatly relieved – and agreeably surprised – by his choice. The following summer she, too, became engaged to a young army officer, Harry Cantan, whom she had first met in Cologne but who was now stationed at the Fort in Guernsey with the Duke of Cornwall's Light Infantry.

Soon after her return Sibyl went over to Sark to see her father and tell him about her travels. He seemed to have aged considerably even since their last meeting – though a spark of his old fire came back when he told her in no uncertain terms that he disliked her newly-shingled hair. Sibyl often said later that she somehow regretted the change in his personality over the years, for his fiery temperament had always added a spice of adventure to their relationship and given her the enthusiasm which enabled her to enjoy a full life without the "inconvenience" of self-pity.

She stayed on Sark for the summer Cattle Show in July and helped her father to entertain the new Lieutenant Governor of Guernsey and his secretary to lunch at the Seigneurie and shared the duty of presenting prizes at the Regatta with the writer, Compton Mackenzie, who now lived with his wife, Faith, on John Allaire's old island of Jethou. After that, it was back to Guernsey for Sibyl and a further round of social events before a three-week cruise to Greece in October, followed by another short spell in London. It is, perhaps, hardly surprising that her youngest daughter, Jehanne, remembers little of her mother in those days beyond seeing her in evening dress on the way to some function with one or another "Uncle", or saying goodbye to her as she went off on yet another overseas journey. From all accounts her behaviour, generally, shocked those who considered themselves the Guernsey society of the time and her daring exploits included dancing on the table at one of the functions at a local hotel and associating with those who were reputed to be the fast set, who gambled and drank more than was acceptable in polite circles. If she had the reputation of being "The Merry Widow of the Rhine" in Germany it is understandable that there were those who thought she should also qualify for the title in Guernsey as "The Merry Widow of Brock Road".

Her stay in London on this particular occasion was brought to an abrupt end when she received a cable from Nanny Bishop informing her that both Jehanne and Tuppenny had diphtheria and that she must immediately return home. For some weeks her social engagements were few and when the children recovered she took them to Champéry in the Swiss Alps to convalesce. She stayed there until the spring of 1926, then it was back to Guernsey and another busy "season" – bolstered this year by the crews from a large number of visiting foreign warships. Once again she deputised for her father at the Sark Cattle Show and in his official speech on that occasion the Lieutenant Governor expressed his pleasure at taking luncheon at the Seigneurie with the Seigneur and his daughter "who took such a keen interest in the island and anything concerned with the welfare of the people" – a comment which, at the time, some islanders felt was hardly justified, for they saw comparatively little of their Seigneur's elder daughter.

Autumn began for Sibyl with another short cruise with friends to Tangier, Corfu and Palma, before joining her family in London for Buster's wedding to Enid Ripley on 5th October. William Spencer Beaumont had died two months earlier and as Buster had now come into his inheritance he had characteristically lost no time in cabling the news from Iraq to his fiancée and asking her to arrange for their marriage "as soon as possible". The wedding took place at All Souls' Church, Langham Place, with a reception afterwards at the Langham Hotel. Less than two months later it was the turn of Harry Cantan and Amice to marry as Sibyl had told Harry that she did not approve of long engagements. The service was held at eight o'clock in the morning, so that the bride and groom could catch the morning boat to England, but Amice's popularity was such that every seat at the Town Church of St. Peter Port was filled. Sibyl had arranged a wedding breakfast for a few close friends, including the Lieutenant Governor and his wife and the Colonel of Harry's regiment and they all went down to the harbour afterwards to see the young couple depart. Her *Cloud of Witness* book gives at this time a hint, perhaps, that these two weddings may have taken her back to her own and that even in the midst of her busy social life she still occasionally gave a thought to Dudley and the emptiness of her life without him, for with this year's date beside it she had written: *"Le Temps passe, mais L'amitie reste – ."*

The year 1927 began for Sibyl with visits to Ireland and England and on her return she became involved in rehearsals for a production of Richard Sheridan's *School for Scandal*, which was to be performed at the end of April by the newly-formed Guernsey Dramatic and Operatic Club, in aid of the local blind and Children's Aid Society. Lady Sackville-West, the wife of the Lieutenant Governor, and Compton Mackenzie headed the cast as Lady Teazle and Charles Surface respectively. Sibyl, for once, took a comparatively minor rôle as Lady Sneerwell but, according to local press reviews, she acquitted herself well as "a typical lady of the beau monde" and was specially mentioned, with others, as having danced a minuet which had been "rapturously encored" and was one of the "most attractive items of the show". The play ran for five performances and proved a great success. Bouquets and gifts were received by all the members of the cast and even eleven-year-old Tuppenny, who took the part of a page, came in for his share.

Sibyl had fewer social engagements during the early summer, for she had been making more visits to Sark than usual to see her father. He had not been well for some months and had not felt strong enough to attend either of his grandchildren's weddings the previous year. He had allowed his official correspondence to lapse and latterly had not been attending meetings of Chief Pleas. He rarely left the Seigneurie and although he had someone to cook, clean and garden for him, had felt too ill to bother himself with either the collection of his tithes or the upkeep of his property. A visitor to the Seigneurie during the early months of 1927 gave this description of the conditions there: "Neglect reigned supreme. There were not even curtains at some of the windows and outside the overgrown trees and shrubs made the whole place weird in the shady half-light. There were no sinks or taps inside and all the water had to be carried from an outside pump." No decorations had been attempted since Sophia died some twenty years earlier and although the servants did their best the whole house looked seedy and run down.

William had prostate trouble and was convinced that he had cancer of the bladder but the Sark doctor whom he, as Seigneur, had initially been responsible for engaging, was no longer reliable for he had become an alcoholic and spent most of his days in a state of delirium tremens – carrying around a forked stick with which to protect himself against the snakes and monsters conjured up in his befuddled brain. By the time Sibyl crossed to Sark in June to deputise once again for her father at the Cattle Show, William was in constant pain, though he steadfastly refused to take to his bed. A few days after her return to Guernsey, however, he collapsed and his maid sent word that he was unconscious. She at once travelled back to Sark with a nurse and two other doctors but although the Sark doctor had performed a minor operation before their arrival, William died early on the following day – 20th June. He was seventy-five years old.

Despite his eccentricities, Sark genuinely mourned its Seigneur and the funeral a few days later was, according to press reports afterwards, "the most impressive ever seen on the island". The Dean of Guernsey conducted the service assisted by the Vicar of Sark, the Reverend Ernest Nelson Greenhow, and the Lieutenant Governor and other dignitaries from Guernsey also crossed over for the occasion.

Sibyl gave no indication to those present of her feelings at seeing her once wayward father buried beside her mother in the railed portion of the churchyard that was the family grave. Theirs had been a curious love – at times bordering on hate – relationship. Both were equally hot-tempered, strong-willed and impatient with the other's feelings yet at the same time still possessed a strong, if somewhat brusque, affection for one another. Sibyl was greatly touched when she later discovered that he had kept most of the letters she had written to him during her travels. But any sadness she may have felt by his death was no doubt ameliorated by her plans for the future and the realisation at last of her girlhood dream of one day succeeding him as Seigneur of Sark.

She would no doubt have been astonished had she known that the legality of her "assumption of the office" was at that time being questioned by the Home Office in a letter to the office of the Lieutenant Governor in Guernsey. In his reply Sir Charles Sackville-West wrote:

> ... I have consulted the Procureur who, after examining the old charters relating to Sark, informs me that in the case of sons the eldest son takes the Fief and the entire real property in Sark. There seems, however, to be no reference in the Charters to the case where there are only daughters to inherit but the custom appears to have always been and there are precedents for it, that the eldest daughter inherits in the same manner as the eldest son. Mrs. Sibyl Dudley Beaumont is therefore the new Seigneur ...

Over forty years later her right of accession was again questioned and from a quarter which for Sibyl was as hurtful as it was unexpected. But on that June day in 1927 a new, exciting chapter was beginning to open up for her as "La Dame de Serk" – the title by which she preferred to be known and which she hoped would one day become synonymous with her island the world over.

Part Two

La Dame de Serk
(1927–1939)

Chapter 6

ONE OF SIBYL'S first duties – less than a week after her father's death – was to see that a special meeting was called of Chief Pleas, the island's parliament at the Court House, which was also the Boys' Schoolroom.

She showed no signs of nervousness as she took her place on the raised dais beside her chief officials: the Seneschal (President of the assembly and official magistrate); the Prévôt (Sheriff); Greffier (Clerk of the Court) and Treasurer – all of whom she would from now on have the responsibility of appointing. The Connétable (Constable) and his assistant, the Vingtenier, were elected annually to their office by Chief Pleas. During her father's time, in 1922, new constitutional changes had been introduced and in addition to the "tenants" – owners of the forty original "tenements", who were automatically members of Chief Pleas – there were now twelve peoples' deputies, elected by islanders every three years from among the five hundred or so non-tenants. Not all the members of this assembly – Sark-born or "English" (as those few non-islanders who had purchased tenements were often termed) – attended meetings regularly, but Sibyl was aware that those who did were often sharply divided in their opinions as to what was best for Sark. Some hoped that she would join them in voting for what they felt to be much-needed changes and improvements, while others were ready to fight anything that altered a mode of living which they considered had served the island well enough in the past and were viewing with suspicion this woman who, in a generally male-dominated community, was now in command.

Sibyl said afterwards that she felt very conscious of her responsibilities and slightly overwhelmed by the occasion as she stood up to make her carefully prepared reply, in French, to the official welcome from the Seneschal, Frederick de Carteret:

> Tenants and inhabitants of Sark. I should like to thank you for your sympathy towards me and for the respect and affection you have shown in your remembrance of my father.

I do not ignore that, in becoming Dame of Sark, I am investing myself with an office that carries great responsibilities. I am but a woman among you, but at heart I am *"un vrai Serquais"* and with the help of God, I shall do my utmost for the good and prosperity of the island.

I place myself at the disposal of all: any person having cause for complaint has only to come to the Seigneurie and speak to me about it. I promise to listen to all and not be influenced by anyone. I shall act according to my own conscience. I hope that at all times I shall receive your help and goodwill and wish for the favour of the King and the consideration of his representatives.

The assembly was obviously moved by her stirring words and apparent sincerity and she resumed her seat amidst loud applause. Then came the first business of the day – the removal of the Medical Officer of Health and the appointment of his replacement. Sibyl had seen enough during past weeks to realise that her people's health was suffering at the hands of their present physician and agreed to serve notice of dismissal upon him personally. Improvement to the island's sanitation was the next subject for serious discussion, following upon a letter from the Lieutenant Governor showing his concern, and then came another major item – that of the proposed harbour extensions. Despite lively debate on both topics, no useful conclusions were reached and it was three hours before Sibyl's first meeting as Dame of Sark came to an end.

Her subsequent interview with the doctor at his home was something she always remembered with distaste. After she had pressed the unshaven, flabby and sickly man to tender his resignation he had fallen on to his knees and tried to kiss her hand. Disgusted by his action she had moved quickly to the door but he had shuffled after her, still on his knees. It was the last she was to see of him for he left the island soon afterwards.

For the next few weeks her time was spent commuting between her Guernsey home at Brock Road and Sark, seeing to the sale of some of the surplus furniture and effects from the Seigneurie and having discussions with an architect over her plans for the building's renovation. She planned to redecorate the neglected house throughout, install electricity, central heating and a proper indoor water supply. A bathroom, new dining room and a modern dairy were also to be added and she was prepared to spend much time and thought over the whole project in order to make the Seigneurie a comfortable, permanent home and a manor house for the island of which both she and the Sark people could be proud. But for the time being it was in no condition for her family to move into and for that first summer she rented the house belonging to her old friend Ernest Platt, later in the year moving into furnished lodgings in the Avenue – the island's main shopping street. It was at Brock Road or the Seigneurie, however, that she usually conducted her many interviews with the press over her accession.

The journalists appeared to find her an ideal subject, intelligent, alert and with an instinctive knowledge of the kind of information they most needed for their articles on the "woman feudal ruler of a tiny kingdom" – as many termed her. Sibyl, for her part, saw these interviews as a means of publicising not only the uniqueness of her situation but of the island itself. She told the reporters that she was hoping to take up permanent residence at the Seigneurie some time the following year after its "extensive renovations" had been completed and that she then proposed to continue the custom of opening its grounds to the public each Monday. She also intended to supervise personally the affairs of the home farm as she had, she told reporters, "experience of dairying and was interested in cattle". To this end she had already engaged a farm bailiff – Nanny's brother, Leonard Bishop. A year later he married and his wife, Jenny, also came to the Seigneurie to work.

Most of the early press reports quoted Sibyl as saying that she had no intention of changing the island's policy and that "as far as possible with modern conditions" she would do her utmost to preserve the autonomy of the Sark Court. The *Daily Mail* of 2nd July, 1927, described her as "a middle-aged, dark, active woman" who wanted everything to be carried on "absolutely in the old way, to conform to the old regime", and who would continue to exclude motor cars "which would spoil the island entirely, hooting round every corner". *The Times* devoted a whole column to the beauties of the island, even "commending to Mr. Churchill" Sark's way of successfully raising revenue – by charging landing tax to its visitors. The local *Guernsey Press* thought that "Sark should be congratulated on its lady Chieftain" as in her the island would "have a ruler of broadened outlook on affairs in general and a practised guide in those political and legislative matters which may come within the purview of the administrators of its public affairs". She was proud, the newspaper reported, of Sark's continued prosperity under Home Rule and was quick to point out that the island had no public debt and "doubted whether any part of the Empire could make a similar claim".

Several of Sibyl's friends who came to Sark for the August

Regatta, of which she was now president, expressed concern that she had undertaken the expense of such extensive alterations to the Seigneurie, in addition to the taking on of a position which they felt would bring her great responsibility but little revenue in return. Many of her old feudal rights as Seigneur stemmed from the island's early years as a Fief Haubert.* Each Michaelmas she was still committed to pay to the Crown the twentieth part of a Knight's Service Fee – in 1927, around thirty shillings – as all preceding Seigneurs had done but she was also entitled, as they had been, to a "treizième" or thirteenth of the purchase price should any of the forty tenements change hands. Certain tithes were also due to her for cereals, cider, lambs and wool and a royalty on any minerals mined on the island, plus the small annual property tithe payable in a live fowl "poulage" for every chimney on each of the forty houses. Her father had let most of these lapse over the years and the "treizième" by no means occurred frequently enough for her to rely upon it bringing her in a regular income. Money from the Seigneurie furniture sale and property left in her father's will and marriage settlement with Sophia helped, but she had already mortgaged some of this in advance to help pay for her trip to India and Ceylon in 1924. This left her little beyond her annual income from the Beaumont estate to pay for the work to the Seigneurie and to continue to live and travel as she had been doing, in circles where money was more easily come by.

In later years an old friend commented that Sibyl always seemed to cultivate people of wealth and position – which may or may not have been true – but many of these acquaintances became firm friends and there is no doubt that it was due to their generosity that she was able to stretch her income further. When asked they willingly gave her financial help and she was invariably such good company that many invited her to travel with them as their guest on their journeys abroad. She accompanied one such woman friend on the SS *Oransay* for a Mediterranean cruise in early September, 1927. This was the first time she had travelled any distance since becoming Dame of Sark and she took every opportunity of advertising the island and making her position known to those on board.

One of her fellow passengers was the Governor General of Eire, Tim Healy, whom she had last seen in 1903 when she had visited the House of Commons and watched him as he had taken part in a stormy debate on Irish affairs. She reminded the politician

* See page 17

of this and after talking together he invited her to visit him at his residence in Phoenix Park next time she was in Dublin and he gave her a book in which he wrote: "From the Governor of one island to the Governor of another" – which pleased her greatly.

She returned to Sark in time for the Michaelmas Chief Pleas meeting at which the appointment was announced of the new doctor whom she had engaged before she went away.

Refreshed by her holiday, she took up her affairs with renewed vigour, bicycling around the island armed with a small notebook to jot down anything she felt needed further investigation or attention. Plans were now in hand to raise funds for the projected new harbour and for a war memorial to commemorate those from Sark who had died in the 1914–1918 war. She had also announced her intention of seeing to it that the neglected roads were made good and that the dilapidated windmill was repaired. The Sark correspondent of the *Guernsey Press*, reporting this in October, wrote of her additional interest in providing better housing "for the working classes of Sark" to counteract "the growing practice of strangers, who do not support the island in any way, occupying cottages during the summer season and taking profits that should accrue to the Sark people themselves". It was not surprising that most of the islanders felt that once again they had a Seigneur who truly had their interests at heart.

But not all of her improvement plans for Sark were as well received. In the late autumn notices were posted under her name at the entrance to the church, giving warning that many old laws and customs which had long since lapsed into disuse were to be reintroduced. Seigneurial tithes of crops were once again to be paid in kind, rather than money – particularly with regard to corn – "in order to increase the amount grown on the island" and the old law forbidding games of chance or payment of entrance fees to any entertainment, such as whist drives and dances, was also to be re-enforced. As these admission fees often went towards "the provision of Christmas trees and summer outings for the Sunday School children" – according to the *Guernsey Press* correspondent, many Sarkese saw no advantage in such a restriction. Those who no longer cultivated their land did not take too kindly either to the prospect of once again having to provide crops from their tenements in order to give the required tenth – "dîxieme" – to the Seignory and their grumbles drew the attention of the international press, many of whose members made much in their reports of the woman ruler who wielded such feudal power.

So began her first year as Dame of Sark. This was to be the

forerunner of so many others in which the introduction of new policies or the renewal of old caused some, both in and outside the island, to view her many well-intentioned actions with mistrust. About this time she told a woman friend that she would have liked to have "smartened up" the whole of Sark in the same way that she was tackling the Seigneurie, but there was "always too much dust in the corners that new brooms can't reach" and, years later, in commenting upon that period, she wrote:

> It was a difficult and discouraging task trying to benefit the island after its long spell of neglect, but I was determined to get prosperity, health, education and all the good sides of progress going and yet never let the island lose its real security which lies in its freedom, character and peaceful sense of well-being...

Her private life was, as usual, not without its excitements. Douce, whose schooling had been as chequered and erratic as that of her elder brothers, had already been expelled from a number of other educational establishments before joining the daughter of one of Sibyl's Guernsey friends at a Wimbledon finishing school. She had grown into a very beautiful young woman with a perfect figure, large, dark eyes and skin "the texture of a magnolia" – according to one description of her during those middle 1920s. Frank Cadogan Cooper painted her portrait several times and one of these had hung in the Summer Exhibition at the Royal Academy. She had the same intense sexual drive that her mother appeared to possess but, unlike Sibyl, was not always in control of her emotions. For some years now she had managed to gather around her a large circle of male admirers and these, with Sibyl's men friends, had been frequent visitors to the house in Brock Road. She, as much as her mother, had enjoyed the press interviews and the razzamatazz over the accession and was delighted when she was sometimes termed the "Princess of Sark" and saw her photograph appear with that of her mother and younger sister, Jehanne, in many of the glossy journals. Perhaps of all Sibyl's children, Douce was the most like her. She was exuberant and lively, highly intelligent, courageous, a fine swimmer and horsewoman and gave the impression that she was capable of successfully turning her hand to almost anything that came her way. If Sibyl had not felt that the social strictures of that time prevented it and had been able to direct her beautiful daughter's abilities into an absorbing career, the pattern of Douce's life from then on might well have been very different.

As it was, although she occasionally helped with some of the island's social events, there was little for her to do but seek out fresh admirers to add to those she already dangled on a string.

It was while Sibyl had been away on her Mediterranean cruise, she told friends later, that Douce had met Major William James, a tall, handsome ex-army officer in his middle forties, who had recently arrived in the Channel Islands and that when she returned in the autumn, her daughter could not resist telling her of this latest conquest. According to Sibyl, this had immediately prompted her to engineer a meeting with this middle-aged man, who appeared to be so interested in the young girl. Some islanders, however, say that it was not to Douce but to a Sark hotel-keeper's daughter that the Major had first paid court and that it was he who, on having Sibyl pointed out to him in one of the shops on Sark's Avenue, had gone out of his way to make her acquaintance. But whatever the circumstances that led to their first meeting, the fact remains that on 22nd October she entered in her diary – "Dined Pullings – Meet Major James", the first of many such references from then on to "J" or "Jimmy", as he very quickly became known to her. Before the year was out he, too, had moved into the furnished lodgings on the Avenue and it soon became clear that his intentions were now focused upon Sibyl alone and that this time she was treating the relationship as a serious affair.

Douce meanwhile had evidently found herself several other men, nearer her own age, to dance attendance upon her and did not appear in the least concerned over the loss of one of her admirers.

That year of 1927 ended with two more important events for Sibyl. On 18th December, Amice gave birth to a son, Peter, and two days later in Egypt – where Buster was now stationed with the RAF – John Michael was born, Sibyl's grandson, who as Buster's heir apparent, would one day inherit Sark.

After Christmas with her family at Brock Road, Sibyl returned to Sark and she and Jimmy James saw in the New Year of 1928 alone together – among the workmen's tools and paints – at the partially refurbished Seigneurie. For the next fortnight, however, her time was mostly taken up with island affairs as the Chief Pleas meeting, fixed for the middle of the month, promised to be lively, following upon her announcement in October that Seigneurial charges on contracts and tithes would in future be paid in kind.

There had been continuous discussion on the island and correspondence in the local newspapers since the first notices were posted – the main comment being that the Sark people did not wish to avoid any legal payments but to "pay their dues in the most suitable manner according to present-day conditions". The *Guernsey Weekly Press* correspondent remarked:

> ... In some instances it would be impossible to make payments exactly as required by Seigneurial contracts and leases* – (cash in Tournois for instance) nor is it possible in the present day to comply with all the conditions contained in such leases as, for instance, that a tenant must keep a soldier with his musket and ammunition always on the premises ...

But, despite all the criticism, Sibyl remained adamant that she had decided to take such action in order to safeguard agricultural interests and in her press interviews, was quoted as saying that agriculture had deteriorated "to a shocking state" owing to the occupation of farmhouses by English residents who "neglected the cultivation of formerly tilled land, some of which had been allowed to run to waste". Sarkese, she maintained, generally preferred to pay in produce rather than in cash and, as far as she was concerned, the returns were insufficient anyway to occasion either gain or hardship either way.

The fact that there was no milling on the island was, she felt, also to be deplored – particularly as the growing of corn had previously been well established. With no bakery, either, Sark was wholly dependent upon Guernsey for bread and she recalled how on one occasion during the 1914–18 war, the island had been threatened with starvation through boats being unable to cross to Guernsey. There was an "urgent need", she told reporters, to encourage and safeguard agriculture – particularly the growing of cereals and she proposed to install a milling plant on the island, not in her own personal interest but "with a view to making Sark more self-supporting". Many years later the Sarkese were to be reminded very forcibly of these words when their need to be more self-sufficient became even more vital. As it was, she was surprised and a little hurt by some of the critical reaction her first efforts received. Even the officials outside the island were not as helpful as they might have been.

Early in January the Lieutenant Governor of Guernsey wrote to C. G. Markbreiter, Assistant Secretary at the Home Office:

> ... Mrs Dudley Beaumont, la Dame de Serk, is anxious to go and see a suitable official at the Home Office in regard to her

* See Appendix One.

> island. I have told her to write to you and make an appointment. You will find her tenacious of her "Seignorial rights" but in the meantime she is doing a great deal to improve the organisation of the island. I should be grateful if, after her interview with you, you would let me know the points she raises . . .

In a further letter a week later, he explained more fully Sibyl's reasons for requesting such a visit and this also gives an insight into how the officials in Guernsey viewed her actions in those early years as Seigneur of Sark:

> . . . What Mrs. Beaumont says she wants to talk about is the agitation in the press, generally, regarding her insisting on her rentes being paid in kind and not in money. Personally I expect she wants to put herself on the map as being *"la dame de Sercq"*. She is full of her position but as she is at present working up the island and pushing on needed reforms, I see no objection to her making love to you or anyone else in the Home Office! I think her attitude as regards the wheat rentes is justified. The only people who object are certain foreigners who have bought land in the island for houses and gardens and not for agriculture. By "foreigners" I mean not Sark born . . .

At the Chief Pleas meeting she told the assembly that no alteration could be made to the existing ancient laws without a petition to the Privy Council and pointed out that where it was not possible for farmers to grow the required grain they could purchase it from some other source. She nevertheless took the opportunity of putting her case to Sir Malcolm Delevigne at the Home Office at the end of the month when she was over in England for the christening of her grandson, Peter. She also arranged a meeting with her London solicitors, at which Jimmy James was present, to discuss arrangements she had made with Buster over her future income from the Beaumont estate.

Under the terms of her settlement, Sibyl received £1,500 a year but there was a proviso, should she re-marry, that this would be reduced to £300 – an amount on which she felt it would be quite impossible for her to live as Dame of Sark. She had intimated as much in a letter to Buster – reminding him at the same time that she had settled some of his previous debts and pointing out that he was not only the main heir to the Beaumont estate but would also one day inherit the Seignory from her. He had immediately agreed to the deed being changed so that she should receive a fixed annual income of £900, with no conditions attached, and the solicitor was in the process of drawing up the necessary papers.

By this time it was becoming increasingly obvious to her family as well as her friends that she and Jimmy were proposing to marry.

Chapter 7

Most of Sibyl's friends had been as charmed by Jimmy James on first acquaintance as she had been – though some thought him a shade too suave for their taste. To several people on the island she had introduced him as her cousin but most realised that the relationship was closer than she would have them believe. From the first he appeared to take a great interest in Sark and even persuaded Sibyl to write and have printed privately a booklet about the island entitled *Notes on Feudal Tenure** and to have a special seal made for her personal use. He also gave her practical help over the renovations at the Seigneurie, suggesting ideas for furnishings and generally making himself useful. Sibyl was glad to be able to leave him in charge while she went about her other island affairs and entrusted to him the payment of the men's wages. Sometimes he wheeled barrows for them as he supervised their work and generously gave them pipefuls of tobacco or cigarettes, behaving – as one man remarked later – "as if he was already the 'gaffer' ".

The early months of 1928 were busy for Sibyl for she was preparing to move out of her Brock Road house and endeavouring to get the Seigneurie ready for occupation by the beginning of May. Jimmy had made himself responsible for the purchase of some additional furnishings and had already been to England several times for this purpose. Sark affairs were also taking up a considerable amount of her time, for her duties now ranged from semi-official functions such as the christening of the Rowing Club's new racing gig to committee meetings about corn tithes or the projected new harbour. She had recently experienced at first hand the problems of the present harbour – Creux – for she had waited there for two hours on a stormy day in late March for Jimmy to return to the island after one of his furniture-buying visits to England. So rough was the sea that no boat could put in or out

* Few copies of the booklet were sold and the bulk remained in the attics of the Seigneurie.

on that or the day following and on the third day, although one did manage to cross from St. Peter Port, the high seas and exposed conditions of Creux Harbour prevented the landing of either passengers or cargo and, after an abortive attempt to use the old Eperquerie landing stage to the north of the island, the steamer returned, with all on board, to Guernsey. When at last it did manage to discharge its passengers on the fourth day, Jimmy was not aboard but, according to Sibyl's diary, "the *Joybell I* [the Sark boat] brought a wire later. Thanks Be." She gave no reason for his delayed return but he was back the following week in time to attend the Easter Sunday church service and meet the Vicar of Sark, the Reverend Ernest Nelson Greenhow who, before coming to the island two years earlier, had travelled as a missionary to many parts of the world.

Mr. Greenhow was uneasy when Sibyl informed him that she and Jimmy were proposing to marry, for he was certain he had met this prospective bridegroom somewhere before – and, what is more – under similar circumstances. When he intimated as much to Sibyl the following day, Jimmy having once again left the island for "business in London", she was furious that the clergyman should dare make such a suggestion and even more so when he told her that he would not feel happy about the proposed marriage until he had satisfied himself that he had not, in fact, married the gentleman before. The very notion that the vicar of her small island should have met – let alone married – Jimmy, in some distant part of the world was, she felt, altogether too ridiculous. Brushing aside any uneasiness she may have felt, she tried to concentrate instead on the Easter meeting of Chief Pleas to be held the next day, at which the urgent matter of the new harbour was again to be raised. There was feeling in certain quarters that the Sark authorities had been "dilly-dallying" over getting the work started and this had been the subject of considerable debate on the island.

After a lively session of Chief Pleas at which it was decided that further advice should be sought over the cost of the harbour, Sibyl departed for England and Jimmy met her the following day in London. Whether she told him of the vicar's suspicions is not known but after spending a long weekend with her, he again took his leave on the Monday morning, pleading "urgent business" in Plymouth. This sudden departure came as something of a surprise to Sibyl for that very same day – 16th April – the national press carried the announcement of their forthcoming marriage. *The Times* reported:

The marriage between Major William James, M.C., son of the late Major H. R. and Lady Ann James, and Sibyl, Dame de Serk, daughter of the late Seigneur of Sark, will take place at St. Peter's, Island of Sark, early in June.

Her first qualms of uneasiness began to grow when next day she visited the large store where Jimmy had allegedly been buying furniture on her behalf, with money she had advanced him over a period of some weeks, and found that her account was still outstanding. She told her solicitor what she had discovered and, according to her diary, he was "most unpleasant" – presumably because she had entrusted Jimmy with such large sums on so short an acquaintance – and suggested that she should try to contact her fiancé without delay. This she attempted to do but without success, although she was able to ascertain that he had now reached Exeter. She returned to Sark an anxious woman.

The next few weeks must have taken on nightmarish qualities for her. Her diaries, for once, give some evidence of her feelings. She had undoubtedly been in love with this man and had been completely taken in by his charm, entrusting to him close on £400 of her money towards their future home – a sum she could ill afford to lose when considered with the other expenses she had already incurred over the Seigneurie. She became sick with worry and, very unusual for her, spent a few days in bed during which time, according to her diary, Jimmy sent her two telegrams from Weston-super-Mare and Weymouth, followed by a letter giving no address.

"Still feeling wretched and worried", she wrote on 29th April, and "No news at all – very anxious" on 30th. Somehow she still clung to the hope that there was some logical explanation of his behaviour but, after more than two weeks of uncertainty, a woman friend in whom she had confided and who was now with her on Sark, urged her to return to London and put the matter in the hands of either the police or her solicitor. Reluctantly Sibyl agreed and arrived in England on 7th May. Three days later, after enquiries had begun, she wrote in her diary this single, significant sentence – "Worst fears justified". The following day with her solicitor and a friend she visited the War Office and was there able to identify a photograph of Jimmy and to learn something of his previous activities.

Jimmy, for reasons known only to himself, continued to write to her though he was always careful not to give his exact whereabouts. Under the circumstances it must have been heartbreaking for Sibyl to receive these love letters, particularly as she knew the police net was closing in on him in the West Country. The announcement that the marriage would not now take place appeared in the national press on 22nd May and on 26th she returned to Sark.

She had told no one on the island of what had occurred, save two very old English farming friends, and when she had been asked earlier in the month, by the social columnist of the *Guernsey Press*, why her fiancé was not with her, she used the same excuse that Jimmy had given for his protracted absence. Thus it was that on 12th May the columnist had written:

> Major James, R.E., whose engagement to the Dame de Sercq was recently announced, has suffered a heavy bereavement in the loss of his only sister in India, and has since been laid up with a very bad attack of influenza but is now about again and hopes to return to Sark during the next few days.

After it became known that she had broken her engagement, however, another piece appeared in the Sark News section of the paper – on the very day that a much subdued and mentally exhausted Sibyl returned to the island:

> Much regret and surprise is being evinced on the island on the announcement of the breaking off of the engagement between La Dame de Serk and Major William James, M.C., R.E. The event was being looked forward to with great pleasure and satisfaction and subscriptions of between £80 and £100 had already been collected towards a wedding present in appreciation of the event. Madame Beaumont is not in residence in Sark at present but is expected to return shortly . . .

For someone whose pride had already received a punishing blow this undoubtedly added a few more bruises. She must have realised that sooner or later the whole story would become known around the island but for the moment she had no intention of revealing her reasons for breaking off the engagement. Nor was she prepared to give Mr. Greenhow the satisfaction of hearing that he had been right after all. With her usual courage and practicality she set her mind upon tackling some of the island's problems and trying to untangle the complicated financial knots she had managed to get herself into.

She had supposed that, once they were married, Jimmy would

share some of the expenses she had incurred over the Seigneurie and now that the work was almost complete she knew that there would be heavy bills to settle. Once again her friends rallied round and lent her money to help tide her over some of her immediate financial difficulties. But Sibyl was only too aware that this relief could only be temporary and that somehow she must raise more money from other quarters – particularly now that her regular allowance from the Beaumont estate had been reduced by the deed she herself had requested from Buster earlier in the year. She decided that first and foremost she must move herself into the Seigneurie, whether it be completely finished or not, and so with Nanny Bishop and Jehanne took up her official residence there on 9th June. That same evening came a telephone call, which she must have received with mixed feelings.

Earlier in the week she had again heard from Jimmy who now appeared to be in Exeter – though, as usual, his letter carried no address – and through this, police were able to locate him and make an arrest on a warrant that had been issued against him three years earlier. Sibyl's telephone call was from a solicitor to say that Jimmy had been arrested and would be taken to London to appear before a magistrate at Bow Street the following week. She travelled to England and made a further statement but was naturally not anxious to become more involved than she need be. When it transpired that Jimmy was to be brought to trial at the Central Criminal Court later in the month her friends, as usual, came to her aid and made sure that she would be out of the country. She was invited on a cruise to Las Palmas, Tenerife and Cadiz but even this could not take her mind off what was happening at home, for among her forwarded mail she received – according to her diary – yet another letter from Jimmy, the contents of which she did not record.

By the time she returned to Sark, the trial was over and Jimmy had been sentenced to three years' penal servitude. The charges on which he had been arrested had been comparatively minor, concerning sums of money ranging from £15 to £100 which he had illegally obtained from various London money-lenders, but he had admitted to other crimes of a far more involved nature. His story was long and complicated. During the hearing it was revealed that his real name was Douglas James, he was forty-five years old and had already been imprisoned in 1922 when, as an officer in the RAF, he had embezzled £720 of "public funds". According to press descriptions of him at the trial he was a "tall, well set-up man with a close-clipped military moustache" who wore "a smartly-cut suit of plus fours and a neatly-tied bow-tie" and gave every appearance of being a "typical ex-officer". (A description which would have fitted so many of Sibyl's previous men friends.) Despite his "birth and breeding" and "educational attainments of no mean order", he had fraudulently acquired thousands of pounds from many innocent people both in England and abroad, had tricked at least three women into bigamous marriages and several others into supposed "engagements" for the sole purpose of obtaining money from them. Sibyl was not described by name, only as "a woman from the Channel Islands owning a landed estate" who had discovered before the date fixed for the wedding that he was already married, but by that time had already lost £400 of her money to him.

It was a sordid, unsavoury tale and his sentence only served to add to Sibyl's worries. She knew that Jimmy must realise her involvement in his arrest but expected his term of imprisonment to be much longer and it is easy to understand her genuine uneasiness when she admitted to a woman friend that she was worried about what he might do, on his release, if he were to find her "all alone at the Seigneurie" – although she brushed this off by adding, half in jest, "I'll just have to find another husband".

She returned to Sark on 10th July – two days before the house-warming garden party she had planned at the Seigneurie. It was a perfect day and although the interior work was not fully completed, the garden, as one of her guests recalled later, was looking "quite splendid". Sibyl, wearing a long beige lace dress with fur-trimmed matching coat and a large salmon pink picture hat, carried off the whole proceedings in her usual courageous manner, knowing only too well that by now most of those present were fully aware, through local gossip and the national newspapers, of what had occurred at the Old Bailey the previous week. Jimmy was not mentioned by her then – nor, indeed, to many afterwards – but knowing what the whole affair must have cost her, both in pride and heartbreak, it is clear that her father's hard training once again stood her in good stead.

The following week she had to face more of the Sark people at a special meeting of Chief Pleas where, among other matters, a recent and much criticised action by herself was discussed at length.

For some weeks she had been exploring ways of raising the money she now so badly needed and had already decided – along with several other schemes – to reclaim the Manoir tenement which, although it had been used for some two hundred years as a rent-free vicarage, was still Seigneurial property. The roof leaked, the staircase needed attention and she could see no way of effecting the necessary repairs other than letting it to another tenant on a repairing lease – or so she intimated to the Bishop of Winchester in a letter dated 28th May, adding: "... The situation financially means a great deal to me as the revenue for the island has practically become nil owing to neglect ..." In a further letter to him on 12th June she wrote:

> You will understand that I have no personal feeling in any way against Mr. Greenhow, but I consider it a matter of urgent necessity that the Church here should be properly established and no longer exist as a sort of Seigneurial charity ...

But those who knew of her acrimonious encounter with Mr. Greenhow over her ill-fated, proposed marriage – aggravated by the fact that he had then made his suspicions known to the Dean of Guernsey – could not help but wonder if her reasons for taking up the matter of his house at this particular time were other than financial. Quite understandably, her written notice for him to quit within three months, served upon him on 23rd June, came as a great shock to the clergyman. With a wife and five children to support on a small stipend, he had little enough to spare for renting a house elsewhere on the island, even in the unlikely event of one large enough for his family being available. Most of his congregation were sympathetic over his plight and some who knew what had previously transpired said openly that they thought her action was her way of "hitting back" at their vicar for being proved right over Jimmy James. The outcome provided yet another setback – not only to Sibyl's purse but to her pride – for after much discussion the Sark Court of 30th July rejected her claim to the house because of the terms of her father's letter of engagement to Mr. Greenhow when he had first been given the living. But although she publicly treated the clergyman with courtesy, as she felt befitted her position, she by no means let the matter rest there. Meanwhile, however, she had other plans in hand to increase her capital which she hoped might bring about greater returns.

Early in July, while passing through London after her cruise, she had signed a petition at her solicitor's office which she proposed to lay before the Privy Council regarding "leave to sell or mortgage the Island or any part thereof" to a British subject or "corporation". Her action created a considerable stir both at the

Home Office and in government circles in Guernsey and for several months there was much correspondence and discussion between all the parties concerned.

After the Privy Council Office had made its comments on her petition to the Home Office, Markbreiter wrote to Charles Sackville-West – now Lord Sackville – in Guernsey:

> I suppose that Mrs. Beaumont desires to leave the island and to realise her assets, or, as indicated to raise money thereon . . . There is not, however, any precedent for a) a sale to a corporation and b) a sale of part of the fief, nor a mortgage, since 1354 . . .
>
> For the present, Mrs. Beaumont only wants to mortgage her property and to preserve all rights and privileges as Seigneur. No one would wish to prevent her from realising her assets, if she should find a suitable purchaser, but the question will arise as to whether her position as Seigneur in the Constitution of the Island can be continued if there is anything less than a complete sale to an individual capable of succeeding as Seigneur on the transfer of the property . . . It is also a question as to whether it would be right for Mrs. Beaumont to continue as Seigneur if she intends to leave the island permanently.

Further discussions between Lord Sackville and the Home Office followed, in the course of which Lord Sackville said that he did not know if Sibyl intended to leave the island, or of her plans for disposing of her interests there. He thought she might want to sell only part. The Home Office intimated that it would not agree to this and suggested that Lord Sackville should once again approach Sibyl over the matter and at the same time discuss with the Law Officers in Guernsey the opportunity the situation might give of doing away with "the constitutional functions of the Seigneur" – something the Bailiwick had long envisaged.

Back from Guernsey came the astonishing result of Lord Sackville's meetings with Sibyl. He wrote on 14th August:

> She informs me that all she wants is to be able to mortgage Sark in its entirety to her youngest son as she cannot do so by will. He could then foreclose on the property and become Seigneur at her death, I remark that this is what she says, and I can bear no responsibility as to what she may do in the future (!) This being the case can you tell me what is to be done next and how I am to advise her? The youngest son is a minor. Mrs. Beaumont claims that certain portions of Sark such as

Little Sark and the Island of Brecqhou do not form part of the original manor of Sark.

To which Markbreiter replied, somewhat sceptically, on 17th August:

> The proposal to mortgage to her youngest son in order to get round the legal objections to leaving it to him is a novel one, which could not have been deduced from the form of the Petition. We shall probably have to ask you to obtain the opinion of the Law Officers upon the propriety of the expedient.
>
> As regards your final paragraph, I presume that if Mrs. Beaumont's contention were established she would ask to be allowed to sell the outlying portion of her property separately and upon this we would wish to have the Law Officers' opinion.

A further letter from him five days later asked Lord Sackville why Sibyl should want to divert Sark from her eldest to her youngest son and had her eldest son "given his permission"? Further observations from the Law Officers were also needed, he felt, both with regard to her claim that the property on Little Sark and Brecqhou were not part of the Seignory and to her proposals generally.

Discussions with the Law Officers in Guernsey followed and in a letter to the Office of the Lieutenant Governor, dated 27th August, she gave her reason for selling Brecqhou as being her need to "adequately repair" her cottages on Sark itself, which her father had "left in a derelict state". She also wrote:

> ... I wish to explain that I am anxious to be in a position to ensure the succession of my youngest son to the Seignory. My eldest son has his own interests in the Beaumont Estate, entirely in England and does not care for Sark. My second son has disappeared in Australia and I am endeavouring to bring up the youngest, now thirteen years old, to be fitted to the life here in every way ...

In October she added, in a personal note to Major Dugmore, Secretary to the Lieutenant Governor, further reasons for her decision. She was writing from her club in London having just undergone "some exhausting electric treatment" for an unspecified complaint:

> ... I feel if my insides finish me off I'd like to secure my young

son's succession. My eldest son has now chucked the RAF and is looking for a job! and the second has now gone to the New Hebrides. Heaven knows what he will do there. For heaven's sake contradict any rumours about another fiancé! It's not as bad as all that!!! Once bitten twice shy! and I'm not making a habit of it!!! ...

After further discussion and correspondence with the Home Office, Lieutenant Governor and Law Officers, she submitted a slightly reworded petition in December for "a general licence" to mortgage but this, again, was unacceptable. She had not included the name of the proposed mortgagee for approval by the Crown and it was also felt that the mortgage should only be granted on the *whole* island and limited "to such sum as His Majesty thinks fit to decide". And so the matter dragged on into the new year of 1929 with nothing being resolved, complicated even further by her refusal to disclose whether or not she had discussed the matter with Buster. The Home Office officials, however, were given some inkling as to the situation between Sibyl and her eldest son when they received a letter from Buster's solicitor which told of the alterations to Sibyl's marriage settlement agreed between mother and son prior to her "engagement". According to the solicitor, when her proposed marriage did not take place, Buster refused to let her revert to the £1,500 annual allowance (or £300 on re-marriage) she had previously received, and this had caused a "feud" between them.

On learning of this, Markbreiter wrote to Lord Sackville that it would be "most undesirable" if her only object in mortgaging was to serve the purpose of some family feud or disagreement. But it is likely that Sibyl had other reasons for wishing to make Richard (Tuppenny) her mortgagee.

It is certainly true that he was her favourite son but, knowing that money was uppermost in her mind at the time, it is far more probable that, despite what she wrote to Major Dugmore, finance was the main purpose behind her action. As Richard was still a minor, she would have had some access to his share of the family trust, settled upon him and the other children by Dudley. If this "loan" was taken out on his behalf this would have provided her not only with the capital she so badly needed but would also guarantee – if only for the time being – that her position as Dame of Sark would be secure, whereas some other mortgagee might decide to foreclose, take over the island and become Seigneur in her place. She had already made it clear, in one of her letters to Major Dugmore, that she had no intention of considering an "outright sale" to Richard until she knew for sure how he would "turn out".

But the complications entailed in the petition and, indeed, the whole scheme itself, proved too great and she decided to concentrate instead on the sale of two of her properties, which she now believed was possible without permission from the Crown, providing she made grants of them as "tenements". By early March, 1929, she had already sold Brecqhou in this way, transferring with it the tenement rights and consequent seat in Chief Pleas originally assigned to La Moinerie de haut – a property which had belonged to the Seigneurs for over ninety years. She was also making plans to sell other property she owned on Little Sark by the same means.

The swiftness of her action took the Home Office officials by surprise, involved as they still were over the legality of the proposals set out in her previous petition. Their immediate enquiries, however, brought prompt reassurance from Lord Sackville that:

> ... the sale formed no part of her recent petition to be allowed to mortgage the island of Sark and was only countenanced after it had been established by Crown Officers that she had power to dispose of it without consent of the Crown ...

But neither the Office of the Lieutenant Governor nor the Home Office was entirely happy about the situation and it was becoming increasingly clear to all those who had dealings with her that here was, in the words of one official some years later, "a lady of unusual personality" who was making it her business to learn all she could about the complicated, often obscure laws of her island, in order to put them to work in her favour – or even "bend" them in some cases to suit herself. It also became apparent as time went by that far from shrinking from confrontations with these senior officials, she enjoyed pitting her wits against theirs as much as she enjoyed testing her strength with other adversaries on her island or in her private life. For their part, despite their awareness of her sometimes dubious machinations, many of these same officials became lifelong friends, often visiting her on Sark or entertaining her to lunch or dinner when she was in London.

The Sark people, meanwhile, were unaware of all the discussions that had been taking place over the mortgaging of their island. With the exception of those who thought she had treated their vicar unfairly over the matter of his house, most islanders saw only changes for the good beginning to take shape around them and appreciated much of what she was trying to achieve.

Thanks to her publicising Sark's need to mill its own flour and bake its own bread, a Guernsey baker – Hubert Lanyon – was now installed in premises on Seigneurial land at the old mill and the islanders also appeared to be adopting her suggestion that they should grow more of their own produce instead of importing from Guernsey or Jersey. Some took up the invitation made at the time of her accession, that they should seek her advice on any matters that troubled them and those that visited her at the Seigneurie found her to be a kind, dispassionate listener, ready to help where she could. The Sark correspondent of the *Guernsey Press* wrote glowingly in the summer of 1928 of her "personal generosity" and hard work in helping to reintroduce, after a lapse of some years, an island sports day for which she later provided tea at the Seigneurie.

In the autumn the same Guernsey newspaper devoted a full column to the "new beauty" and "charming effect" that the architect, Mr. Stanley Collins, and Sibyl herself had achieved over the renovations to the island's "manor house" which were, according to the reporter:

> essentially derived from Madame Beaumont's own taste and efforts. The skilful, painstaking adaptation of modern comforts to old-world charm is everywhere in evidence. No old beauties have been sacrificed; no new ones obtruded out of place. The antique pieces retain their essential character amid the most luxurious of the new. The old structural features whispering history and mystery, stay in happy harmony with all that has been added. There are rare delights in store for many a future guest of the Dame de Serk, and the Island's own prestige is reflected in the renaissance of its Seigneurie . . .

The Sark people had an opportunity to see this "renaissance" for themselves when, for three successive Sundays in November, the Seigneurie was opened for them to view – with port wine provided, a thoughtful touch on Sibyl's part which was greatly appreciated.

Lord Sackville was the first to experience the "rare delights" of being a guest, for he stayed overnight at the Seigneurie early in November in order to unveil Sark's war memorial – another project in which Sibyl had been closely involved, having presented the piece of land on which it stood. From her days at Ross-on-Wye, Sibyl was known to be an excellent hostess and there is little doubt that she brought the same meticulous care to the arrangements for his visit that she did to other matters in which she was involved.

The year ended with another enthusiastic tribute to her from the Sark correspondent, when the new hall was opened on a site she had also presented to the island as a public gift. "This entitles her once more," he wrote, "to the acknowledgment and esteem of the people." As Sibyl was away in England at the time of the opening, Douce represented her and, much to the delight of those present, bowled the first ball in a skittles match to mark the occasion. She again represented her mother when the hall had its "official" opening the following summer in the presence of the building's donor, Captain E. G. Marden, a former resident.

Douce, Richard and Jehanne were all at home to spend their first family Christmas with Sibyl at the Seigneurie and to see the New Year in together. Nineteen-twenty-eight had brought little in the way of happiness for her and a considerable amount of disillusionment but, characteristically, she now gave every appearance of putting it behind her and looking to the future and her plans for the island. Whether she gave a thought to the previous New Year's Eve – alone with Jimmy in the semi-renovated Seigneurie – is a matter for speculation but, according to her diary, she did think back over the years on at least one occasion during those past twelve months, which indicates that, despite all that had happened since, Dudley was by no means forgotten. On 24th November, the anniversary of his death, she noted – quite simply – "Ten years".

Chapter 8

NOW THAT THE Seigneurie was a comfortable home, Sibyl began to do a great deal of entertaining and, although she kept this from her family, some of her guests helped her to eke out her expenses by paying for their stay. Several men friends visited her during the early months of 1929 and in June Buster and Enid brought Michael to the island for the first time. Although Buster still refused to alter the arrangements over Sibyl's marriage settlement, the pair were no longer estranged. There is no record as to who made the first move towards a reconciliation but it seems probable that the easy-going, warm-hearted Buster would not let the matter go on for long, nor would he be likely to refuse any invitation to stay at the refurbished Seigneurie which, contrary to what Sibyl had told Major Dugmore, he hoped one day to inherit. Soon after Buster's visit, Amice arrived with her young son, Peter, and for many years to come the house was the venue for happy, family holidays.

From the first, Sibyl had made it clear that her grandchildren were to be strictly confined to the nursery – so much so, that in later years one child was heard to remark, looking down from the top of the stairs, that it was "Granny's house down there". Young babies bored her as much as they had always done and she showed little patience, either, for the concern some of the young mothers showed over their infants. "What does it matter if he goes off his feed?" she once remarked to a friend. "These young women nowadays have no *guts*. He'll start eating again sooner or later if she lets him alone. All this hysteria . . ." She nevertheless soon discovered that, since becoming a public figure, people appeared to be as interested in hearing about her family as about herself and the fact that she was a mother and a youthful-looking grandmother was usually taken up by those who interviewed her for the world press. Occasionally, however, their interest in some of her children proved an embarrassment.

One member of her family that she rarely mentioned in these interviews, if she could help it, was Astley. When he had disappeared in Australia in 1924, Sibyl had continued her efforts to trace him through the police and was eventually able to establish that from Sydney he had sailed to Vancouver, but it was not until two years later that she heard, through her London solicitor, that he had returned to Australia. The solicitor had received a letter from him saying that he had been ill with a heart condition but had married and was earning a living quite successfully. In reply the solicitor told him of the death of his grandfather Beaumont and that, as he was now twenty-one, he was entitled to a share in the estate once affairs were settled. Later investigations showed, however, that Astley had already been borrowing money for some time against this very eventuality and, despite warnings, continued to do so. During 1928 – when Sibyl had enough worries of her own – there had been a great deal of correspondence between solicitors in Sydney and London over various difficulties in which Astley had by then found himself and cables arrived from him several times during the year, asking for money to be sent out to settle various debts. It appeared that he had lost his job, owing to illness, and had been living on money obtained from money-lenders – first by mortgaging his interests on his grandfather's estate and then from the sale of his interests on his father's estate which would only revert to him on Sibyl's death. By late 1928 he had found himself in prison over a hire-purchase arrangement on a car and had only been released after Sibyl had arranged for his debts to be paid. She also bought back the reversionary interests he had sold to the money-lenders for some £1,700 – a sum which at that time she could ill-afford – and with the use of the small additional capital she thus acquired had been sending her errant son a small weekly allowance to try to prevent him from once again getting into the hands of the money-lenders. She continued to pay this until the autumn of 1929, by which time she decided to try to enlist the help of other members of the family.

She saw her solicitor about this in early September when she made a brief visit to England with a party of friends to see the Schneider Cup Air Race from aboard the *Orantes* in Southampton Water. She also took the opportunity of visiting Richard at Bradfield College – the Berkshire school at which he had been a pupil for the past year – and of seeing Buster and Enid who were now settled at their new home at Weybridge in Surrey. Buster had left the RAF after trouble with his eyes whilst in Egypt. When there had been no improvement after six months' sick leave in England, he had been told that he would have to be grounded. The idea of being in the RAF and not flying was not to his liking for he was a fine pilot and, very regretfully, he had decided to leave the service and start a business career, using the Beaumont family money he had inherited to form a small company.

Sibyl returned to Sark for only a few days after this visit for she had been persuaded by one of her friends, Mrs. Lily Speke, to accompany her to New York for a short holiday at her expense. Although the Michaelmas meeting of Chief Pleas came in the middle of the proposed visit, Sibyl thought this opportunity of seeing America too good to miss and she hurriedly made her preparations. Another old acquaintance, Mona Linton, arranged an introduction in London, two days before she sailed, to "a charming, amusing American" – Robert Hathaway. "You will like him," she said to Sibyl, "and he will be able to give you an introduction to his family in New York."

This first meeting with Bob Hathaway was a great success. They lunched together at the Piccadilly Hotel and Sibyl was instantly attracted to this lean, bespectacled man whose sense of humour more than matched her own and she was at her sparkling best. He, in turn, appeared so captivated by her that he insisted on sending long, enthusiastic cables about her imminent visit to his family in New York and, when she arrived on board the liner, she discovered that he had arranged for her cabin to be filled with flowers. Almost every day while at sea he sent her a wireless message and one of these informed her that his eldest brother, Stewart, and his sister-in-law, Helen, would meet her when the *Olympic* docked in New York. They were there as arranged and, according to Sibyl afterwards, "overwhelmed" her with kindness from that moment on.

Her four crowded days in the city convinced her that she would like to return – so hospitable did she find everyone – though she often spoke afterwards, with amusement, of the prohibition laws in force at the time. She had always been used to a cheap and plentiful supply of alcohol on Sark and was surprised by the number of speak-easies she encountered and the secret hoards of whisky in the various offices she visited between dinner and the theatre. She stayed at the Biltmore Hotel and on the first night shocked a waiter by smoking a cigarette in the lounge – something "lady" guests did not do, he had told her, a trifle coolly. According to her own account of the episode, his manner indicated that "only ladies of joy loitering for no good purpose" would consider doing such a thing and she had stubbed out the offending article with annoyance, restraining herself with difficulty from giving him a "sharp reproof". During her visit she went to the theatre with the Hathaways to see Oscar Hammerstein's *Sweet Adeline*, saw most of the city sights, including Wall Street, and was invited to the offices of the *New York Sun.*

The American press found her an intriguing personality – one journalist referring to her as the "Queen of the 'Pearl in the Silver Sea'" – and with her penchant for making full use of any opportunity to publicise both herself and her island, she provided vivid and highly-dramatised versions of her rôle on Sark. One journal quoted her as saying that life on the island was "sweet and pastoral". There were no poor and no rich: "... everybody seems happy and satisfied. The people refer almost every possible problem or perplexity to me for a solution. I love it ..." Another referred to the twentieth part of a knight's fee she paid to the King of England for the privilege of her title and it appealed to Sibyl's sense of humour when this was misquoted as "half a *night's* fee".

She was surprised, and rather flattered, when Bob Hathaway sent more messages to her on the homeward journey, one of which asked her to dine with him at the Berkeley Hotel on her return to London. That evening of 18th October, 1929, proved to be memorable for them both. In her own words:

> ... Before the end of dinner that night it had become clear that this tall, lean Yankee was not only an entertaining companion but a very determined man. I am a strong-minded woman, but this time I had met my match ...

Although at no time had she been short of male admirers, after the affair with Jimmy James she had not unnaturally been hesitant about letting herself become seriously involved with any man, but Bob's persistence and the introductions to his family – whom she had liked immensely – quelled any misgivings she may have had. After spending as much time with each other as possible throughout every day of the following week, she took Bob to meet Richard at Bradfield and the next day introduced him to Buster, Amice and Douce, who happened to be staying with Amice at Farnborough. The family were delighted, if at first a little stunned, when she told them that she had decided to marry this impetuous, charming American and that the engagement would be announced within a few days. In fact some of the weekly journals only wrote of the engagement of that "very popular and delightful woman" after her wedding had actually taken place, for the pair were married in London – at Holy Trinity Church, St. Marylebone – on 5th November, less than a week after the first announcements had been made. Some thirty relations and friends were present at the ceremony, which Sibyl insisted should be just a "quiet family affair". Buster gave his mother away and Douce was in attendance. According to the newspaper reports, Sibyl looked "very attractive" in a "blue crêpe de chine dress with a tweed coat of flecked blue and white, collared with oppossum and a blue felt hat". Small wonder that the whole affair – five weeks in all from their first lunch-time meeting – was inevitably referred to by most of the reporters as a "whirlwind courtship".

Sibyl was now forty-five years old – Bob some three years younger. If he and Dudley had ever met it is doubtful whether they would have found anything in common. Bob was not in the least artistic and his culture, not unnaturally, was more of the new world than of the old. He was a keen sportsman, being a first-class golfer and tennis player and usually enjoyed gregarious living with an ample supply of gin – one of the reasons, he jokingly told Sibyl, that had made him decide to leave America on the introduction of prohibition. He had been born in East Orange, New Jersey, and was one of three sons of a Wall Street banker whose family interest was in publishing. He had graduated from Yale in 1913, worked for a time as a film projectionist and on the outbreak of war had, on an impulse, signed on with some university friends at the New York recruiting office of the British Royal Flying Corps, giving his nationality as Canadian. He was sent to England as a flying instructor after training in Toronto and remained there for the rest of the war. After a brief spell back in America he returned to England to work with the London branch of the sports firm, Spaldings – a job which, according to him, he only took because it provided him with free golf balls – and he became a naturalised British subject. He now appeared to be quite prepared to give up his job, his comfortable bachelor life in London and his golf (there being no room on Sark for a course) to become Sibyl's "consort" – as one journal described him – and live on the small island he had never seen. He was unprepared, however, for the extent of Sark's welcome to the honeymoon couple.

Sibyl had been pointing out some of the beauty spots to him as the small steamer from Guernsey sailed in under the rugged cliffs when she noticed with delight that a number of flags were flying from the houses above. Passing the lighthouse at Point Robert, they were startled by a "feu de joie" from several sporting rifles and as they entered the small harbour, waiting for them with her youngest daughter, Jehanne, were most of Sark's leading officials and as many islanders as could crowd themselves on the quay. The tenor bell of St. Peter's Church rang out a welcome and handkerchiefs were waved from every doorway as Charlie Perrée – Sark's mailman, coalman, lighthouse supply man and general carrier – proudly took Sibyl and Bob in his best carriage along the tree-lined roads to the Seigneurie and another welcome from the staff there. Later the couple, in the traditional island way, took wine and cake to every house.

But Bob's greatest surprise came later when Sibyl told him that by his marriage he had become Seigneur of Sark "in right of his wife" – a fact which she had confirmed with Guernsey historian, Edith Carey, her friend and adviser on many matters dealing with island law. The situation is explained in a letter on the subject some years later from H. A. Le Patourel, the Attorney-General in Guernsey, to Martin Jones at the Home Office:

> ... Under Sark law, such as it is, Mrs. Hathaway by her marriage incurred a drastic modification of status, there being nothing in the nature of a Married Women's Property Act there.
>
> Her husband, by the marriage, acquired in law the control and administration of her real estate and absolute rights over her personal estate. A pre-nuptial contract or settlement, if it exists, may have modified the situation as regards the personal estate but it is somewhat doubtful to what extent it could have done so in respect of the real estate. At all events we regard Mr. Hathaway as now the Seigneur in right of his wife, and thus vested in the rights and committed to the duties attaching to that position, and I do not think Mrs. Hathaway herself has ever contested the point.
>
> In fact, and unofficially, her status as Dame of Sark is still conceded to her but, officially, she disappears.

Sibyl had made it clear from the beginning that she had no intention of "disappearing" from island affairs. It is, perhaps, a measure of both personalities that from then on the Hathaways generally sat side by side at Chief Pleas meetings, with Bob as the figurehead and official spokesman but with Sibyl very definitely in control, explaining any point he did not understand, translating French when it was used, advising him on how to vote and continuing all the while to air her own views – albeit illegally according to Sark law, which prevented married women from appearing in the Court of Chief Pleas or having a "voice". The press and those outside the island continued to refer to her as the "ruler" of her domain and she, and Bob, were happy to leave it that way, though in later years this situation was to give rise to some dissatisfaction among islanders and government officials alike.

The speed of her remarriage had caught the Sark people unawares and it was not until early the following year that she and Bob were presented with their official wedding gift – a cheque towards a pair of wrought-iron gates which were to be erected at the entrance to the Seigneurie grounds, with a suitable plaque to commemorate the event. The Seneschal, Frederick de Carteret, in presenting the gift to Sibyl at the new recreation hall, said that since her father's death she had "identified herself with everything essential to the welfare of the island". Certainly during the previous twelve months, despite her travels outside Sark, she had given evidence of her involvement.

Many in the hall remembered how last winter with Ethel Cheesewright, a local artist friend, she had taken turns for several days and nights to nurse a sick lighthouse keeper, critically ill with meningitis, until he could be removed to hospital in Guernsey. As the lighthouse was situated halfway down a bleak cliff, reached by a flight of about sixty granite steps, her journeys to and fro during those foggy days were difficult enough, let alone the rigours of nursing such a case in a confined space. Sibyl never forgot her first sight of the poor fellow. She wrote, years later, that she had found him:

> . . . curled up on one side, facing the wall. His head was retracted in a horribly rigid fashion and he was already mildly delirious, muttering to himself . . . The slightest sound or touch made our patient twitch convulsively and we knew that the noise of the siren would provide unthinkable torture. There was nothing to do but watch and wait for the dawn . . .

The man, Rippon, recovered and soon let it be known how grateful he was for the ministrations of Sibyl and Miss Cheesewright who had undoubtedly helped to save his life.

It was actions like these and her obvious interest in island activities – whether by raising funds for the hall, opening the first public hard tennis court (on which she played the first ball) or her keen application to matters before Chief Pleas – that helped her to create a good impression upon most on Sark. But, naturally enough in such a small community, she still had her critics who were more apt to remember her shortcomings than her successes. On that happy occasion in the hall, however, everybody looked kindly upon Sibyl and her new husband and as she gave thanks for their wedding present she received their cheers when she said that she felt sure the future would see both her family and the Sark people "working together for the common good".

The next few years seemed, if only on the surface, to prove her words and were, on the whole, happy for Sibyl. There was no mistaking Bob's love for his wife nor his pride at being her husband and he began to show a great interest in island affairs. When his widowed mother came to stay at the Seigneurie during the summer of 1930 he proudly showed her around and this energetic old lady thoroughly enjoyed her carriage rides with him, absorbing all that she saw and heard. When she finally returned home to the States, after making what even Sibyl termed "a hectic visit" to the Continent with her son and new daughter-in-law, she carried back with her a fund of stories about the beauties and delights of Sark and the resultant publicity in the American press led to many tourists from across the Atlantic coming to see the island with its "American Seigneur".

Meanwhile some of the "English" residents who wintered abroad and returned to their Sark houses each spring, were beginning to take a fresh interest in the social life of the island – particularly as Sibyl had started to give an annual "At Home" during the summer months, when she usually had her own large family house-party at the Seigneurie. The Sark people themselves were not normally included among the guests on these occasions – few expected to be – but the fact that Sibyl seemed to entertain only the "English" and not even the Sark-born officials at her social gatherings was to rankle in some quarters, particularly as she liked to refer to the whole community as "one big family". She continued to let it be known, however, that the Sarkese were always welcome to approach her at the Seigneurie with their problems and those who took her up on this invariably received a sympathetic hearing. Nevertheless as time went on what some saw as her apparent favouring of the English residents only served to widen the gap between the two distinct factions that existed on the island.

Outside the Seigneurie she encouraged her family to take as much interest in the Sarkese as she tried to do herself and Douce, especially, seemed to go out of her way to gain the islanders' goodwill. During the early 'thirties she joined wholeheartedly in many of their social gatherings, drinking with them in the bars and organising annual entertainments and dances in aid of the British Legion, the horse parade or for the upkeep of the new hall, of which she soon became a committee member. The reintroduction of the annual horse show had been her idea. With so many horses on Sark and being a good rider herself, she had suggested that one way of making sure their owners would keep them in fine fettle throughout the winter months would be to have a parade for them in the spring at the start of the carriage season. This proved very successful and continued as an annual event from then on. Her good looks and charm, as always, won her many admirers and on several occasions her enthusiasm and that of her mother persuaded some of the guests staying at the Seigneurie to take part in one or another of the fund-raising activities in which they were both concerned. An example of this was the successful entertainment she organised in the spring of 1930 in aid of the horse show parade, for which Sibyl produced four short plays – recruiting her cast from among those at the Seigneurie and a couple of the English residents. It turned out to be a spirited family affair in which even the eleven-year-old Jehanne took part. Sibyl, whose love of theatricals had not diminished over the years, was in her element and gave herself two parts – as a prima donna, in which she appeared with Bob, Douce, Richard and others in a state of dishabille outside "a mysteriously locked hotel bathroom door", and as a passenger on the SS *Riduna* crossing in bad weather from Guernsey to Sark. The following year Buster also took part in a similar family entertainment organised by Douce and showed some of his home movies taken in and around the island. But after that it was to be some time before his sister was to organise any more fund-raising activities on Sark.

In the August of that same year of 1931, Douce was presented with a travelling clock by islanders, in recognition of her work for the British Legion, and she had no reason to doubt the promise she gave then that, after a projected journey to India later in the year, she would be back to help run more dances for them in 1932. Instead, within a few months, she was married and had left the island in circumstances that brought about a temporary estrangement between herself and her mother. That summer – by no means for the first time – she had become involved with a young Englishman holidaying on the island and by the early autumn discovered that she had become pregnant. An outraged Sibyl had immediately arranged a marriage in England between twenty-one-year-old Douce and the father of the expected child refusing, however, to attend the wedding herself. It was not that she had been unaware of Douce's behaviour over the years. She had left all her children to lead their own lives in their own way. But that it should now inevitably be made known both in and outside the island and involve Sibyl herself in a certain loss of prestige as a result, was difficult for her to accept. The whole affair caused strong feelings between mother and daughter and Douce's later actions by no means helped to mend the breach.

After her departure from the island, it was left to Jehanne and Richard to deputise occasionally for their mother at some of the Sark events during school holidays and to help at the annual Cattle and Horse Shows or with the Sports Day at the Seigneurie. Richard also donated a cup to be competed for annually by the newly-formed Junior Football Club in which both he and his mother showed great interest and he usually made a point of watching the matches when he was home. All comings and goings at the Seigneurie and the household's participation in island affairs continued to be noted weekly by the Sark correspondent of the Guernsey newspapers and these columns helped to create the impression that Sark was, as Sibyl so often claimed, a happy "family" unit, presided over and cared for by herself – its matriarchal head.

Chapter 9

Ghost stories connected with pirates and monks have always abounded on Sark but more circulated after a woman visitor early in 1930 claimed to have encountered a Dominican friar near the Seigneurie, who incanted a Latin text and then disappeared. Sibyl mischievously encouraged the suggestion made later that the "monk" had returned to protest at the demolition of some of his old priory buildings during the renovation work on her house. In fact she knew all along that the original "apparition" was a practical joke perpetrated by Douce just before her departure from the island, and a friend, John Campbell. Nanny Bishop's old grey cloak had been borrowed to clothe the "friar" and his incantations had been nothing more than the repeating backwards of his Latin school grace as he carried a copy of *Winnie the Pooh*. Sibyl enjoyed the whole escapade – and the ensuing publicity – as much as everyone else at the Seigneurie and when visiting journalists arrived to follow up the story, seized the opportunity to pass on several more of her own, including some of the island tales of witchcraft and superstition. These soon found their way into newspapers and magazines in many parts of the world and she repeated many of these stories again in an article she herself wrote about Sark for the *National Geographic Magazine* in the summer of 1932. She did not reveal, however, two of her own personal superstitions which dogged her throughout life. She was convinced that if she wore green it would bring her bad luck, and her seemingly irrational fears over crossing that narrow strip of water between Guernsey and Sark were due, she confided to close friends, to her belief that – after both her grandfather and father had been involved in shipwrecks upon it – she, as third in line, would be the one the sea would claim.

To her joy, she was spared this crossing just before Christmas, 1932, when she flew from Guernsey to Sark in Puss Moth GABVX, thus becoming, she proudly told reporters, the first woman to land on the island by aeroplane. Only a few months earlier, amidst great publicity and excitement, the very first flight had been made to Sark by Lord Sempill. Since her Cologne days, Sibyl had claimed a special affection for airmen and aeroplanes and had been delighted when Lord Sempill had telephoned on that August morning to ask if he and his passenger, writer James Wentworth Day, might land in a field near her Seigneurie to lunch with her on their way through to Jersey. She had promptly agreed and supervised all the preparations for the landing – seeing to it that nearby telephone wires were covered with sheets and a smudge fire built in readiness. On several occasions after that she had the opportunity to accompany Lord Sempill on short flights around England and later in the year eagerly accepted an invitation to a dinner at the Royal Aeronautical College at which he introduced her to several other famous airmen of the day. The following summer he again flew to the island to pick up a ten-day-old calf she had given him for his herd. After several other landings by young airmen during the next few years, Sibyl and Bob considered a regular service, but when the suggestion came up for discussion before Chief Pleas both agreed with the majority decision – that such traffic would not only be impracticable but would almost certainly change the peaceful image of the island.*

In the summer of 1933 in an editorial dealing with the considerable publicity the "miniature state" had been receiving in America – the result of several interviews with Sibyl – a Guernsey newspaper commented, a trifle sourly, that generally Sark's news was of an "unexciting nature". But at the beginning of October it reported:

> Sark, the Island Where Nothing Ever Happens is still right in the news! Sark, the Serene and Unperturbed has been thrilled with the strangest riddle its inhabitants have had to face in the present century . . .

For two days running a local fisherman had seen a bundle of clothes on the rocks at Port Gorey, a small bay in Little Sark. The Constable had made enquiries at local hotels and boarding houses but no one had been reported missing, nor had anyone since claimed the garments. A thorough search was made of the surrounding caves and bays but without success. By chance, a guest staying at the Seigneurie remembered seeing an "unhappy-looking" couple on the boat from Guernsey to Sark who were wearing clothing similar to that found and was able to make a

* Some twenty years later she flew from Guernsey to Sark by helicopter with a view to introducing this form of air traffic but again had second thoughts when she discovered that such craft were not suitable for landing in all weathers.

positive identification of the garments and help the police in Guernsey who had now taken over the case. At this stage the national press descended on the island and Sibyl once again enjoyed their attentions as, this time, she played detective. When a woman's body with appalling head injuries was washed up in a cave some days later, there was great speculation as to whether she had been a murder victim, but Sibyl thought not and was widely quoted as saying that it would have been impossible for the man concerned to have left the island without being seen. While efforts were being made to identify the body, Sibyl twice had to forbid the funeral on instructions from the police and this prompted further publicity for her with such headlines as "She holds up her lily-white hand and stops a burial". When the interment was finally allowed to take place, she sent a wreath and many of the islanders turned out to see the mysterious woman buried in Sark churchyard. Three days later, however, a man's body was washed ashore, thus proving the local fisherman's theory upon which Sibyl had based her own conclusions: that if the couple had been drowned near to where their clothes had been found, their bodies would circle the rocks before rising to the surface some days later – the woman's first. Sibyl had maintained all along that it had not been a case of murder but a suicide pact and her opinion was supported by the subsequent inquests.

News of a more cultural nature from Sark was provided that same year by the opening of an art gallery during the summer and the formation of a small "Sark Group of Artists". Sibyl was asked to perform the official opening and in doing so said that she welcomed the opportunity it gave of providing the artists living on the island with a means of showing their work. Those like Ethel Cheesewright and William Toplis, who had made Sark their home for some time, were already well known but there were several younger artists exhibiting who had only recently arrived and she wished them equal success with their work. Among these was a young man of twenty-two, Mervyn Peake, whose paintings made a great impact at the exhibition and were later to gain even more acclaim for him elsewhere. It is doubtful, however, if Sibyl was aware of this young man's potential, or of any other talent displayed at the gallery for neither she nor Bob was ever particularly interested in the work shown – nor, indeed, in the cultural arts generally. Although she initially gave the venture as much support as she gave other activities on Sark, she was really – according to one close friend – "only interested in the work of artists or writers when they became famous". She had a good eye for colour, chose her clothes and house furnishings with taste and skill and displayed a talent for embroidery, but paintings, music and the literary world meant little to her. Far more exciting for her was her first radio broadcast in October, 1934.

She was on one of her visits to London and, as such, was "one of the interesting people . . . IN TOWN TONIGHT" – in the words of the announcer's introduction to the popular BBC Saturday night programme of that time. She spoke of the peace of Sark, where there were only "the sounds of the sea or the cries of the seabirds", and she compared the island with the "glare of flood-lights and noise of motorcars and trams on the mainland". After talking of the happiness of "being a landowner in a place where there is no income tax", she finished the broadcast with a message to her people in patois – the first ever to be heard on the air – which greatly pleased those Sarkese who gathered to listen. On this same visit to London she also divulged her plans for a project which she thought might prove interesting both for herself and the island.

Baroness von Hutten, a friend then living on Sark, had suggested that a historical story with the island as its setting would make a good subject for a film and, fired by her friend's enthusiasm, Sibyl had started to make a few notes for the story. A *Sunday Express* article told of her "negotiations with British producers" over the idea and she was quoted as saying that she "would not have a picture made by Hollywood for a million pounds". It was to be "a story of our own islands and has to be made over here". She hoped to do for Sark "what Robert Flaherty has done for the Isle of Aran in his recent picture [*Man of Aran*]". But the writing took a great deal longer than she anticipated and it was only after a French friend, Pierre Pannier, had helped her to put into shape her story of "love and adventure set in sixteenth century Sark", that the script became a reality. It was all but complete when the New York publishers, D. Appleton-Century, with whom Bob's family were involved, made Sibyl an offer for it, on condition that the script was translated from its original French. Bob's niece, Cynthia Hathaway, agreed to do this for Sibyl and, although the story was never filmed, in 1939 it finally appeared in book form under the title *Maid of Sark*, illustrated by reproductions of paintings of the island alleged to have been executed by Turner.*

Meanwhile Buster, who had always been interested in films and

* After Sibyl's death these were not positively established as having been painted by the artist, although the style is similar and he is believed to have visited the island.

had now formed his own company, had been on location in Sark in the late summer of 1936 to make a screen version of Victor Hugo's *Toilers of the Sea.* A small fishermen's village was built at Creux Harbour, an old drifter was converted into the paddle-boat *Durande* and an attractive young actress, Mary Lawson, with Clifford McLaglen (one of two famous actor brothers) headed the cast. Although some objected strongly to the buildings erected at the harbour, most people, including those who were taken on as extras, enjoyed having the film made on the island – and Sibyl, as always, welcomed the resultant publicity. When filming was completed, several members of the company took part in a charity entertainment at the hall, the main item of which was a play, *Murder in the Island,* written by Selwyn Jepson, one of the directors. Sibyl was the producer and cast herself – much to everyone else's amusement – as "the dreadful old mother" who was "a prime mover in the murder schemes". Douce, who was on her first visit to the island for some years, was the "vain, film-struck daughter", Jehanne – the "little girl, Elsie" – and other parts were played by guests at the Seigneurie.

That year of 1936 turned out to be quite eventful for Sibyl. She had already travelled to Burma in the spring to bring home her old friend, Gladys Richardson, who had been taken ill in Rangoon and had wired for Sibyl to join her. As always on her journeys overseas, Sibyl had made the most of the occasion and in Colombo, where she stayed for only a few days in transit, her arrival and departure were noted and a piece about her and Sark had appeared in the *Ceylon News.*

She returned to London with Gladys early in July – in time to present Jehanne to the new King Edward VIII at a Royal garden party at Buckingham Palace, before going home to Sark to pick up the "season" there – very much enlivened for her later by the arrival of Buster's film company. This Royal garden party was the second of only two held by King Edward VIII and the forerunner of many other such afternoon "Courts". Sibyl, always a traditionalist, regretted the passing of the brilliant evening Court occasions she had known in the past. Only the year before, she and Bob had taken part in the island's jubilee celebrations to mark the twenty-fifth year of the reign of the King's father, George V – when Bob had worn his Royal Flying Corps uniform and she her Red Cross nurse's cap and apron and, on horseback, had led the procession which preceded the festivities. The new King had been a much-loved Prince of Wales then and Sibyl had arranged for some of the Sark children to go over to Guernsey to see him when he made an official visit to the Channel Islands that summer. Bob, Sibyl and island officials were also presented to him at a reception in Guernsey and during this same visit she received from the Prince the King's Cup for the best bull on Sark at the Guernsey Farmers' Show. She now had great hopes that his next official visit to the Channel Islands, as King, might also include Sark, for Sibyl had a great respect for the monarchy and all that it stood for.

In November the Hathaways crossed the Atlantic on the *Queen Mary* to visit Bob's relations for the first time since his marriage. From their arrival in New York to their return on the *Berengaria* nine weeks later, Sibyl and Bob were overwhelmed by invitations which took them to so many different places in so short a time that one Californian newspaper was moved to remark that they had covered the countryside "in a way to make even the natives gape in amazement". As always, they received publicity wherever they went – curiosity having been aroused beforehand by several articles about them, including an international *Believe it or Not* by Ripley, who had visited Sark the previous year in order to feature Sibyl and her island in his series.

Dictators were very much in the news at this time and one New York journal described her as:

> ... more powerful than Mussolini or Hitler as far as Sark goes ... But Mrs. Hathaway is far from being a dictator. Frocked in a chic black cloth tailored suit and a white crêpe blouse, with a silver fox scarf about her throat and a small, very Parisian, black felt hat on her smartly-dressed grey hair, she looked more like a lady from Park Avenue than the ruler of a windswept Channel Island ...

Between her many social engagements during her brief stay in New York, Sibyl managed to fit in a broadcast on NBC and a lecture engagement, to accompany Bob to two Yale football games – against Princeton and Harvard – and even some sightseeing. She said later that she found the air of the city "so vitalising" that she never felt tired there but found the "extremes of wealth and poverty appallingly evident".

After a few days in Washington and a luncheon with the British ambassador, the couple flew to Los Angeles but had to spend the night in a hangar at Columbus, Ohio, during a snowstorm. A tour of California followed, taking in, among other places, San Francisco, Pasadena, Palm Springs, Death Valley and Hollywood, before going on by air through Fort Worth, Dallas, Atlanta and Spartanburg to stay with Bob's old Yale university friend, Maurice (Lefty) Flynn, at Tryon in North Carolina – where they were to meet for the first time a young British film actor, David Niven.

Bob and Sibyl had been lunching at a restaurant in Los Angeles when they heard a radio announcement that King Edward VIII had abdicated and according to Sibyl's account afterwards, a well-known actress sitting next to Bob had spoken of the King's "wonderful sacrifice for love" as she dabbed her eyes with a handkerchief. Sibyl could barely refrain from telling the star to save her "celluloid emotions and glycerine tears for a Hollywood epic", for she had "just heard one man sacrifice the loyalty of millions". Adolph Zukor had made a similar comment to that of the actress when the Hathaways visited him later at the Paramount Studios in Hollywood and Bob – who had as great a respect for the monarchy and as strong a sense of duty as Sibyl – startled the film-maker by rapping his fist smartly on the desk and asking him how he would feel if his highest paid artist "walked out without a scruple" in the middle of his most costly production.

Christmas found the Hathaways back in New York attending a reception in their honour at the English Speaking Union and involved in another hectic round of social engagements before boarding the *Berengaria* early in the New Year for their homeward journey. Bob went straight to Sark from Southampton but Sibyl spent a few days in London and Guernsey "recuperating", before travelling home for another busy year which was to include celebrations for the coronation of the new King George VI early in May.

Sark people had a natural gift for celebrating an occasion and that Coronation Day of 1937 was no exception but there was some indignation when it was suggested shortly afterwards at the Bailiff's Court in Guernsey that Sark should introduce a "Black List", as drunkenness was very prevalent among its younger people. When Sibyl was approached by the press on this she said that some of the twenty thousand visitors that annually came to the island set a bad example. She knew that there was some drunkenness but it was generally limited to "only a few of the young people" for the average Sark man was "hard-working and well behaved". She had nevertheless tried to introduce a Black List two years earlier but her suggestion had been turned down by Chief Pleas. Her further attempt later in the year was also rejected.

It was not so much for the older generation of Sark people that Sibyl wished to introduce such a list. She knew that – like Bob and herself – most were quite capable of occasional hard drinking, on an island where liquor was always cheap and plentiful, but she genuinely wanted to protect the younger members of the community who, with Sark's increasing prosperity, had more money and time for leisure than their elders had enjoyed previously – and therefore more opportunity, she thought, for over-indulgence.

She was already seeing an example of this within her own family, for Douce had for some years been drinking to excess to the detriment of her own life and the unhappiness of those around her. She had left her husband some years before, and it was largely due to Sibyl that arrangements had been made for their baby girl to be taken to the home of the father's parents where she was to grow up happily in Nanny Bishop's charge. After divorce and a series of lovers, Douce had now remarried and for the moment seemed reasonably content, though her drinking habits had not changed. This time Sibyl approved sufficiently of her daughter's choice to attend the wedding in London and now had hopes that with a happy marriage her still beautiful daughter might at last settle down. But Douce was not the only member of the family to be a source of some anxiety at this time.

Richard's escapades since he left school had frequently involved his mother in discussions with the family solicitor and in unfortunate publicity both at home and overseas. Bob had lost patience with his wife's continued attempts to help her favourite child and from the outset of their marriage had made it clear that he had little time for his youngest stepson, so after a while she took to assisting him without Bob's knowledge. The relationship between the two men had not improved over the years and Richard had not visited the island since his twenty-first birthday party in September, 1936.

By 1938, Buster was also estranged from the family. He had left his wife and two young sons and in the late June of that year, after his divorce had been made absolute, had married Mary Lawson – the actress he had first met during the making of "Toilers of the Sea". The film – as with most of the ventures Buster undertook – ran into financial difficulties before it could be completed and his affairs, generally, were in a bad way. It had not taken him long to discover that the Beaumont Trust was by no means inexhaustible – and the breakdown of his first marriage had been partly due to the financial worries he had caused his wife, Enid, from their earliest years together. Sibyl had heartaches enough over her children, but Buster's remarriage was also creating problems as far as Sark was concerned, for divorce was not recognised on the island and he was, after all, her heir apparent. On hearing that divorce proceedings were being started Sibyl had made a special visit to London to try to bring about a reconciliation between Enid and Buster, but matters had already gone too far. There is evidence that she then sought to avoid what might have developed into a tricky situation by this time considering selling or mortgaging the island to Amice, so that there would be no possibility of it eventually passing to Buster, but she encountered the same difficulties as before and the matter was not pursued.

Sark, too, was going through an unsettled period. Outwardly it was becoming increasingly more prosperous and Sibyl liked to think that this was due in no small way to her own efforts on its behalf but she was well aware, also, of certain dissatisfied factions among the island people. The situation then prevailing is aptly described by Alan and Mary Seaton Wood in their book *Islands in Danger*:

> ... Like many another strong personality she [Sibyl] aroused violent antagonism as well as loyal admiration. The six hundred inhabitants of this tiny island were all feuding between themselves with the bitter feeling which only small communities know. These two main camps were sub-divided in turn by subsidiary feuds and counter feuds, the members of each faction being ready to tell the most scandalous tales concerning the other ...

Arguments were still taking place over the new deep-water harbour, the construction of which, by the spring of 1938, was about to start after numerous suggestions and plans had been rejected by Chief Pleas. A jetty was to be built off a concrete foundation on the seabed at Maseline Bay, north-east of the original Creux Harbour. A new tunnel approach road would be required and the cost of the whole scheme was expected to be in the region of £45,000 – a heavy charge on the small island but one which Sibyl and the other members of the harbour committee hoped would be offset by the additional accommodation it would provide. Larger steamers would soon be able to land passengers direct in all weathers, instead of having to transfer them to small boats and this, Sibyl felt, would inevitably lead to more tourists being attracted to the island. The poll tax had for some time been put aside to help defray some of the costs and the harbour committee were anxious for work to be started, despite the continuing assertion by some fishermen and others that the jetty was being built in the wrong place and would still not provide the all-weather and all-tide landings that were claimed for it.

A *Sunday Dispatch* article in June put forward other reasons for disquiet. Headed "Sark is scared", it reported that some residents thought the new scheme would not just bring revenue to the island. A bigger harbour would mean, they thought, "bigger boats and cheaper people – the tripper – and Sark had always tried to avoid this type of visitor". The islanders, according to the article, foresaw an unwanted change and the regular visitors were also objecting:

> ... So quaint is the present tiny harbour, peaceful in the hollow of steep, frowning cliffs, that the yearly visitors, artists and writers, cheerfully pay the Sark boatmen the demanded sixpence for the privilege of being landed on the island from a rowing boat...

Sibyl scoffed at what she termed this "romantic nonsense" but the wrangling continued and, as so often happened, she became the scapegoat for much of the dissatisfaction.

She was also conscious at this time that there were some who were far from happy over the way she had been dealing with other Sark matters for which she bore more personal responsibility. Chief among these was that of the Church and its incumbent. Even before Mr. Greenhow had left to take up another living in Guernsey, early in 1932, she had let it be known that she was determined to try once more to regain possession of Le Manoir, despite this house having been the residence of the vicar for some two hundred years. She also proposed to take the opportunity of withdrawing or at least reducing her share of the new incumbent's stipend – some £100 a year – and free herself from other Seigneurial obligations to the Church. As the Seigneurs of the island had up to this time been the patrons of the living, there followed much discussion between the ecclesiastical authorities, the Home Office and officials in Guernsey and Sark as to the legality of her proposals. A letter from the Office of the Lieutenant Governor in Guernsey to the Home Office in January, 1932, observed:

> ... As far as I can ascertain there is no obligation on the part of the Seigneur to appoint a parson at all! The first vicar, if he could be called such, was really a private chaplain to the Seigneur who perhaps had the spiritual welfare of the islanders more at heart than the one now reigning! ... I cannot even be certain as to whom the church belongs!! Apparently it is divided into parts each of which belongs to a different individual ... The present arrangements are not satisfactory and it is a pity that they cannot be put on a proper footing, but what steps could be taken to effect this I do not know ...

Sibyl wrote to the Bishop of Winchester shortly afterwards:

> ... As regards any moral liability, it should not be overlooked that the Seigneurs have been very generous always, my grandfather built the chancel and gave a cemetery and my father during his years as Seigneur actually paid over £4,500 and gave a house free, also land for a new cemetery and I have already paid nearly £500 and given the use of the house ...

She was nevertheless prepared, she told him, to offer a "valuable" site and the stone for a house but thought the time had come for the churchgoers themselves to help for they had not contributed "one farthing to the upkeep of their church or their minister for years – either by pew rent or otherwise".

By the Church Contract of 1823, Sark tenants were supposed to rent their pews for an annual payment of fivepence a sitting which, together with an additional twenty shillings a year provided by the Seigneur, constituted a repair fund for the church. Anything required in excess of that amount was to be shared equally between the pew-owners and the Seigneur. Sibyl maintained that these fivepences had not been paid for thirty-four years and she also wanted to be released from her responsibility for both the annual twenty shillings and half cost of repairs. But the conservative islanders were not prepared to agree to any scheme which relieved their Seigneur of his responsibilities and the question of where the money should come from rumbled acrimoniously but inconclusively on for some time. A Home Office report gave one view of the position in the late autumn of 1933:

> ... The tenants think La Dame is wealthy (this is not so) and that she would pay for the repairs. The islanders are very obstinate and ignorant and La Dame, who is a clever woman and is anxious to do all she can for the island within her means

has not so much influence with the tenants as her father had. The Seigneur, Mr. Hathaway, is completely under the influence of his wife and being an American is not very popular though he too is anxious to help . . .

By the spring of 1934 one Sark faction, backed by the Medical Officer, Dr. Pittard, who was head of the church council, thought that the best course was to bring influence to bear on Sibyl by some form of legal action and for a while feelings ran high between his and Sibyl's supporters. Unperturbed, she went ahead with her own plans and by the autumn had already sold Le Manoir to her friend, Gladys Richardson, for £2,400 – a transaction which did little to help her cause.

An uneasy settlement was finally reached, with Sibyl retaining her responsibility for the appointment of incumbents but cleared of her share in providing their stipend. She was still required, however, to make her small contribution of twenty shillings and her pew rent towards repairs. A new vicarage was built in 1936 on a site provided by her, close to the church, half the money being provided by public subscriptions and the remainder by the Ecclesiastical Commissioners. But although she continued to attend church occasionally and, in public at least, generally kept her feelings to herself, none of the vicars who followed Mr. Greenhow felt that they had either her approval or support. Between 1933 and 1938 Sark had five different clergymen and when the fifth, the Reverend R. H. Phillips was installed in April, 1938, the Dean of Guernsey, as he had done at each previous induction, expressed once again the hope that the occasion would not be repeated for some years. A *Guernsey Press* correspondent who reported the service and had also been present at the previous ceremonies, referred to a tablet on the church wall beside him commemorating the Reverend J. L. V. Cachemaille, who had been Vicar of Sark for some forty-two years. "*Autre temps, autre moeurs,*" he commented wryly.

But most of Sark came happily together in the recreation hall the following month, in response to an invitation by Sibyl to meet the radio producer, Francis Dillon, who was preparing a documentary about the island to be broadcast later in the year. Listening-in to the radio was a popular form of entertainment on Sark, particularly during the winter months, and there was great excitement among those who crowded into the hall, at the prospect of taking part in a programme themselves. Some months earlier rumours had circulated that Bob and Sibyl had been approached by speculators interested in operating a commercial radio station on the island and some had welcomed the idea. Others viewed the suggestion rather differently, particularly after William Hickey had hinted in his column of 13th January, 1938, in the *Daily Express* that "... the least pleasant feature of the scheme will be that some of its backers are wealthy businessmen known to be closely in touch with Fascist sympathisers". In the same article, Bob was quoted as saying that "the agreement, if any, would contain a clause barring religious or political propaganda not Seigneurially okayed by the Dame". "But what," asked the newspaper, "would she okay?" Post Office officials, however, soon put paid to any ideas Bob and Sibyl may have entertained by saying that the 1934 Act of Parliament would, in any case, forbid transmission on the island, and as it later turned out this was just as well, for William Hickey's fears had not been unfounded.

On that May day in the island hall, however, a party atmosphere prevailed as Sark people danced, sang old Norman French songs and chatted to Francis Dillon about their lives. Sibyl, who had provided refreshments and acted as hostess for the occasion, appeared to enjoy herself as much as her islanders and even demonstrated one of the traditional dances that she had learned as a child. Other recordings followed and the documentary *Welcome to Sark* was eventually broadcast early the following year on the National Programme of the BBC. With an introduction by Sibyl, who also explained various historical aspects, the programme depicted island life throughout the seasons, with recorded voices of fourteen of Sark's main personalities, some speaking their own patois, and the venture brought in its wake a fresh wave of publicity for the island. Sibyl, however, was not at home at the time of the broadcast for she was again on the other side of the Atlantic, helping to promote her small island even further.

On her last visit she had been approached by the National Geographic Society and asked if she would return the following year to give a lecture. She had agreed and had spent part of the summer of 1938 preparing for this. A friend, Arthur Radclyffe Dugmore, whose films on African wild life were well known, had agreed to make one about the island for her and the Geographic Society had also sent a photographer to take pictures for coloured slides, both of which were to be used to illustrate her talk. Quick to grasp the commercial possibilities of such an undertaking, Sibyl had asked an agent in New York to arrange other lectures for her while she was in America and so a tour had been organised.

She sailed in the *Queen Mary* for New York on 10th December and as her first engagement was not until the New Year, she spent

Christmas in Arizona with friends at the Circle Z Ranch at Patagonia, riding and relaxing generally before going to Cleveland, Ohio, early in January for the first of her three lectures in that city. After a few days in New York she went on to Washington where she was asked to speak at a luncheon at the Women's Press Club of America. Then came the main lecture to the National Geographic Society on the evening of 27th January to an audience of close on two thousand people. Sibyl showed no signs of nervousness and looked, according to press reports, "very regal in a lovely ivory lace evening dress" – but she confessed later to having had a "bad attack of stage fright". Bob had reassured her by telling her that there was nothing about Sark that she did not know better than anyone else and, as always, once she was on her feet her confidence returned and her personal charisma and the superb film she showed kept even that large audience enthralled.

The impression that Sibyl often gave on this tour, that Sark was rather more feudal and its people more subservient than they in fact were, annoyed some of the islanders when her remarks were later relayed to them by visiting Americans. But she had long ago discovered that such exaggeration of her position not only increased the interest in herself but in Sark as a whole – particularly in those countries without monarchies of their own.

Her tour also included lectures to the Foreign Policy Association in Boston and the English Speaking Union in Chicago. She broadcast nationwide from New York and visited Congress in Washington, where she was introduced to the Speaker. She and Bob also managed to spend five days visiting Jack Hays-Hammond – another of Bob's old friends from Yale – at what she called his "strange museum house", Abbadia Mare, at Gloucester, Massachusetts. Its Norman keep, moat and drawbridge, Italian abbey and fifteenth-century French house which had been transported brick by brick across the Atlantic greatly intrigued her and she often spoke of it later when recalling what had been altogether a most memorable few months.

With promises to return for another lecture tour in the autumn, she and Bob boarded the *Queen Mary* in New York on 11th March, 1939, for their journey back to Europe. After two days in London she flew on to Paris to give yet another lecture – this time in French – to the Société de Géographie at the Salle d'Iena and finally arrived back in Sark on 1st April in time for the Easter Chief Pleas meeting the following week. Island affairs then kept her busy for most of the early summer, with visits from the Bishop of Winchester and other official guests, and the task of finding a replacement for Dr. Pittard who had decided to retire from his position as Island Medical Officer – a post he had held for as long as she had been Dame of Sark.

She had need of a doctor's services herself soon after her return from America – and in circumstances which might well have had extremely serious consequences. She was accompanying two friends in a carriage to the harbour to put them aboard the evening boat when the horse suddenly bolted and the carriage, swaying from side to side, careered down the steep harbour hill. The horse was only brought to a stop when it ran into the workshops which had been erected for the new jetty and which, fortunately for Sibyl and her companions, stood between them and the sea. Although the carriage was completely smashed, its occupants – and the horse – miraculously escaped with only a few cuts and bruises but the incident might have ended otherwise and a very different pattern of life on Sark might well have emerged over the next few years.

Despite the island seeming at times to be far away from the troubles of the world outside, by early summer Bob and Sibyl were only too aware of the mounting tension as Hitler made further demands in Europe and Britain prepared for what now seemed to be the inevitable confrontation. Sibyl saw evidence of this in early August when she accompanied her American sister-in-law, Helen Hathaway, and her daughter, Val, on a tour around England. This had barely been completed when Neville Chamberlain made his historic broadcast on 3rd September informing the nation that war had been declared. Helen Hathaway and her daughter returned to America and Sibyl to Sark where, although she was not to know it at the time, her greatest challenge awaited her.

Part Three

Occupation and Aftermath
(1939–1954)

Chapter 10

A VISITOR TO Sark in the mid-1930s was said to have remarked that, should a war ever be declared, that island would be the place in which she would most like to be, for it was always so peaceful it was unthinkable that it could ever be touched by conflict. Certainly the first few months of war did little to change this image. Many of the summer visitors had already left before August was out, for some had been urgently recalled to duties elsewhere and September was a quieter month than usual with only a few remaining to enjoy the late season. Among these were Douce, her barrister husband and their baby daughter who had been living on the island since July. By the end of the year, however, he had left to join the army in England and, at Sibyl's suggestion, Douce and her little girl, Jane, had moved into the Seigneurie.

Soon after war had been declared, Sibyl had written to the Canadian Prime Minister, Mackenzie King, offering the Seigneurie to his government to use as a convalescent home for officers, in memory of her mother, and he had replied that he would keep her offer in mind should the need arise. In the meantime she had been busying herself in other ways about the island, trying to organise first-aid classes and some form of committee to deal with the various problems that had arisen with the advent of war. Unlike most people in the United Kingdom at that time, no one on the island had been issued with a gas mask, nor indeed had any air-raid precautions been taken beyond some rather haphazard black-out restrictions. At her suggestion, an extraordinary meeting of Chief Pleas was called in late September to look into these problems and a War Emergency Committee was appointed with herself as President, other members being the Seneschal, William Carré, the Constable and five other members of Chief Pleas, who each made themselves responsible for such things as petrol, coal, bread, fish and other food supplies.

By the end of the year everyone appeared to be settling down to the pattern of life they thought would continue until the war came to an end – a pattern which at that time seemed little different from usual. Work on the new jetty was proceeding well, the "Corvée"* was in operation as usual during the winter months – Bob, as Seigneur, together with his officials having inspected the roads selected for attention. Perhaps there was more activity than usual centred around the hall for it was here that, under Sibyl's leadership, a Red Cross Depot had been set up by the Women's Branch of the British Legion, and throughout the island women were knitting and sewing items of clothing for hospitals and servicemen. By the beginning of January, Sibyl was able to announce proudly that this band of workers had collected £200 for the Red Cross and contributed over a thousand hand-sewn or knitted articles. She had managed to enlist the aid of some of her American friends in this enterprise and their donations had helped to buy some of the wool and bales of flannel used.

During that first winter of the war, heavy snow fell on Sark – unusual for that generally temperate island. So snowbound did it become that Bob and one of the hoteliers put their tractors to work to help out the carters who were unable to use their horses. Tractors at that time were only allowed to be used on the farms and just three years before, Bob himself had been fined half-a-crown by the Sark court – at his own suggestion – for taking his tractor out on the island roads, in order to avoid the delay there would otherwise have been in obtaining formal permission to tow a stone-crushing machine up the steep harbour hill.

Apart from the snow, the winter passed with nothing for the Sark people to worry about, beyond heated discussions in the bars as to whether ormers (the popular Channel Island shellfish) could now be collected on a Sunday – the island Sabbath having always been very strictly observed – or if it were feasible to cultivate more ground and grow more cereals and main-crop potatoes, as had been suggested to them by the Guernsey States Emergency Committee.

The island was even looking forward to having summer visitors, for it had been announced in the House of Commons, early in March, 1940, that passports or visas would not be needed for visiting the Channel Islands and travel agents were already suggesting the area as being "ideal for holidays away from the war". By early May, however, Norway, Holland and Belgium had all been rapidly invaded and as German troops advanced towards

* The Corvée bound every Sark man to work on the island roads for two days each year or pay a tax for maintenance – in 1939 this was around eight shillings.

the French coast, Sibyl and Bob, listening to the news at the Seigneurie, realised – perhaps for the first time – the horrifying possibility that their small island, with others in the Channel, might soon be exposed to attack. Sark life nevertheless went on as usual and there was even disappointment when Sibyl, after a small committee meeting at the Seigneurie, decided that "owing to prevailing conditions" the annual Sports Day at the Seigneurie would be cancelled – with the exception of a few children's races. Plans were optimistically allowed to go ahead, however, for the annual Cattle Show on 4th July, over which she hoped to preside as usual.

But by 9th June the heavy pall of smoke from burning oil storage tanks on the French coast, brought it home to most Channel Islanders that the war really was on their doorstep. French fishing boats full of refugees were daily putting into one or another of the Sark bays or Creux Harbour, hoping to pick up food and water, and the islanders did what they could to help. Sibyl and Douce organised baby clothing and comforts for one particular yacht with twenty-five people on board, whose ages ranged from that of a three-week-old baby to a man of seventy-two. They had no clothes except those they wore, no stores and no charts as they had, on impulse, decided to steal the boat at Le Havre. Sibyl found them an old chart of the Brittany coast and they went on their way, but she always wondered what became of them.

On the 15th, she went over to Guernsey to take stock of the situation there and to make sure that, whatever happened, her youngest daughter, Jehanne, would have some form of celebration for her twenty-first birthday three days later. Although she was not to learn of it until later, at this very time discussions were taking place in London on whether troops should be withdrawn from the Channel Islands and their people evacuated. As it turned out, the day following Jehanne's celebration party at the Royal Hotel in Guernsey, it was announced that children of school age, younger children accompanied by their mothers, men of military age and "all others" would have to register for evacuation that evening. No one fully understood the order and it was not clear if everyone was meant to leave. Amid great confusion evacuation began the following morning. Sibyl, still being in St. Peter Port, was able to witness the panic and indecision of many as to whether they should stay at home and face the possible terrors of Nazi rule or go to England where they might encounter other dangers in the shape of air-raids or a possible invasion. She saw the queues of anxious people drawing money from the banks or harassing officials at the States Office and often recalled afterwards her encounter there with one young man, Louis Guillemette – at that time the Bailiff of Guernsey's secretary – who, amidst all the chaos around him was dealing efficiently with the situation in a calm, good-humoured manner. "I caught his eye," she later told a friend, "and could not resist giving him a big, fat wink."

After making arrangements to buy up some of the stores from the evacuated Elizabeth College she said her goodbyes, in her hotel room, to Amice and Jehanne who were about to leave on one of the evacuation boats. Amice and Harry had been living in a small farmhouse on Guernsey since Harry had left the army some years earlier and, now that he was again a serving officer, Amice had decided to join him and their evacuated children in England. Jehanne, who had been helping her sister with last-minute haymaking and packing at her farm, proposed to leave in order to take up some form of war work. While they were saying their farewells to their mother, Sibyl received a telephone call from Sark and for the first time in her life, Jehanne heard her mother swear, for the call was to tell her that the island's Medical Officer had left, with other English residents, aboard a private yacht. That the island should be deprived of its one and only doctor at such a time was, she considered, unpardonable and said so in no uncertain terms. But whatever thoughts she may have had, as she later bade her daughters goodbye, she kept them to herself and returned early the following day to Sark and the situation that she knew she must tackle there.

According to her own account, on the return journey she thought back over all that had happened in Guernsey and of how, as she later wrote to a friend, "no one took any lead and *explained*". She decided that this must not be allowed to happen in Sark. From the outset she and Bob had seen it as their duty to remain on the island, despite telegrams from friends and relations in England and America urging them to leave, and nothing that had happened since had changed that view. Should Sark be occupied – a prospect which at that time she thought to be unlikely – she saw no reason why the islanders, providing they went about their work as usual, should be molested in any way. In her view Sark had always been a close-knit community caring for nothing and nobody outside and she could not believe that its people would really wish to leave their homes and land which, in many cases, had been passed down to them from Helier de Carteret's original "forty". If the Germans should come, she felt confident that she would be able to keep some form of control and it would help that she could speak and read their language –

thanks to her German governess and her year in Cologne. Since that time she had also acquired a few German friends and knew that her name was now included in the Almanach de Gotha, which she considered might give her a certain standing with what she termed the "upper-class Germans". If the "lower classes" made any attempt at bullying she was sure that neither the islanders nor herself "would show any signs of cringing".

She discussed the whole matter with Bob on her return from Guernsey and he agreed that a special meeting should be called the following evening after church so that the people might be made fully aware of the situation.

There had naturally been a certain amount of general uneasiness on the island over what had been going on in Guernsey and Sibyl's apparent air of confidence as she stood before those who crowded into the island hall on that momentous Sunday evening of 23rd June, did much to quell their fears. It was almost exactly thirteen years since that summer day in 1927 when she had made her first speech to Chief Pleas after her accession, and she told Bob later that she felt she was reaffirming her promise made then that, whatever happened, she would continue to do her utmost for the good and prosperity of the island.

She began by saying that she doubted if the Germans would even come to Sark for it offered little of importance to them but – if they did so – she, as head of the island, would greet them and make the best terms she could for everyone. There was plenty of food and stores had been acquired from Guernsey but all waste land should be brought under the plough, as it was unlikely that food for the islanders or their animals would, from now on, be imported. Sark would not starve if this was done for it had better chances than the other islands – "we are one big family and must live as such. Each must help the other, we must all help each other." There were enough cows to provide an ample ration of milk and butter and enough land to grow the food needed. The fishermen could provide all the fish that could be consumed and there were rabbits in abundance to shoot or snare, ormers on the beaches and even limpets and winkles. She then added a word of warning:

> If any of you "outsiders" spread rumours or untrue tales, I'll have you sent off the island. [Loud Sark applause] . . . and if any of you Sark people should do so, and I know you won't, I'll have you . . . [pause] . . . locked up.

There was again loud laughter and applause. It was Sibyl at her best, swaying the audience by the sheer force of her personality. She went on to tell them that whatever happened, she, Bob, her daughter Douce, and grand-daughter Jane, would remain, although transport could be arranged for those wishing to leave. She made it clear, however, that she thought such evacuation would be unwise. The tension could be felt in the hall as she asked those assembled:

> Do you think I would keep my grand-daughter here if I thought it unsafe for her? You, who are thinking of going away, where are you going? You will be going to towns that will be bombed. No town in England will be safe from bombs.

She nevertheless advised young men of military age to join up, with the exception of those who had a stake in the land, whom she felt should stay to safeguard it.

By this time all were obviously moved by her words and there was a burst of applause as she ended dramatically: "Britain must win! Britain will win!"*

The Seneschal, William Carré, and other officials later toured the island asking for the names of those wishing to be evacuated but the response was small. When Louis Guillemette later telephoned from Guernsey to see if any special boat would be required for the island, Sibyl felt quite justified in taking the matter into her own hands and voicing what she honestly thought at the time to be the true feelings of her islanders. "Why should we leave?" she asked. "We are perfectly all right here." She also wrote to a friend in England that, whatever happened elsewhere, "we shall stay and see this island through" and by "we" she meant the Sark people also.

That she came to this decision on her own there is no doubt, for some claimed afterwards that they would have gone should a boat have come over for them, but as ordinary mail boats were still operating between Sark and Guernsey and Guernsey and England for some days afterwards, there appeared to have been nothing to stop those who really wished to leave from doing so. As it was, all Sark-born people remained. In the light of what happened during the next few years it would seem that her action was right and that if Sark had been evacuated, the small island would, within a short time, have been in a very sorry state – as

* Reports of her speech are conflicting but this account has been based on the memories of those present and from notes taken by local pressmen, and embraces most of the main points.

the history of nearby Alderney suggests.* Her handling of the whole situation at this time ensured that there was little, if any, panic and with Sibyl very firmly in control the majority of islanders seemed content to stay and some were heard to say that she might even be a match for the Germans, should they arrive.

Meanwhile she took it upon herself to keep the Home Office informed of all that was happening. Work was proceeding normally and all was quiet. Most of the English residents had gone and 471 people were left. The crops were good, there were plenty of cattle and pigs and a fair amount of wheat:

> Officially Guernsey has forgotten us and we have not had any instructions as regards the situation at all. The responsibility of advising people to go or remain falls on me and I should be thankful for any assurance or hints from you. Personally I remain unless ordered to leave, and all the Sarkese remain also.

But lines of communication between the various authorities during those days appeared to be chaotic and there was delay over informing the German government's representative that the Channel Islands had, in fact, been demilitarised and on the evening of 28th June, German aircraft attacked Guernsey and Jersey. Bob and Sibyl saw three aeroplanes flying low over the Seigneurie garden and a few minutes later heard the explosions as bombs dropped on St. Peter Port. She learned later that the petrol tanks of lorries loaded with tomatoes ready for shipment at the harbour, had caught fire and some of the drivers were burnt to death. Horses and cattle which had just been disembarked from the Alderney boat stampeded and confusion reigned as injured and dying lay in the midst of it all on the quay. Haymakers in the fields and an ambulance carrying the wounded to hospital were machine-gunned, as were some of the Sark fishermen and the Guernsey lifeboat crew – a spatter of bullets killing the son of the lifeboat's coxswain. In this and another raid on St. Helier in Jersey over forty people lost their lives.

These raids naturally alarmed everyone on Sark and few people slept that night for fear their island would be the next to be bombed. The fishermen were wary about putting out to sea again

* At the end of hostilities the people of Alderney returned to find destruction of property boundaries, rusty barbed wire; water-logged bunkers; ruined farms, infested with rats; weed-covered streets and demolished houses.

the following morning and no one on the island could settle down to normal work. Two days after the air-raid, the Germans occupied Guernsey and all communication then ceased between Sark and the larger island and everyone waited for the next move. On 3rd July it came. Philip Carré, whose farm overlooked the stretch of water between Sark and Guernsey saw, through his binoculars, the old lifeboat from St. Peter Port crossing the strip of water between the islands, with a white flag flying and what appeared to be uniformed men on board. He immediately telephoned the Seigneurie to alert Bob and Sibyl that the Germans were on their way and the news soon spread round the island. Sibyl quickly sent word to the Seneschal, William Carré, to go down to Creux Harbour to meet the Germans and escort them back to the Seigneurie. The Seneschal was never one to hurry himself and he took his time, calling first at one of the bars for a bolstering drink and, with his usual measured gait, his return from the harbour with the German officers was slow, which gave Sibyl ample time to make her own preparations.

According to her account of this first meeting with the Germans, she had suggested to Bob that they should "take a leaf out of Mussolini's book" by sitting on two high-backed chairs behind a large, solid oak writing table, which she placed at the far end of her drawing room. Being a long room she knew the officers would have to walk the full length to greet her, which she thought would give Bob and her a certain psychological advantage. Cecile Bouget – daughter of Sibyl's old nurse (Nana) – who had been working at the Seigneurie since the early thirties, was also brought into the play-acting. "When the German officers arrive," Sibyl told her, "announce them as if it is an everyday occurrence to have them call upon us." She and Bob were determined, she said later, that Sark should "present a front of firmness and dignity".

She always enjoyed telling the story of that meeting with Major Albrecht Lanz, Guernsey's first Commandant, and Dr. Maas, his Chief of Staff. She had been reassured on hearing them wipe their feet on the hall doormat after their long, dusty walk from the harbour, and felt even more confident when she heard them ask Cecile if she had a brush for their boots. This Sibyl regarded as a gesture of respect for the house and she had turned to Bob and whispered that she felt sure that it was "going to be all right". Bob left it to her to greet the Germans officially and she received their introductions with the regal dignity of a queen, graciously condescending to grant an audience to her subjects. Her confidence increased when neither added the customary "Heil Hitler" to their salutes. Major Lanz, who she decided looked a fair-minded, intelligent man, spoke no English so Dr. Maas acted as interpreter. A printed order was produced from the "Commandant of the German Forces in the Channel Islands" which gave notice that, among other things, a curfew would be introduced between eleven p.m. and six a.m.; all firearms were to be handed in; no boats were to leave the harbour without permission; no more than five people were to assemble in the streets and no wines or spirits were to be sold or bars to be opened. To the officers' obvious astonishment, Sibyl told them, in fluent German, that she would see that the orders were obeyed and suggested they stayed for lunch. By the time they left for Guernsey in the afternoon she had managed to establish her position so well that Lanz had suggested she carry on administration "as usual" – Bob throughout having kept a low profile – and that should there be any difficulties she should send her complaints direct to the Commandant's office in Guernsey. From then on she took every advantage of this suggestion and found that such contact with the High Command gave her, in her own words, "a very valuable weapon against any petty tyrannies by local officers". The precedent she had created on this first occasion, of the occupying force coming to her rather than she to them, was also to stand her in good stead, for at no time after that was she expected to alter the procedure. A sergeant and ten men formally occupied the island the following day, 4th July, American Independence Day – 'A hell of a date to be taken over by the Huns," Bob commented – and Sark entered yet another phase of its long and varied history.

The War Emergency Committee which had been set up the previous year, with Sibyl at its head, now came into its own and using the powers that had been vested in it by Chief Pleas, set about organising the island's resources so that they might be used in the best possible way should the occupation last for some time. Groceries, clothes and other items were requisitioned from the vacated houses and put into store for later distribution. At Sibyl's suggestion, materials from the Red Cross workroom were also removed from the hall and taken to the Seigneurie, where she later set up a "special aid committee" with the idea of making up replacement clothes for islanders as new ones became more difficult to obtain.

Most of the troops seemed anxious to create a good impression and generally their behaviour was exemplary. The German mark was fixed at just over two shillings and they soon began spending their money in the island's shops and bars, for the ban on the sale of liquor did not last long. In their usual hospitable way, some of the Sark people were soon exchanging drinks with the young German soldiers or inviting them into their homes, while at the Seigneurie visiting officers were entertained in a similar friendly manner by Sibyl and Bob.

Only two incidents ruffled the calm of those early occupation days for Sibyl. The first came about soon after the arrival of the German troops when two young Frenchmen and a Pole landed on Sark from a dinghy and were brought secretly to the Seigneurie. Sibyl and Bob arranged for them to have a meal but could think of no way for them to leave the island again without being seen, for all the fishing boats were under constant German surveillance – as were the small motor passenger boats the Germans allowed to run between Guernsey and Sark. It had been the young men's intention to make for England but Sibyl, as she later recorded, regretfully advised all three to give themselves up. On an island as small as Sark there was, she decided, nowhere that they could hide with safety, and their presence might only create more problems for the islanders.

The second incident occurred shortly afterwards when Amice's cowman came over from Guernsey, officially to consult Sibyl about her daughter's property – La Cour de Longue at St. Saviours – but, in fact, to tell her that two young British officers, Second Lieutenants Philip Martel of the Hampshire Regiment and Desmond Mulholland of the Duke of Cornwall's Light Infantry, were sheltering in the house, having been landed by submarine some days earlier, as an advance party for a commando raid. The main operation had been postponed for forty-eight hours and, due to mismanagement, the whole affair had become a fiasco. Although landings were effected, other launches went off course and little had been achieved. Martel and Mulholland had been unable to make contact with either the raiding parties or their pick-up boats and they had been forced to seek shelter where they could with relatives and friends. They both knew the Cantans' house, as they had served with Harry in the Guernsey Militia, but Amice's cowman was plainly worried for himself and the animals under his charge, for he knew that if it was discovered that he had been harbouring British officers, he would be liable for deportation and a spell of penal servitude. Both men were dressed in civilian clothes and, having no ration cards, were short of food.

Sibyl managed to convince the Germans that she had severe toothache and was in need of a dentist in Guernsey – there being none on Sark – and crossed to the larger island on Friday, 19th July, cautiously visiting the farmhouse the following day with some tins of food she had managed to smuggle over with her. The young men were frightened for their families, with whom both had made contact, and were anxious to get back to England as soon as possible – by fishing boat from Sark if Sibyl could arrange it. Once again she had to explain that these were closely watched and even if a boat were able to slip away, it was unlikely that there would be enough fuel on board to take the pair safely across the Channel. She could only suggest they found a way of giving themselves up and left two crestfallen young men behind her at the farmhouse.

By the time she returned home, after spending the rest of the weekend with friends in Guernsey, Martel and Mulholland had decided to take her advice and give themselves up. They had presented themselves at the home of Major Ambrose Sherwill, the Guernsey Procureur and President of the Controlling Committee, who had managed to smuggle out suitably doctored militia uniforms for them from the Town Arsenal, and in this garb they were able to present themselves to the German authorities as serving British officers. Had they been caught in civilian clothes they would have been regarded as spies and liable to execution, instead of the prisoners of war which they then became.

No doubt Sibyl would have liked to have done more for all these young men, but any action she might have taken in finding a boat for either party would have put the Sark people at risk also and it is understandable that she hesitated over saving a few, when suffering might so easily have been brought to many by a hasty decision on her part – particularly as relations between them and the Germans were at that time good. She had an extremely difficult task in doing what she thought was best for Sark and its people and at the same time retaining the respect of her position from the occupying force, which she considered was necessary to achieve these ends.

Dr. Charles Cruikshank in *The German Occupation of the Channel Islands* prefaced his book by saying that the occupation confronted all islanders with the same problems that faced other men and women in larger occupied countries, namely:

> How far to collaborate with the enemy, what to do about resistance and sabotage, how to endure isolation from friends and allies, how to tolerate extreme hunger and cold, how to face illness with inadequate medicines, how year after year to sustain morale when there was no certainty that they would ever be liberated.

All these were Sibyl's problems also, in addition to her self-imposed responsibility for the welfare of her island and there is no evidence to show that she did anything but face up to this challenge with her characteristic courage and fortitude. Stories of her "fraternisation" with the Germans soon began circulating on Sark and it is true that the senior officers were usually entertained at the Seigneurie while on official business and that, with her sense of history, she gave them her visitors' book to sign, in which they wrote such pleasantries as "Always delighted with nice reception" and "Many thanks for lovely afternoon", but there is no doubt that she was at all times regarded by them with great respect. There was nothing to be gained, she felt, by opposing the occupying force openly or "being rude" to them. On the contrary, through these social occasions the Germans were often gently nudged into bestowing favours not only upon herself but upon Sark also and her attitude generally could possibly have accounted for the occupation there being later described as "the most benevolent in the Channel Islands".

An early example of her strategy occurred shortly after her return from her weekend in Guernsey, when Bob and she once again entertained Major Lanz and Dr. Maas to lunch at the Seigneurie, before accompanying them to the field beside the house for the "children's only" island sports, which Sark had planned prior to the occupation and had decided should still take place. Throughout the afternoon Sibyl appeared to her islanders to be "graciously hospitable" to the two officers yet at the same time sufficiently aloof to command their obvious respect – an imperious manner which later earned her the title among most of the occupying forces of "*Königin*" (Queen). There is no record on this occasion of any discussions having taken place at the Seigneurie over lunch, but was it purely coincidental that a few days later certain concessions were announced allowing Sark fish to be taken once more into Guernsey and special facilities were arranged for those wishing to visit the larger island?

The Michaelmas Meeting of Chief Pleas also took place, as planned, in October with no restrictions of any sort being imposed by the occupying force. The islanders' only concern appeared to be over the law passed at that time, after a great deal of heated debate, to enable work to be undertaken and football to be played on their strictly-kept Sunday.

By the close of the year, the Emergency Committee found it necessary, as a precautionary measure, to tighten up their controls on butter and meat and to introduce rationing of bread, flour, tobacco and clothes. Later Sark was given help over some of its supplies from the purchasing commission for the Channel Islands based at Granville in Normandy and Guernsey's representative –

Agricultural Officer, Raymond Falla – made periodic visits to consult with Sibyl and other members of her Emergency Committee over the island's needs.

Food generally did not present too great a problem at first. The island had, in fact, more milk cows per head of population than Guernsey and there was usually a reasonable amount of dairy produce available, although some Sarkese later indulged in black-market activities with the Germans when rationing came in. Later on some of the fishermen found that they could get a better price for their fish outside the island and this too caused bitterness in some quarters. But most islanders were now growing their own vegetables and, where possible, keeping pigs and poultry – as they had been urged to do from the beginning. A few, including Sibyl, decided to keep tame rabbits, but for those that did not, there was always an abundance of wild ones to be shared. Flour was more difficult to obtain, for there was not enough room to grow sufficient grain for Sark's needs and much of this had to be imported from France but the island baker did his best and the food controller saw to it that after grinding at the Seigneurie mill, everyone had a fair share of what flour there was from local crops.

Raymond Falla later described the whole food situation on Sark as being similar to that he found in any of the small rural Normandy villages he often passed through while in France for the purchasing commission. There was "always someone with something to share", which helped rations to spread further and this often included the carcass of a slaughtered animal for, as there was no cold storage on the island, the Germans would generally agree to the meat being distributed. Later on, when there was a surplus of milk one summer, Sibyl asked him if he could procure more salt – a difficult commodity to come by – so that the islanders might preserve their butter for the winter and this request, he considered, was typical of Sibyl who, with her Seigneurie staff, provided a perfect example of good husbandry. They tended to their cattle and animals in a sensible manner and always made sure that every scrap of land was utilised and that summer fruits and vegetables were preserved.

During that first occupation Christmas, however, there were few who could say that they went short of either food or liquor and the season was celebrated in a manner little different from that of normal years, particularly as the Germans decided to throw a party for the Sark people and lengthen the curfew to three a.m. Sibyl also organised a special entertainment for the children, to which most people subscribed, and cards and letters were sent around the island. Despite the depressing war news in the German-controlled newspapers, Sark, it appeared, had accepted the whole situation in its customary unperturbed manner.

Among correspondence that Sibyl and Bob received at this time were letters from some on the island who realised the difficulties of the task she had set herself and appreciated all that she was trying to do. One of those was from a retired serviceman – Major John Skelton – who with his wife, Madge, had come to live on the island shortly before the occupation and was now president of the agricultural committee:

> La Rondellerie, Christmas, 1940.
> ... We wish to send to you and your husband a less conventional greeting this Christmas than of yore. Again we would wish to express our genuine admiration for the courage and competence with which you have dealt with a situation so abnormal and difficult as that in which Sark finds itself. With my large experience of men and affairs I at least appreciate the marked ability shown by you in so many ways. I hope that not only all in Sark but those outside will show a proper realisation of what they owe to you in the years to come. I would be proud to have it said of me – as happened last week – "Whenever we go to the Seigneurie for advice or assistance, we are always helped and never sent away. No one could be kinder than Mr. and Mrs. Hathaway."

But, as was expected, not everyone shared the same views and there were those on the island who were already hinting that Sibyl was not being strictly fair over the distribution of certain items that came her way and there was talk of stores from vacated houses and elsewhere being retained at the Seigneurie for the occupants' own use. Some foodstuffs and bottles of wine and spirits there undoubtedly were, but there is no evidence to suggest that most of these were not kept by for emergencies or distributed later as the need arose. If Sibyl sometimes did not extend this help to those whom she thought were not making the most of their resources or to those she personally disliked, perhaps, in the circumstances, her attitude was excusable. She, also, suffered in the years that followed, for people under stress often require scapegoats and she was frequently to carry the blame for the frustrations and deprivations of others.

Chapter 11

THE YEAR 1941 started quietly. By this time the improvised administration set up by the occupation forces had ended, for the war had not finished at Christmas, as the German troops had been confident it would do, and more long-term plans had to be put into operation. Major Lanz and Dr. Maas had both left the islands and a military government had taken over the civil administration. The Seigneurie then became, according to Bob, "like the Information Bureau at Grand Central Station" as more officials from the new command arrived daily, demanding a variety of statistics. Most of these men Sibyl scathingly described afterwards as being "nothing more than jumped-up peacetime clerks and office workers, in spite of the uniforms they wore". Never one for figures, she was confused by the demands for balance sheets and "estimates of future revenue", particularly as at that time Sark bore the cost of maintaining the troops, whose numbers fluctuated daily.

Of particular annoyance to her were the officials who endeavoured to introduce regulations on the growing of crops or those who tried to limit fishing to certain hours. Because a crop grew successfully on the Continent, she told them, it did not follow that it would flourish on the Channel Islands and the farmers alone knew what suited their conditions best. When the local Commandant complained to her that the fishermen were not keeping to the hours that had been laid down for them and that the armed guards detailed to accompany them waited for them in vain at the harbour, she retorted caustically that fishing depended "more upon tides than times" and that the fishermen could scarcely be expected to waste their precious, rationed petrol by putting out on what they knew would be fruitless trips. Eventually, after further appeals, the fishing regulations were lifted and the fishermen were allowed to fish when they chose, so long as they were accompanied by their guards. Sibyl was amused later, however, when she heard of how they had sometimes deliberately stayed out in rough weather to watch their guards gradually succumb to sea-sickness in the choppy Channel waters.

In early May, 1941, unknown to Sibyl at the time, reports were circulating in Britain and America that she had been taken to a concentration camp in Germany and this had naturally created a great deal of worry for Amice, Jehanne and the rest of the family in England. Fortunately, within a few days of the reports appearing in the British press, Sibyl's first Red Cross message arrived from Sark, with the information that both she and Bob were safe and well and her daughters were able publicly to refute the rumours, which were believed to have originated from German sources.

Sibyl was also unaware, until some weeks after the event, of another item of news which this time, sadly, was correct. Earlier that same month Buster, who had rejoined the RAF on the outbreak of war, was spending a few days' leave at the Adelphi Hotel in Liverpool with his second wife, Mary, when they were both killed in an air-raid. As the United States had not yet entered the war, Amice had approached their Embassy in London to ask if they could relay the news to her mother through diplomatic channels, and a message was duly sent via the consulate in Berlin to the Military Commander-in-Chief of the Channel Islands – Colonel Graf von Schmettow. He at once telephoned the Commandant on Sark and thoughtfully instructed him to tell Bob first so that he might be the one to break the news to his wife and this kindly action did much to lessen the shock for her. A few days afterwards, von Schmettow himself came over from his headquarters in Jersey and called at the Seigneurie personally to express his sympathy. Sibyl had already met this German aristocrat – whom she later described as "a soldier of the old school" – and had great respect for him. But this visit presented her, she admitted, with "one of the most difficult moments" of her life, for she had to steel herself to "accept with calmness and dignity the enemy's condolences", despite von Schmettow making it easier for her, by saying that his sympathy was "for mothers of all nations who grieve in the same way for their sons". Two years later, when his own son died on the Russian front, she remembered his kindness to her and sent him a message of sympathy in return.

She was very upset at the news of Buster's death, for despite their differences, he was, after all, her eldest son and for once the iron control broke and the vulnerable woman beneath showed through. Cecile Bouget who, perhaps of all her staff, knew her best, was astounded to see her normally stoical mistress unable to hold back her tears as she passed on the news she had just received from her husband.

Through the same diplomatic channels that Amice had used

and until the United States had entered the war, she and Bob were able to send messages to his relations in America and it was in this way that they were to learn of the death in the late autumn of Bob's mother whom Sibyl had always admired. Her death meant a large inheritance for Bob but it was to be some time before either he or Sibyl were able to enjoy it.

Brief messages through the Red Cross were by now being regularly exchanged between Sibyl and her family – the maximum twenty-five words' allowance presenting no great problem for an inveterate letter-writer like herself. She had always been able to keep up a vast correspondence with her many friends in peacetime – thanks to her gift for being able to pack the maximum of news into the minimum of words.

Sibyl was never short of work on the island for Chief Pleas and other committee meetings were still being held regularly and she continued to take a special interest in the schools and the children's welfare. With her food committee, she made sure that those under sixteen were given a special ration of chocolate and that all were adequately clothed and fed. As time went on clothing became more difficult to come by but this situation was greatly eased by the workroom she had set up at the Seigneurie, which helped to provide growing children and others with clothes made out of blankets, tablecloths or curtains. When shoes also became unobtainable, toes were cut out of old ones so that there was still room for young feet to grow and presentable slippers were made from the underfelts of carpets.

In the late autumn of 1941, she thought it sensible to take up the suggestion of the Feldkommandantur in Guernsey that German lessons should be started for the twenty-two Sark children between ten and fourteen years of age and wrote to the German official concerned asking for textbooks. Some weeks later she was able to inform him that "we are well satisfied with the instruction book and the children study with enthusiasm and tell stories and sing a few songs . . ." Characteristically she took the opportunity of mentioning that lessons had been difficult in winter because of the inadequate heating in the schoolroom which, she claimed, hampered the children's concentration – hoping, no doubt, for an extra allowance of fuel – and added: "Won't you come over yourself, or with a few of your gentlemen and hear the children?" Friendly overtures such as this undoubtedly went a long way towards ensuring a sympathetic response to her approaches on other, more urgent, matters – an example of this being her later request for medical aid.

Earlier in the year she had inaugurated an Island Sick Benefit

Fund – initially to help those who could not afford medical treatment for their children – and many islanders had been moved to organise concerts and other activities on its behalf. Since the departure of its former Medical Officer just prior to the occupation, Sark had been without a regular doctor, although two had helped out for a short time and the elderly Dr. Pittard, who had retired some years earlier, did what he could. Eventually a married nurse from Guernsey was engaged but even her ministrations were not to last for long for it soon became apparent that she was expecting a child. Much to everyone's surprise – including that of Sibyl who was summoned to help Dr. Pittard with the delivery – early in 1942 the nurse gave birth to twins and it was obvious that alternative medical care would have to be found. As a last resort, Sibyl appealed to Prince von Oettingen, who was in charge of the civil administration in Guernsey, and he forthwith made arrangements for the Sarkese to be looked after by the German army doctor quartered on the island. This arrangement proved invaluable and the men who held this position gave their services willingly and unstintingly at any hour. Sibyl had cause to thank one of these doctors herself for some years later he skilfully brought her through a sharp bout of bronchitis.

Prince von Oettingen was always a welcome visitor at the Seigneurie. He was a wealthy and much-travelled Bavarian landowner and it was not long before he and Sibyl discovered that they had mutual friends. She commented afterwards that they used to talk to each other "as friends do" and always found it incredible that at the time they were "enemies", particularly as – but for the war – they might so easily have met through one or another of their acquaintances.

But the reminders that the Channel Islands were in a strategic position between England and France were with the Sarkese daily – apart from the field-grey uniforms to which they were now becoming accustomed. Aeroplanes from both sides passed constantly overhead and anti-aircraft gunfire could often be heard. On one occasion Sibyl and Bob were awakened by the sound of an aircraft circling and Len Bishop, the farm bailiff, who lived with his wife, Jenny, in the Seigneurie, climbed the tower just in time to see the pilot make a forced landing close by. The German patrol had also seen it and as he watched, the bailiff saw the troops hurrying to the scene. Much as Sibyl would have liked to have gone too, the strict curfew prevented it and it was not until afterwards that she learnt that the plane was an RAF Lancaster bomber returning from a raid on Stuttgart. Three of the crew had landed safely with the machine after the others had baled out over France. As they were later escorted on to a boat at the harbour, en route for their prison camp in Germany, the airmen all waved to the watching fishermen and gave the "thumbs up" sign. Never one to miss an opportunity, Sibyl managed to persuade the sentry guarding the aircraft to let her have some petrol from it for her cigarette lighter, in exchange for what she later termed "an inferior bottle of kirsch" from her larder.

Both she and, more particularly, Bob, who was normally a heavy smoker, found the strict rationing of tobacco one of the most difficult privations to accept and took to using all kinds of dried leaves, including those from the Seigneurie vine and clover heads, in order to get some kind of smoke. As time went by, substitutes were also found for other goods in short supply. Rose and blackberry leaves or pea pods were used to make tea and an ersatz coffee was concocted from a mixture of dried sugar beet, parsnip and barley. Grapes from the vine were also dried and used to make what the staff at the Seigneurie thought was quite a passable pudding for their second occupation Christmas – though with the war news from all fronts being singularly depressing, particularly now that Japan and America were also involved, the season on Sark was hardly one of good cheer.

By this time the beaches and cliffs had been wired and mined and boats were no longer allowed to land except at the harbour. For the first time in history, Sark roads were – as some islanders put it – "desecrated" by cars, lorries and motorcycles for, small though the island was, the troops felt they needed some form of mechanised transport to take them about. Sibyl disliked these changes as much as everyone else and warned the children, who were excited at seeing cars – in some cases for the very first time – that the vehicles could be dangerous. But if she and Bob thought conditions had deteriorated in 1941, the deprivations of that year were negligible compared with what was to follow.

The new year had scarcely got under way when a building on Sark that had held many happy memories for her, from the days when Dudley had stayed there before their marriage, was burnt to the ground – the first fire on the island in most people's memory. German soldiers had been occupying the Bel Air Hotel at the top of Harbour Hill and sparks from their stove set fire to the thatched roof of the building. Within two hours there was nothing left but a black stone shell and another familiar landmark for her had disappeared.

Not long afterwards the island experienced another "first", when the only murder Sark people could remember was reported. In the early spring, the German doctor was found dead in his bed with gunshot wounds to his head and his gold watch, wallet and other articles missing. He had been a popular man both with the troops and the Sark people whom he had tended and only a week before his death had played in a scratch soccer match against the island team. But the Gestapo officers who had been called in to investigate were certain that an islander was responsible for his death, despite Sibyl assuring them firmly that Sark people did not commit murders. The curfew time was brought forward to seven p.m., which in early May meant that people were shut into their homes during daylight, and special permits had to be granted by the German Commandant to allow farmers to attend to their cattle. Shortly afterwards it was discovered that the doctor's batman was also missing and from then on every man from sixteen to seventy years of age was required to report twice a day to the German headquarters. Every house and cottage was searched and the whole population was threatened with deportation to France unless the criminal owned up. It was only after the batman's body was discovered at the bottom of the well – still being used without adverse effects – at the doctor's billet that the restrictions were lifted.

At the time it was assumed that the batman had committed suicide after murdering the officer, but Sibyl heard later that another soldier had subsequently confessed to the killing. The real murderer was said to have been a malingerer, bent on avoiding service at the Russian front, and the doctor had certified him fit to go. He had taken his revenge by murdering the doctor and left early the following morning with his draft. It was after he had been wounded at the front and lay dying that he was alleged to have confessed. Sibyl firmly believed this story and that the batman had thrown himself down the well after being worked on by the Gestapo but other stories circulated and the true facts were never to emerge.

The murder affected everyone on the island and for a while the generally good relations that had existed between the occupying force and the people were shaken and this situation was not helped by a German order some weeks later announcing that all radio sets were to be confiscated. Until this time, with the exception of a few weeks in November, 1940, when sets were temporarily called in as a reprisal measure for the landings on Guernsey, Channel Islanders were allowed to listen to British programmes and details of these were, surprisingly, printed in the German-controlled local press. That June, however, radios were again ordered in and several people, including the Hathaways, decided to keep theirs back, despite the threat of heavy penalties for doing so. At Sibyl's suggestion the Seigneurie set was hidden in a trunk which she kept in a small upstairs boxroom with other cases belonging to friends who had left the island. Thereafter she and Bob, with Len and Jenny Bishop, listened-in each night to the BBC's nine o'clock news and between them worked out a drill should they be disturbed by visiting Germans. She knew that her two large poodle dogs would always bark if they heard a noise near the house and trusted that this would give them sufficient warning. The idea was that she should then make her way downstairs, using her lame leg as the excuse for her slowness, and take her time quietening the dogs before opening the door. This, she considered, would give sufficient time for the others to return the set to its hiding place. Fortunately she never had to resort to such tactics nor was she or anyone else ever penalised for listening-in although the Germans were later informed of those who were receiving the British news.

In mid-September Sark was shocked by the announcement that all "English" male residents and their families between the ages of sixteen and seventy, with the addition of others caught by the war on the island, were to register for deportation. Bob and the Bishops were three who fell into this category, together with others whom Sibyl felt should remain on the island and she immediately wrote a letter to the Feldkommandantur in Guernsey appealing against the order. Translated from the original German, it reads:

Seigneurie de Sark
via Guernsey
19.9.42.

Dear Mr. Brosch,

I take advantage of your kind offer of help and advice in difficult matters. Please free the following men and declare them as absolutely indispensable and necessary for existence and administration.

1) L. Bishop aged 45	Is the island miller for baker's flour and cattle food, as well as being an engineer and expert in repairs of agricultural machines and electrical matters. He also drives the tractor for the German garrison.
2) J. H. Skelton aged 63	President of the agricultural committee. Could not be replaced as no farmer on Sark has the knowledge to organise and control the agricultural cultivation and its harvest.

He is the only member of the Sark Emergency Committee who speaks and reads German. He also meets all the demands put by the German garrison in agricultural matters.

3) R. H. Phillips aged 65	Vicar of Sark. No marriage could be pronounced valid as we recognise no other ceremony other than the religious.
4) R. W. Hathaway aged 55	Seigneur of Sark. The parliament could not sit without him and the whole civil administration is illegal without his presence. His signature is absolutely necessary on all official documents. Our ancient feudal system does not allow me, as a married woman, to have special rights in the absence of my husband.

I count on your influence and your goodwill to help me.

Sibyl Hathaway

Most of her other letters appealing against the deportation of several elderly people and of a Mrs. Sharp – who at that time was the sole teacher at the girls' school – were successful. For the time being Bob and the vicar were also allowed to stay but Bishop and Major Skelton were to go. The Sark Commandant wrote to the German Command in Guernsey that Major Skelton had only arrived on Sark the day after the bombardment of St. Peter Port. He was a former Major in the Royal Engineers, known to be anti-German and possessing enough knowledge to evaluate Sark's defences. When the minefields were being laid he was said to have asked for information on the exact position of mines, so that he might be able to clear them after the war. All this, wrote the Commandant, made him a security risk should he remain. Bishop's work could, he felt, be taken over at any time by other men. What he did for the German troops was "minimal" and he often caused trouble. He therefore saw no reason why his name should not be added to the list.

For reasons that are not explained in the records, though it seems likely that Sibyl had a hand in this, Bishop was not, after all, among the eleven people ordered to assemble a few days later at Creux Harbour where they were to board a boat for

Guernsey, en route for France and internment camps in Germany. John and Madge Skelton, however, were. Sibyl went down to the harbour to see the deportees off, having done what she could beforehand to see that they were all adequately provided with food and warm clothing for the journey, and was disturbed when – after what seemed a long wait – there was no sign of either the Major or his wife. The day before, they had called at the Seigneurie to ask if she would take charge of some jewellery and letters which, they told her, they were reluctant to leave behind in an empty house and they had clearly been very worried by the deportation order. She and Bob sympathised as best they could but there was nothing more either could do. Because of John Skelton's background, the German Command had been adamant that they should go.

The boat finally left without the Skeltons aboard and Sibyl told Bob later that she marvelled at the calm way its passengers had left for their unknown destination. Meanwhile the German Commandant and his troops were searching for their missing deportees and that evening islanders were questioned and their houses searched, but no one appeared to have seen the couple for several hours.

After a sleepless night Sibyl was called from her bed at dawn by a German soldier who bade her go with him at once as the Skeltons had been found near their home and Madge was asking for her. Although she realised by his tone that the matter was serious she was totally unprepared for the shock that awaited her. John Skelton was dead, having slashed his wrists, and his wife, with whom he had made a suicide pact, was seriously wounded, having stabbed herself in several places after vomiting back the poison they had both taken. All Sibyl could do was to talk soothingly to her and hold her hand until the German ambulance arrived and she was put aboard the boat for Guernsey where she was then, on Sibyl's instructions, taken into the civilian hospital. A short while afterwards she contracted pneumonia and became desperately ill so it was some weeks before she could be questioned further.

Meanwhile Sibyl was doing her best to persuade the Gestapo, who had now moved in to deal with the case, that John Skelton was not a British agent. The officers arrived at the Seigneurie soon after Madge had been removed to hospital and began questioning her closely about documents or papers they thought she might have in her possession. Having no idea of the contents of the letters which had been entrusted to her, she thought it best to tell them that she had been given only jewellery for safe keeping and, according to her account of the affair, as soon as they had gone, she hid the letters in the straw of one of her rabbit hutches at the back of the Seigneurie. Within a few hours the Gestapo returned, this time with a letter which they told her they had found in the Skeltons' home addressed to her. In Sibyl's own words "the most aggressive of them" thrust it towards her and pointing to the words, "You have our last messages," demanded an explanation. Her quick brain provided one. "In English," she said, coldly, "*messages* mean words spoken and not written. The messages I have are only connected with the jewellery and to whom it should be sent should they not return." The Gestapo were evidently satisfied with this and troubled her no further. Madge Skelton eventually recovered and came back to Sark, where Sibyl kept a kindly eye on her for the rest of the occupation. The letters turned out to be quite harmless messages of farewell, but at that particularly crucial time on the island, Sibyl could not have been sure.

German officials were still presenting themselves with regularity at the Seigneurie and almost every week the local Commandant brought notices of new orders – generally concerning requisitions or demolitions – which he wished her to sign, put on view and see enforced. It is to her credit that at no time did she agree to put her signature to any of these insisting that, as they were German orders, the Commandant should sign them himself. Shortly after the deportation he arrived with yet another notice which he wished to be circulated and Sibyl was outraged by its contents. In an attempt to control venereal disease in Guernsey the chief German Medical Officer for the Bailiwick there had ordered that all women undergoing treatment should be handed the following notice:

> Sexual relations, with either German soldiers or civilians, are strictly forbidden during the next three months. In cases of non-compliance with the order severe punishment by the occupying authorities is to be expected, even if no infection takes place.

Unfortunately, by the time the notice reached Sark the briefing that it was to be handed only to women under treatment had been forgotten – hence Sibyl's reaction to the suggestion that the notice be exhibited as usual. She had, she told Bob later, looked the Commandant "squarely in the face", with no attempt to hide her disgust and said, "I will not publish anything so insulting to my people." Bob's reaction was to treat the whole affair as a huge joke, saying that he thought it "a highly indecent communication for a German officer to present to a lady" and that "they must be having a lot of fun and games in Guernsey which is more than can be said of Sark".

Early in October of that same year of 1942, Sark was to experience "fun and games" of another sort with the first of two British commando raids on the island, which was to bring about far-reaching results in other theatres of the war. The raid was led by Major J. G. ("Apple") Appleyard, who had spent several holidays on Sark before the war. Sixteen men were landed about midnight from a motor torpedo boat between Dixcart and Derrible Bays to the south of the island and, cutting their way through the barbed wire defences, they climbed the steep Hog's Back headland separating the two bays. On reaching Dixcart Valley they made for a small house – La Jaspellerie – the home until his death four months earlier of the retired Medical Officer of the island, Dr. Pittard. Breaking a pane in the french window they gained access and explored the downstairs rooms, disturbing Mrs. Frances Pittard who now lived alone. She answered the commandos' questions as best she could, giving them a map of the island and copies of the German-controlled Channel Island newspapers containing the recent deportation order and told them that the nearest German soldiers were those billeted in the annexe to the Dixcart Hotel – for which the men made on leaving her. At the hotel they overpowered the German officer and his four men, whom they found sleeping, and after securing their hands, bundled them outside with the intention of taking their prisoners back to England. Once in the open the Germans realised how small the raiding party was and tried to raise the alarm and free themselves. In the struggle that ensued, the German officer was shot and stabbed to death, two privates were wounded – one dying later – a third escaped altogether and only the fourth was finally taken aboard the waiting boat.

Sibyl knew nothing of this until early the following morning, when a soldier came to the Seigneurie with an order, issued by the Commandant, for all civilians living in the centre of the island to vacate their homes by midday. The Junior School was also to be cleared as all these buildings were to be used for housing German troops. As Chairman of the Education Committee she immediately made her way to the school where, with the aid of one of her farm hands, Philip Le Feuvre and the Seigneurie's horse van she supervised the clearing of books and desks out of the building, without any clear idea of why the Commandant should have come to such a sudden decision. It was only when the van was commandeered to take the bodies of the two Germans down to the harbour to be shipped to Guernsey, that the full story came to light.

The incident proved serious enough to merit a full report to the German High Command in which it was suggested, much to Bob and Sibyl's amusement, that the commandos must have been in contact with agents on Sark by means of carrier pigeons dropped by aircraft. Consequently it was decided that for their own safety, troops would only be billeted in the centre of the island, defences generally would be strengthened and vigilance increased.

But the report of the raid had other repercussions outside Sark. When Hitler heard that the prisoners' hands had been tied, he immediately ordered the shackling of nearly 1,400 Allied prisoners captured during the Dieppe landing. This was immediately countered by the British with a threat to shackle an equal number of German prisoners of war if theirs were not freed and the Germans then followed this by replying that should such measures be taken, they would increase the numbers tied threefold. This brought about an explanation from London that in Sark the prisoners had been bound merely "so that their arms would be linked with those of their captors" and that when they had tried to escape they had to be shot to prevent them raising the alarm. As the Geneva Convention did not cover any ruling about hands being tied, though it did forbid reprisals, the matter was finally dropped, but not before the German propagandists had said that the British government "had taken refuge in flimsy excuses" and by arguing that "humanity varies according to circumstances". This small raid on Sark was also held to be partly responsible for another order issued by Hitler some weeks afterwards which decreed that:

> In future, all terror and sabotage troops of the British and their accomplices, who do not act like soldiers, but rather like bandits, will be treated as such by the German troops and will be ruthlessly eliminated in battle, wherever they appear.

In commenting on the raid many years later, Sibyl said that its severe repercussions "seemed a heavy price to pay for the capture of one prisoner and a copy of the *Guernsey Evening Press*" – and many who were with her on the island at the time agreed, for Sark was to suffer severely for this one action. Shortly after the incident, General Muller, Corps Commandant in Guernsey, visited the island to investigate for himself the reason for his troops' lack of vigilance. A seven p.m. to eight a.m. curfew was enforced upon its people, fresh barbed wire and landmines were laid – leaving only the areas inland and the way to the harbour clear – and the garrison itself was strengthened by the addition of two tanks which, Sibyl protested, scarcely helped the condition of the roads, which had not been built for such heavy transport. But by far the most distressing result of the raid was the deportation order in February of the following year for another sixty-three of its people drawn from most parts of the island, from young children to elderly people.

Although neither Sibyl nor the islanders were aware of it at the time, the Germans' first plan was to evacuate the whole of Sark as they still believed that British agents were operating there, but after Mrs. Pittard had been questioned closely by the Gestapo about her part in the raid, it was concluded that there was no such activity. A senior officer is also reported as having advised against complete evacuation as such a move would, he thought, only leave the troops with a "desert" on their hands. Instead, as a security measure, it was decided that there should be further deportations not only from Sark but from Guernsey and Jersey as well and, this time, those listed were:

> Those who had offended against the German regime; Communists and others politically suspect; work-shy people; young men without important work in the German sense; former officers and reserve officers; Jews and high-ranking Freemasons; people prominent in public life; rich men who were considered anti-German; and people on Sark not engaged in agriculture and those living in the centre of the islands.

Sark's list once again included Bob, as a former officer in the Royal Flying Corps, and Mrs. Pittard, whose action in helping the commandos had inadvertently triggered off the whole operation. Some of Sark's oldest families were also ordered to leave and Sibyl protested strongly to the Command in Guernsey against the deportations and pleaded – in some cases successfully – for the release of certain of those listed who were in "key" positions on the island. Her further appeal for Bob to remain, however, was this time turned down after the Germans had given the matter some thought.

A bitter wind was blowing from the sea and rain was falling

as the deportees all assembled at the harbour on the first stage of their journey and Sibyl, as before, provided what she could in the way of food and clothing to help them on their way. She could not believe, she reassured them, that their internment would last for long – and even went so far as to forecast to Bob that, as they had heard from their hidden radios that the tide now appeared to be turning for the Allies, the war would "almost certainly" be over by 1945 – a comment Bob was long to remember.

Although she appeared to be dealing with the whole situation in her usually brisk efficient manner, few gauged her true feelings as she went about among them. She admitted afterwards, however, that the order for the party to board the boat came "almost as a relief" for she always hated long drawn-out goodbyes, and she knew how much she was going to miss Bob. It was not that he had officially given her a great deal of help in the administration of island affairs or with her dealings with the Germans – for whom he sometimes openly showed his dislike – but the fact that he was always there beside her to proffer sound and practical advice when needed gave her a feeling of security whatever the situation. His obvious affection for her and his sense of humour had carried her through many a bout of depression when the outlook appeared bleak and this was particularly so during the winter months when normally, in peacetime, she would have been enjoying a holiday away from Sark. Now she was forced to remain on a greatly restricted island to face the Germans alone and, with her remaining officials, deal with the supplies and other problems of the much-depleted population. Loneliness was something she had not yet experienced but with Bob and most of her friends of similar interests gone from the island, she felt she could not even look forward to the occasional games of bridge that had previously helped to relieve the monotony. Once again the Bishops were allowed to remain with her at the Seigneurie and, with them – thanks to their hidden wireless set in the boxroom – she could at least continue to listen each evening to the BBC nine o'clock news. The courage and determination she had always shown throughout her life when faced with a challenge were apparent as she returned to the Seigneurie from the harbour and began, almost immediately, to tackle the island work awaiting her there.

Bob, at least, had no qualms about her capabilities. The deportees had joined others from Guernsey at St. Peter Port for the next stage of their journey and were met by Louis Guillemette, who had had several dealings with the Hathaways since that seemingly far-off day when Sibyl had winked at him in the Bailiff's

Office before the occupation. "How do you think Sibyl will manage without you?" he asked Bob with some concern. "Manage?" was the reply. "That woman? My dear Louis, she could manage the United States – and *knit*!"

Chapter 12

Sibyl heard later that the deportees had all been packed into "stinking boats and filthy trains". The women and children were then put into makeshift quarters near Paris before being transferred to a camp at Biberach with appalling conditions, which were only alleviated when the Swiss government intervened and the Red Cross set about making improvements. Bob was taken with other men to Laufen, an old Bavarian *Schloss* built originally for the Bishops of Salzburg, where he shared a bug-infested room with nine other men, including Major Ambrose Sherwill, who had helped Martel and Mulholland after their landing in Guernsey at the beginning of the occupation.

At first the Hathaways wrote to each other weekly – Sibyl sending open letters to Bob through the German post and he camp cards or letters to her. Although these were subject to censorship, it was not long before they discovered that – as a prisoner of war – he was able to send and receive letters to and from England more easily than she could on Sark and that, through him, she could obtain more up-to-date news of her family and friends. From then on he often relayed messages through Amice, Jehanne or others, interspersed with his own news of camp life and occasionally both he and Sibyl used a prearranged code-form which only the immediate family would have been able to understand. Thus:

BUZZ (a one-time Seigneurie cat) represented the *British and United States forces.*
LENFRANCIES or *FRANKYS* (an Italian friend) – the *Italians.*
STEWART (Bob's brother) – the *United States forces.*
HARRY (Harry Cantan, Amice's army husband) – *British Army.*
RALPH (Ralph Meek, an RAF friend from Cologne days) or *BUSTER'S FIRM* – the *Royal Air Force.*
PAT (Pat Horan, a British Naval officer, married to one of Sibyl's friends from Ross-on-Wye days) – *Royal Navy.*
BELLA or *BEAU* (Sibyl's French poodles) – *France* or *French.*
LULU (a German woman friend) – *Germans.*

UNCLE MARK (Markbreiter) – *Home Office* or *British government.*

Other names or places were added from time to time, depending on the content of the message. Thanks to the efforts of his stepdaughters in England and to Sibyl, who wrote of all that was happening on the island and of what she had heard on her hidden radio, Bob was able to keep up with everything that was going on, his only other source of news at that time being the German-controlled and propaganda-slanted Channel Island newspapers, which the internees were allowed to receive from home. An early example of how information was passed on is contained within Sibyl's letter to him of 18th July, 1943:

> ... The Franky's are getting very sick of their family and of the fact that Harry and Stewart put them aside so much, and as for Ralph he gives them all they get and more, and is getting the same sort of work done as at Gladys's [Gladys Richardson was now living in London] and is a great help to Harry's farming who gets it done well with his assistance, and Stewart and Pat ... Ask Jehanne also is hair short or long and tell her I shall need a trousseau! What are fashions like? Later: Stewart and Harry have got half their job done now ...

In another letter, a week later, she wrote:

> Everything Buzz is doing at Franky's is splendid, he will soon be starting on Bella's and Spaldings with any luck. Ralph and Stewart have given him a jolly good start anyway, and Lulu is carrying on like before you left ...

Occasionally he was able to pass on news of the war himself, as in the following message to her dated 17th August, 1943:

> ... From Amice: Pat's fishing decreased to practically nothing. Buster's firm very sound position accumulating considerable reserves. Amalgamation with Stewart's friends to open new branches, expect great increase in profits without much opposition ...

Most of Bob's letters to Sibyl remain but only three of hers have been found although he is believed to have brought the complete correspondence home. From those that are left, however, their affection for each other is very apparent and it is obvious from Bob's letters that, whatever his own privations at the time,

Sibyl's welfare was always his primary concern – as his final paragraphs usually conveyed:

> . . . All my love as always to you and you will never know how happy you have made me with your constant kindness and care. I think of nothing but you and bless you all the time . . .
>
> . . . My thoughts are only of you . . .
>
> . . . Take care of YOURSELF before all else . . .
>
> . . . Your comfort and safety are all I care about . . .

Sibyl's "kindness" and "care" at that distance was exhibited not only in her "amusing" letters which, Bob told her, were also enjoyed by his room-mates who found her style "unique" but in the other, thoughtful little packages which she sent him as often as she could. Among the items she parcelled up for him were pots of honey, home-made jam – made from plums, saccharine and carrageen seaweed – Seigneurie farm butter, onions to flavour his tasteless camp stew, matches, and, to Bob's particular delight, what she referred to as "Zeus". Knowing how much Bob missed what he called "a real drink", she sent him on several occasions small bottles of whisky and brandy which she hid away among the onions and other items. The whisky she labelled "eye-wash" and the brandy "sleeping draught" – much to the amusement of those of his companions who were let into the secret. Although Bob always assured her that he was "leading the life of Riley" and at no time hinted at the true state of affairs, Sibyl could usually guess when matters were not going too well for him and this was generally the signal for her to send him another small bottle of "medicine" to cheer him up.

Life on Sark after the deportations went on very much as before, though there were occasional moments of excitement to lift the endless monotony of living on a small island with ever-increasing shortages. Two months after Bob's departure the Channel Islands were threatened with drastic food cuts following an attack on German food ships plying between Granville and the islands, and Sark was forced to reduce both its bread and meat rations, despite Sibyl's protests to the local Commandant. Even so the island was still better off for farm produce and fish than either Jersey or Guernsey. Most people continued to grow their own vegetables and, where possible, to keep farmyard animals, feeding them on what scraps they could. Wild rabbits, however, were proving a pest as they came out at night from the mined areas around the cliffs, where they multiplied undisturbed, and ate up many of the carefully nurtured and much-needed crops.

In March the island had a sharp reminder of the dangers of venturing too close to this barbed wire area which now encircled the coast, when the local Commandant, known to everyone as "Papa" Hinkel, was killed by one of the mines laid on the beaches by his own troops. He had been directing some naval officials who had gone out in a boat to retrieve a drifting sea-mine when he had accidentally walked into the minefield ashore. Sibyl was as shocked by his death as everyone else, although she had always tried to have as few dealings as possible with the Sark Commandants – preferring to deal direct with the higher command in Guernsey.

During the summer she asked one of these senior officials if permission might be granted for two women friends from Guernsey to stay with her for a few days and he had readily agreed. She had been very lonely since Bob and so many of her English friends had been deported and she eagerly listened to the news her guests brought her of relations and friends in Guernsey, whom she had not seen for some three years. She also cheered herself up by swapping clothes with one friend to make a change after wearing the same dresses for the past few years and even managed several games of bridge, recruiting the German army doctor to make up a four. The pair stayed for nine days and Sibyl heard afterwards – much to her amusement, if not to theirs – that they had been mistaken for German prostitutes on the boat going back to Guernsey, so unusual was it for women to travel unaccompanied between the islands during those years.

By the autumn, Bob was passing on certain other cryptic messages which, sadly, cannot be transcribed fully as only he or she would have understood their exact meaning. In his November letters he several times mentioned "Jim's call on Raymond" and that she was to inform the latter of "Jim's imminent visit" – which may or may not have related in some way to Agricultural Officer Raymond Falla.* But there is no doubt about the implications behind Bob's message, dated 14th December, 1943:

> . . . Permission granted to send you a present soon – hope you will like it – NOTHING to do with Jim's call on Raymond, which will probably be Feb. Harry is visiting Gladys's old home above Allright's farm. Water power for my batteries ONLY, one horse power all necessary. Fred, Fear and the Ewe must all visit relatives . . .

* Mr. Falla was unable to recollect anything that might throw some light on this.

As neither spoke of it afterwards – for fear, perhaps, of implicating others – it is still a mystery as to who in England passed the information to him and thus on to her. But it clearly related in some way to a commando raid which did, in fact, take place on Christmas Day, within eleven days of his letter being sent. Transcribed from what is known of the code, it reads that the army (Harry) would be visiting Le Manoir (the German HQ and Gladys Richardson's old home) above a farm in Dixcart Valley, close to where the "Ewe" (Lamb), "Fear" (Colonel Fear) and "Fred" had all lived – though Bob would have known that by that time all had left their homes for one reason or another and that the area had already been evacuated. There is no evidence that she received the "message" in time as Bob's letters generally took about ten days to reach her, or even that she understood it, and it is difficult now to understand why he should have passed such information on to her at all. There was nothing she could have done to help. Indeed, had she realised its implication this would surely have added even more tension to her already stressful life.

As it was, the raid, when it came, turned out to be disastrous. The first attempt to scale the Hog's Back from Derrible Bay, where the men landed on Christmas night, proved unsuccessful and the party of five, led by Lieutenant A. J. M. McGonigal, were forced to make a further attempt to climb to the summit two nights later. This time they managed it and, using the gorse as cover, made their way towards Dixcart Valley as planned, unaware that they were crossing a minefield until two of the mines exploded. The men then quickly retraced their steps, only to trigger off more mines. Two Frenchmen in the party were killed and two other commandos were wounded who with the one uninjured member managed to make it back to the boat, leaving as they did so a trail of blood to the shore. From out at sea they saw flares from the German patrols investigating the explosions but it was only the next morning that the two Frenchmen's bodies were discovered. Speaking of the raid afterwards, Sibyl said that although the commandos had failed, their action had served to undermine the confidence of the occupying force and they became uneasy and constantly on the alert. It also did much, she maintained, to raise the morale of both herself and the Sark people, for it made them realise that, small though it was, their island was not forgotten.

During the weeks that followed, Bob's letters showed his concern for her welfare:

Jan 4th, 1944 . . . Cannot tell you how worried I am about you. No details of any kind yet known about your latest trouble. Are you at home as usual? . . . Praying for letter from you soon, as nothing else counts until I know you are all right. All Eng. post delayed, so nothing to tell, and no one knows whether Alvar* has mentioned you . . .

However, his letter of 11th January, having heard from her in the meantime, was more cheerful and he told her that "the tenants of Gladys's old house" would be giving up their lease before the summer, but "may move much earlier" – information which he said had been passed on by his "solicitor J. Beaumont" (Jehanne). But it was to be some months before the Germans finally vacated the island, and Sibyl had many Sark problems to solve before then.

In early spring, the island baker and general storekeeper, Hubert Lanyon, was taken by the Germans to Guernsey and imprisoned there for his part in helping to distribute an underground news-sheet known as GUNS (Guernsey Underground News Service), started in 1942 when radio sets had been confiscated, so that people might still be kept informed of the news bulletins issued by the BBC. Its creator, Charles Machon, and four others who had helped to bring out the sheet in Guernsey, were also imprisoned and deported to Germany. The Gestapo tried to force Lanyon to say who else on Sark handled the sheet but he steadfastly refused to implicate others and was sentenced to a term of six months' imprisonment. Fortunately, his father and others were able to carry on baking bread for the Sark people, but Sibyl had yet another place to fill on her Emergency Committee for he had also been in charge of the distribution of bread and flour and his enforced absence from the island coincided with the beginning of the worst food crisis it had yet had to face.

On a night in early June, Sibyl's sleep was disturbed by the continuous drone of heavy aircraft overhead and the next morning the German doctor, Dr. Wolfgang Schubert, who was by now a good friend, called on her while she was at breakfast and broke the news that the Allied forces had landed on the French coast. With great excitement, she and the Bishops for the first time risked listening-in to their hidden radio set during daylight hours and heard the doctor's news, that D-Day had indeed arrived, confirmed. Those at the Seigneurie and others on the island who had secretly kept their radios or had made crystal sets for them-

* Alvar Liddell – wartime news-reader for BBC radio.

selves, found it difficult not to discuss what was going on in Normandy, from which sounds of battle could now be clearly heard. Wild stories circulated about German troops already leaving Guernsey for fear of being cut off and Sibyl was not alone in thinking that the islands would soon be liberated. She knew that she was unlikely to hear any news from England for the time being and was surprised when a letter arrived from Bob on 22nd July, written a month earlier:

> June 13th, 1944. Yours May 14, 16, 22, 29 here. Wonder if you will ever get this one. Letter from Jane (*Jehanne*) dated Mar. 28. No more air mail allowed from Eng, so correspondence will be VERY slow. Will send on all you requested ... Glad you got tractor back and new bull good. Spend TWICE as much on drink if you can get it. Delighted your weight more normal ... All much worried about your welfare at present – lots of rumours but nothing authentic ... We hear Stewart plowed [*sic*] Buster's field in Guernsey, but was quite rough about it ... Do take care of yourself at ALL times; not much more time left. All well here and Buzz all over the place. All my love to you as always. Tobacco and cigs all right – saving all BEST for you. No end of love as ever ... All hope to see you soon,
>
> No end of love, R.

Sibyl had suffered a bad bout of bronchitis during the previous winter and had lost a great deal of weight but her staff at the Seigneurie had managed to build her up again with as much as they could of the farm food. Her extra pounds were not to remain for long, however, for by the late summer Sark, with the rest of the Channel Islands, was suffering from the supply links with France being severed by the Allied landings. The islands were now in a state of siege and troops and civilian population alike were severely affected with medical supplies, fuel and other commodities running desperately short. People stored what they could of their own vegetable harvest in preparation for what looked like being a harsh winter and Sibyl, after a warning by Dr. Schubert that grain and potatoes might soon be commandeered, hid away as many potatoes as she was able in a space beneath a trap-door under her drawing-room carpet.

Conditions grew worse as the year progressed and in October all Sark was shocked when a pretty, four-year-old child, Nanette Hamon, was killed after crawling into a minefield near her home in the east of the island. She was the first – and only – casualty among the island's people and her death came at a time when morale was at its lowest ebb.

Most of the German reserve stocks had by this time been used up and some of the hungry soldiers began stealing vegetables, chickens, calves and pigs to supplement their meagre rations. Others raided empty houses, in search of fuel for their cooking stoves. Sibyl became so incensed by their behaviour that she told the local Commandant that he had not got an army but "a pack of thieves and beggars".

With the additional privations and no letters from Bob to cheer her up and break the monotony of her days, Sibyl said that she went to bed each night at this time "thanking God" that she had managed to get through another day. Her only consolation was remembering the happier times and as she strove to keep warm she would thumb through the photograph albums, which contained pictures of her cruises in tropical climes and she would try to remember the warmth she had experienced in India or Africa.

Christmas, 1944, was one of the loneliest and bleakest she could remember and she wondered how Bob was faring at Laufen and if her family and friends were safe in England, for during the past year the German press had made much of the flying bomb attacks on London and other towns. According to Cecile Bouget, Sibyl was a different woman at this time from the normally self-confident extrovert most people knew, a quieter, more subdued and pensive person who appeared to worry more about the future and be greatly concerned about what was happening to Bob. The arrival of the Red Cross ship, *Vega*, in January, cheered everyone. It brought small parcels of food and other commodities which many had not seen for years. Some of the Sark people took pity on the hungry Germans and occasionally gave them items from their own parcels. But by this time it was apparent that the war was coming to an end and each day it seemed the disheartened troops moved guns frantically around the island or erected iron posts in the fields to prevent gliders landing – wrecking as they did so, much to the islanders' distress, some of the spring crops.

In February, Colonel von Schmettow was replaced as Commander-in-Chief of the Channel Islands by Admiral Hüffmeier – a tough, fanatical Nazi for whom Sibyl had little respect. She heard later that von Schmettow had been accused of being too lenient with the islanders and had only survived after his recall to Germany through the intervention of his uncle, Field Marshal Gerd von Rundstedt. The new Commander-in-Chief made frequent morale-raising tours among his troops but after the news reached them of Hitler's death on 1st May, even Hüffmeier's stirring words had no effect on the totally dispirited soldiers for it was becoming apparent to them all that total surrender was now only a matter of time.

On 7th May the Sark Commandant ordered the first actual requisitioning of island cattle for his starving troops, together with 200 tons of timber but this order was never to be obeyed, for the following day the news reached Sibyl and those others with radios that Admiral Doenitz had surrendered. By eleven o'clock she had given instructions for the Union Jack to be flown from the Seigneurie tower and an excited population gathered at the island hall to hear the Prime Minister, Winston Churchill, broadcast a message which included a reference to the "dear Channel Islands" once again being free. Sibyl later told of the wry smiles this had caused for at that time there were still about 280 Germans on the island and not a British serviceman was to be seen. After the speech Sibyl took it upon herself to thank the islanders for "staying put" and thus sparing Sark and their homes from the "chaotic conditions which obtained in other places where evacuation had occurred". Although the island had suffered to some extent by the "senseless and cruel removal of relations and friends, by the mining and wiring off of large areas of land which deprived farmers of valuable grazing, Sark had come through its ordeal cheerfully". She also paid tribute to the farmers for the "grand work in providing for the inhabitants so fully".

The following day Harold Brache, Assistant Secretary to the States Supervisor, crossed over from Guernsey with the Proclamation of Liberation, which was read out that evening at the school, and the islanders later celebrated their first curfew-free night for nearly five years by lighting a huge "Liberation bonfire" on the cliffs, with material that had been collected secretly for some days. Those who saw the blaze from out at sea or from the other islands thought that the Germans must be engaged in some final act of sabotage before surrendering.

British naval vessels were by this time at anchor off St. Peter Port, but it was not until the afternoon of the next day – 10th May – that three British officers and twenty men made an official landing from a German launch. There had, it appeared, been some concern in Guernsey because the German troops on Sark were not answering telephones and it was decided that a token detachment should cross over to the smaller island to investigate. As soon as the boat was sighted, Sibyl made her way down to the harbour to greet the officer in charge, Colonel Allen, and after informing him that the Germans appeared to have "gone to ground", she offered to act as interpreter for the confrontation with the local Commandant, who had shut himself away in his headquarters at Le Manoir. This was accepted and she took the small party to the house where most of the troops were hiding – "more frightened", one islander remarked later, "of La Dame than of the liberating troops". After accepting the official surrender from the Commandant and satisfying himself that conditions on Sark were reasonable and that the Germans were not likely to give any trouble, Colonel Allen then asked Sibyl if she would mind being left for a short while longer on her own, as he had only a token force in Guernsey and could not spare any of these men for Sark. This prompted her to reply, with some sarcasm, that as she had "been left for nearly five years" she could "stand a few more days", but she suggested to Colonel Allen that he should authorise her to give any necessary orders to the German troops remaining on the island. He readily agreed and she duly translated this to the German Commandant, adding her first order to him, that his men should immediately set about reconnecting telephone lines so that there might be a twenty-four-hour contact with Guernsey.

For the following few days she enjoyed herself hugely. She saw to it that the troops were set to work removing the mines and anti-glider posts, returning confiscated radio sets and rounding up their horses to give to the farmers. It all gave her, she said afterwards, "enormous satisfaction". Only once was her confidence shaken in any way. She had issued an order for the removal of the roll-bombs, which had been hanging precariously over the entrance to the harbour and was, on her own admission, genuinely distressed and shocked when she received a telephone call from the Commandant to inform her that two of his soldiers had been killed in the process. With the approval of Brigadier Snow, who commanded the British force in Guernsey, she gave permission for the soldiers to be buried in the island cemetery with full military honours. Most of the Sark people were sympathetic and many attended the funeral, as a mark of respect for the generally good behaviour and discipline of those who had occupied their island during the past five years. This discipline was no more apparent than when it was discovered that three months' supplies had been laid in at the Girls' School, on Admiral Hüffmeier's instructions, in anticipation of a final stand being made. Sibyl marvelled that the Germans could have left these stores intact throughout the latter days of the occupation when they had been so desperately hungry.

An occasion during the first week of liberation that Sibyl long remembered was her invitation to dinner aboard HMS *Bulldog*, one of the two British destroyers accompanying the liberating forces. She never forgot "that feast of which Lucullus would have been proud", as she later described it, or how white the officers' shirts and collars and the tablecloths appeared to her after the greyness of Sark clothes, which for so long had been washed without adequate soap. The Captain asked her what she had missed most during the occupation and she told him "hot baths and the smell of bacon frying" – though she admitted afterwards that she had never been very fond of bacon and could not understand why that particular aroma should have haunted her when she had been hungry. When the kindly officer saw to it that a special bacon savoury was prepared and set before her, the sudden release of the tension she had been under during past months, the friendly faces around her and the whole emotional occasion were too much for her and it was all she could do to choke back her tears.

Shortly afterwards she went to Guernsey to appear before the Royal Court with regard to, as she put it, "an urgent official matter" which she felt should be settled without delay. Although she had used Bob's position as Seigneur to try to bring about his exemption from deportation, most of the Germans continued to believe that she was really the head of the island. Legally, however, she should not have signed any of the official documents in his absence without his written authorisation making her his deputy – something that had been understandably forgotten at the time of his deportation. All the business that had been passed by Chief Pleas in his absence had therefore to be legalised by the Royal Court, as had her position as Deputy Seigneur pending his return. This was duly arranged but not before Sibyl had taken it upon herself to conduct a correspondence with the Home Office over the rehabilitation of the island and it is obvious from these letters that whatever the legal position, she fully intended to take as active a part in Sark's affairs as she had always done.

By the end of May, mercy ships were plying regularly between all the Channel Islands, loaded with food and other supplies and following quickly upon these and the arrival of the main force of British troops, came the news correspondents and government officials – including the Home Secretary, Herbert Morrison. When the Minister reported his findings to Parliament a Member made an enquiry about Sark and there was much laughter and cheering from the House when the Home Secretary replied that he had seen the Dame of Sark, who appeared to have been "remarkably successful, mostly on her own, in keeping the German garrison in order", a remark which in later years prompted Bob to describe his wife as being "the only woman ever to be cheered in the House of Commons".

Prior to Herbert Morrison's visit she had received an official letter from him as Home Secretary, dated 10th May – the day Sark was liberated:

> Dear Mrs. Hathaway,
>
> I am very glad to have the opportunity of sending you a message of greeting to put on record an expression of appreciation, both on the part of the Home Office and myself, of the courage with which you and your people have faced the trials and privations of the long period of enemy occupation now happily at an end, and to convey to you my best wishes for the future prosperity of the islands.
>
> We have been very glad to receive in the Home Office some news of you, both from yourself and from your husband in Germany, and I hope you will soon be reunited.
>
> Yours sincerely,
>
> (signed) HERBERT MORRISON.

As always, the international press found her a good subject and newspapers all over the world soon carried articles about her wartime experiences. She delighted in once again having interest focused upon her and this encouraged her to provide stories of the occupation which grew with each fresh interview, much to the amusement and sometimes great annoyance of her islanders when the articles appeared. Philip Grune in the London *Evening Standard* of 25th May, 1945, shrewdly began the account of his meeting with her as follows:

> ... To hear first-hand from the Dame of Sark, Mrs. Hathaway, the story of the occupation of this little island, is more like listening to a comic opera ... It seems that most of the 72 odd Germans on the island were the most gullible people in the world and the islanders were so astute that they were able to get away with almost anything ...

The *American Weekly* magazine ended its account of her part in the occupation – as told, presumably, by Sibyl – "... In the succinct phraseology of the GI – 'Some dame!'"

Most of the officials who visited the island reported favourably on her part in the handling of Sark's food and other affairs during the past five years and she was particularly pleased when medical officers praised the condition of the children, whose feeding and general welfare had always been one of her primary considerations. The majority were found to be in a healthy condition and of good physique – only two infants showing slight signs of rickets. The skin ailments which had troubled many were due more, she was told, to the shortage of soap during the occupation than to any dietary cause.

On 7th June, King George VI and Queen Elizabeth made a special Liberation visit to the Channel Islands and in an open-air ceremony in Guernsey's Candie Gardens, Sibyl followed the Bailiff, Victor Carey, in presenting a loyal address on behalf of her island:

> TO THE KING'S MOST EXCELLENT MAJESTY.
> May it please Your Majesty, we, Your Majesty's most loyal and dutiful subjects, the members of the Chief Pleas of the Island of Sark, the smallest legislative assembly by Royal Order established within Your Majesty's Domain, beg leave humbly and respectfully to offer to Your Majesty, and to Her Most Gracious Majesty the Queen, on behalf of ourselves and the other inhabitants of the Island, our deep sentiments of loyalty on the occasion of Your Majesties' visit, and our fervent thanks for the manifestations of Your Majesty's interest in the welfare and comfort of your loving and loyal subjects.
>
> (Signed) Sibyl Hathaway,
> Dame de Serk.
> Sixth of June, 1945.

She took the opportunity, at a private tea-party after the official ceremony, of telling the King about her worries over Bob, for she had received no news of him since the Liberation. The King was sympathetic and promised to see that enquiries were made and Bob's return hastened. Sibyl was not to know it at the time, but a letter was in fact already on its way to her. Dated 9th May, it had been written shortly after the Laufen prisoners had been freed – by the United States Army, much to Bob's delight: "... What a sight to see them speeding down the road towards us – through the front gates and *know* we were free."

Shortly after the Royal visit, she received a telegram from him to say that he was on his way home but it was not until 21st June that he finally arrived back on Sark, a poignant meeting for them both after two years apart and one which Sibyl later described as follows:

> The moment I caught sight of him at the harbour I realised that he must not guess from my expression how his appearance shook me. He had always been a lean man; now he was nothing more than a bag of bones. He had the unhealthy pallor of a man who has been cooped up inside a prison for a long time, and he looked as if he was still suffering from a high degree of nervous tension . . .

She worried that Bob might find her changed also for she, too, had lost a considerable amount of weight since he left, possibly due more to the tensions and worries of past months than to actual shortage of food. Whatever their private thoughts, however, they greeted each other with relief and joy and this time Sibyl's feelings were demonstrated for all at the harbour to see, and there was no doubt in the minds of those present at the reunion of the deep affection between them. It was a long time before Bob looked and felt anything approaching his former self and Sibyl always maintained that he never fully recovered from those two years at Laufen.

By this time she had managed to gather together news of most members of her large family. Now that the war was coming to an end and frequent mention was made of those who would not return, she found it hard to believe that Buster was among them and that she would never again see her eldest son. A consolation to her, perhaps, was that Astley had acquitted himself well during the past few years as a pilot in the Royal Australian Air Force. After an aeroplane crash he had suffered injuries for which he was still receiving treatment but from all accounts he was reasonably well and had kept himself out of financial and other troubles for some years. This had not, she discovered, been the case with her youngest son, Richard, who had tried a variety of jobs throughout the war after failing several medicals for the forces, and whose financial and marital misfortunes were now giving her some cause for concern. Douce was another source of worry to her. When Sibyl had seen her for the first time since the early years of the occupation, at the dinner aboard HMS *Bulldog*, she was shocked by the appearance of her once beautiful daughter. Douce had left the Seigneurie with her young child in late 1940 in order to live with a doctor friend in Guernsey. He had done his best to help curb her drinking habits but to no avail and when liquor became short as the occupation progressed, he discovered she was even rifling his surgery for neat alcohol. His partners, understandably, objected to Douce's continued presence in the house from which their practice was being conducted and Sibyl was trying to persuade her to go to England for a course of treatment.

Jehanne returned to Sark at the beginning of July after working with the Channel Island section of the Red Cross, an organisation for which Sibyl felt special gratitude and said as much, publicly, in a letter to *The Times* on behalf of her people, shortly after the Liberation. Amice was the next to return home – two weeks after Jehanne – and Sibyl went over to Guernsey to meet her and soften her distress at seeing the damage that had been done to "La Cour de Longue" in her absence. Most of the furniture had been wrecked, the silver stolen and the whole house was in a sorry state. Jehanne stayed in Guernsey to help Amice get her home back into some kind of order for her returning family but Sibyl, after making sure that her eldest daughter had material for curtains and sufficient furniture to tide her over, returned to Sark, for there was much work awaiting her there.

Chapter 13

For the first few months following the Liberation, Sark was the scene of great activity. The German troops that remained had been put to work, under the control of British army engineers, repairing most of the roadways which their heavy transport had left in a poor state. La Coupée – that impressive, granite causeway which links the main island with Little Sark – was also strengthened and generally improved and most of the 13,500 mines which had been laid on the beaches and clifftops were cleared. Meanwhile island events were also settling back into a normal pattern. Early in July, the Cattle Show was held in the field adjoining the Seigneurie to which the usual dignitaries from Guernsey were invited and later in the month a special meeting of Chief Pleas took place.

This was Bob's first meeting since his return and he thanked the island for its welcome, telling of how in prison camp his "constant thoughts" had been of Sark. After D-Day he had no way of knowing if the island's houses had been "blasted out of the ground" and he was relieved to discover that there had been few changes. He was glad to be back "now that the Hun had gone" and hoped Sark would soon be able to get down to business again. The obvious sincerity behind his words pleased the islanders and there was further applause when he announced that Sibyl and he had decided "for this year, at least" to continue to waive all claims for tithes – something which they had decided upon at the beginning of the occupation. For the rest of the meeting, as had so often been the case in the past, it was Sibyl's voice rather than her husband's that was more frequently heard and it was apparent to all that she had no intention of withdrawing from her position with regard to island affairs just because Bob – the official Seigneur – was back.

The engagement of a new Medical Officer and a schoolmistress was now high on the list of priorities and Sibyl was closely involved with both. She had long been on the committee dealing with the education of Sark's children and a scheme was under discussion at this time to enable those pupils who had reached a certain standard to attend college or grammar schools in Guernsey at the island's expense. Sibyl was often to claim later that the suggestion for such a scheme came from herself but, in fact, she had shown only a modicum of interest when it was first mooted, declaring that there seemed little point in Sark children having a secondary education, when most appeared to be destined to work on the land or in the house. But times were changing and she now saw the need for broader educational horizons for the island people if Sark was to survive in the tough postwar world and she gave the scheme her full backing. This tendency to take up the ideas of others and pass them off as her own was a trait typical of Sibyl in both her private and public life, so much so that, in later years one Chief Pleas member frankly admitted to starting what he termed a "whispering campaign" in order to make sure a pet scheme of his was pursued with her backing for – sure enough – once the idea had reached her ears it was brought out, in time, as her own.

Changes there undoubtedly were in postwar Sark and not least of these was the attitude of the islanders themselves. Through deportation many had been away from the Channel Islands for the first time in their lives and some of these now viewed their home affairs with critical new eyes. By the end of 1945 the Sark correspondent of the *Guernsey Press* wrote of the "two frames of mind" becoming apparent on the island – one wishing to modernise and the other to hold on to ancient customs. Some felt that, once the military had left, the ban on motorised traffic should be reinforced, as this would be an added encouragement for visitors attracted to the island by "the relief it gave from urban living". Others considered that some form of mechanised transport – if only one lorry – was essential to cart goods to and from the harbour around the island. It was also suggested that the electricity plant which the Germans had installed should be utilised in some way so that electricity could be brought into every home – but others immediately claimed that they preferred to stick to the old oil lamps that had served them well enough in the past. Many did not like the way Sibyl was taking it upon herself to conduct island affairs without prior consultation with Chief Pleas and, for the first time, a few were even questioning her right – as a married woman – to sit in the island parliament at all, let alone have a voice. But despite these whisperings and opinions that were being bandied about outside Chief Pleas, the conservative islanders were greatly shocked when, at the January meeting of 1946, Albert Falle, owner for many years of Stock's Hotel, had the temerity to speak his mind against her.

Bertie Falle was a well-known island personality, a People's Deputy who before the war would probably have termed himself a "pro-Hathaway" in the peculiar divisions Sark always seemed to have over most matters of policy, but Sibyl had recently antagonised him by sarcastically speaking of a personal matter which he felt was his family's own affair. He was further enraged by the stories she had related to the press over the conditions on the island following the occupation. He had worked hard to get his hotel back into some semblance of order so that he might be ready for visitors and took exception to her reported allegations that Sark's hotels had been "ruined" and would take some time to put to rights again.

"Who is Mrs. Hathaway?" he asked the startled assembly. "Is she Dictator of Sark? She takes on too much on her own. Chief Pleas is not consulted on things. There is too much secrecy. Why are we not consulted? Chief Pleas should be told of what is going on. What are we, then – a lot of children who must not be told anything? I'm getting sick and fed up with all this. It's all Mrs. Hathaway." He went on to refer to her comments on the hotels, which she immediately denied having made with regard to either Stock's or the Dixcart. "And what's all this about a new shipping company? Why must we wait until the papers come to know what's happening?" (This was a reference to a recently published article about negotiations Sibyl was purported to be conducting with a shipping company to start up a new and much-needed regular service to the island.) When further remarks concerning her failure to appoint a suitable doctor were followed by those of a more personal nature, Sibyl had had enough. "Since this is the opinion," she countered, her voice shrill with indignation, "I will resign all my appointments, and will have nothing more to do with anything. Chief Pleas will have to find someone else to see to the doctor's affair, the schools and other things." The Constable did his best to placate her, saying that no notice should be taken of "the lies printed in newspapers" and that it was a "foolish argument" but, although agreeing that it *was* "foolish", stern of face and barely able to conceal her fury, she left the building and a stunned assembly.

After a few minutes the meeting continued, though much subdued. At the end of the business a member proposed that Bob, who had remained, should convey an apology from Chief Pleas to Sibyl and that she should be asked to return "to help straighten out affairs" but another said that it was up to Bertie Falle to do the apologising. He refused to accept that this was necessary. "This is the place to talk. You all talk about her outside, but have no guts to speak here." Another heated exchange with the Constable followed, after the official had said in Sibyl's defence: "People are always ready to criticise but not so ready to come forward and help. I propose that Mr. Falle takes on Mrs. Hathaway's work." To which Bertie Falle countered, amid some mild applause: "What has she done? Does she work for the people or for herself? She should tell us what she is doing. There is too much secrecy . . ." But the general feeling appeared to be that he had "gone too far" and he grudgingly agreed to apologise. Bob, who was obviously upset by the whole affair, promised that he would do his "utmost" to persuade Sibyl to return, and added:

> . . . She is a public person wherever she goes – America, Canada, England or France – and is looked to as the owner and ruler of this island. She is greater than any walloping thing that has appeared in newspapers. If it had not been for her, we would not be so well off, neither would we be in such a good position. When she is writing at her desk dealing with correspondence till midnight, don't think she is playing bridge.

It was the longest and most fervent speech he was ever to make on his wife's behalf and the whole incident left a lasting impression.

Of course Sibyl went back – how could she stay away? Whatever her critics may have thought, being Dame of Sark and the promotion and welfare of her island were still of paramount importance to her. Besides which, she was too involved in the many schemes for the future that she had already set in motion to give up at this stage. The legal Seigneur Bob may have been, but his inability to speak the patois was often a handicap and it was generally accepted that without her driving energy and ability to take firm action where necessary, island affairs would have presented a very different picture. As it was, rehabilitation was progressing at a good pace and high on the list of priorities, to her mind, was the completion of the new harbour upon which work had stopped early in 1941, when the materials had run out and the labour force had been taken over by the Germans.

She began correspondence with the Home Office about restarting the work soon after the Liberation and was indignant when it was suggested that the money, which had been set aside for this purpose from the Landing Tax and been profitably invested

La Dame, at her Seigneurie desk, above. Below left, with Lord Sackville, Lieutenant Governor of Guernsey, at the Sark Regatta and, right, receiving the King's Cup for the best bull on Sark at the Guernsey Cattle Show from Edward, Prince of Wales, in 1935.

Sibyl and her husband with a group of German officers outside the Seigneurie during the occupation, above. After the liberation, German prisoners repaired the island roads, seen here at La Coupée, below right, and left, a peacetime visit by Colonel Graf von Schmettow in 1963.

in War Loan, should be diverted instead into other rehabilitation needs. According to her own account of the affair:

> I wrote a firm letter to Mr. Markbreiter at the Home Office telling him plainly that if we used our fund for any other purpose we should be copying the British Government's tactics with their Motor Car Taxes, and I flatly refused to do this.

When she was then politely told that, as Sark was the only Channel Island to emerge from the war with a credit balance, nothing further could be done to help, she let it be known that she thought such a policy harsh in the extreme as "proportionally Sark had suffered just as much as the other islands" and invested what money it had in the war effort. The National Provincial Bank eventually provided a loan on what she described as "favourable terms" and Sark was able to solve its difficulties without any outside grants – which, according to Sibyl, gave the island "a satisfactory feeling of independence for we no longer had to go cap in hand to the Home Office". A good shipping service was essential and she knew that this was unlikely to come until the work on the new harbour had been completed. She had already embarked on negotiations for a possible new service but little progress had been made and for the time being Sark was obliged to rely on various makeshift measures to ship passengers and goods to and from the island.

Other matters had, however, been more satisfactorily settled by the close of 1946. A new doctor, vicar and schoolmistress had all been appointed, the school had re-opened and visitors were beginning to return to the hotels. After a long search for a suitable person to fill the position of Medical Officer of Health it was her sister, Doris, whom Sibyl finally had to thank for finding him. She had telephoned from York, where her husband was stationed with the army, to tell Sibyl that she had found "just the right man for the job". He was invited to stay at the Seigneurie and from their first meeting Sibyl knew that her sister had not been mistaken. Dr. Hewitt – "Hewie" as he was soon to become known to her and Bob – was to prove not only a popular doctor but a valued and useful member of the community. He was also to become one of the few friends for whom she always had a very high regard, whose judgment she trusted and whose counsel she was prepared to heed.

In December the Hathaways left for the United States and Canada, where Sibyl was to give another lecture tour, leaving Jehanne behind in Sark to act for the first time as Deputy Seigneur for the Christmas meeting of Chief Pleas. They spent Christmas at the Ritz Hotel in Boston with Bob's family, whom they had not seen since before the occupation, and Sibyl was to describe this period afterwards as her "first real high, wide and carefree holiday" for seven years. After the rationing and scarcity of luxury goods in the British Isles she was, in her own words, "spellbound" by this new world of plenty. The holiday was also highlighted for her by another visit to Hollywood, where she was able to meet three favourite stars – Bing Crosby, Bob Hope and Alan Ladd.

She began her lecture tour in Cleveland, Ohio, in the New Year of 1947 and from there went to Canada where she was scheduled to speak at the Royal Ontario Museum, an occasion she was not likely to forget for it was one of the very few occasions on which she lost her voice. She had just begun her talk, illustrating it, as usual, with the film of Sark, when she found her normally strident voice failing and within minutes it was reduced to a croaky whisper. There was nothing for it but to push her prepared notes into Bob's hands and motion him to continue in her place. Much to her astonishment – and chagrin – he spurned her typed sheets and launched himself instead into an amusing commentary of his own, which soon had his audience convulsed with laughter. The following morning the press were unanimous in their praise, saying that he was "a new star with a wit as dry as paper". Rather to her annoyance, Sibyl was mentioned only in passing. Her laryngitis forced her to cancel some of the other lectures she had planned but she took the opportunity of seeing, for the first time, Montreal, the city where her mother had been born. Then it was back to the United States and a few days in New York before she and Bob sailed home again at the end of March in time for the Easter Chief Pleas.

In the February, from a friend's ranch at Pasadena, Sibyl had written to Sir Philip Neame, then Lieutenant Governor of Guernsey:

> ...I am sorry the boat service seems delayed. I thought they had promised the MFV (motor fishing vessel) in January. No doubt the fuel shortage delayed the workshop alterations... A boat 247 feet long, carrying some 250 people is to run from Jersey during the summer which should help our landing tax. Judging by the enthusiasm shown here and enquiries about travel after my lectures, we shall have a big influx in 1948 – too soon for this year...

It was not, however, "too soon" for others to visit Sark for on her return she found to her delight that most of the hotel accommodation was already booked for the new season and during the following summer months many day trippers also crossed from Guernsey and Jersey. Among those on holiday in the island was the Labour Minister of Food – John Strachey – and his family. The Minister had never been one of Bob's favourite politicians and rather to Sibyl's embarrassment, he made no secret of his disapproval that planes and boats should have been laid on when, he claimed, the Minister's visit "had no connection with government business". Sibyl reported afterwards that ". . . the atmosphere was strained when I insisted they must be invited to dinner, though I had no more wish to entertain them than Bob had. Nevertheless, it is the business of the Seigneur to entertain all notable visitors to the island, regardless of personal opinions." She chose her other dinner guests with care and told them that on no account were they to raise controversial matters – but in the end it was she herself who allowed her personal feelings to surface. She mentioned her visit to the States and when her chief guest followed her remarks by saying facetiously that he wished England had Roosevelt and the Americans Churchill, she immediately rounded on him for attacking someone for whom she had always had the greatest respect. "Judging by the public applause that greeted Churchill in the cinema newsreels in the United States," she said, icily, "I am quite sure that the Americans would be only too happy to support the idea."

There is no doubt that Sibyl veered more to the right than to the left in her political inclinations but she tried to be equally hospitable to all government officials whatever their party. As time went on, however, it became obvious that some of her guests were made to feel more welcome than others, for her strong personal likes and dislikes occasionally proved too difficult for her to conceal.

During the summer she put up a notice in one of the island's shop windows. Headed, "La Seigneurie, Sark via Guernsey" it read: "Boys and girls willing to count the dîmes for 2s 6d a day are requested to apply: S. Hathaway." Bob and she had decided after all to reimpose the dîxieme, the levy of one-tenth of all cereals grown on the island which they had allowed to lapse since the early years of the war. When some of the farmers protested at its reintroduction, the international press were quick to seize upon the opportunity it gave to attack Sark's feudal system. The *News Chronicle* of 23rd September reported one Sarkese as saying:

We consider ourselves held in bondage in perpetuity. Farmers inherited their farms with their obligations. To refuse would in effect mean disinheritance and to be forced off the island. We in Sark know that Feudal bondage in an age of advancing democracy is a mockery of modern civilisation. We know it should be abolished. We would welcome a Privy Council Inquiry* in Sark...

As was to be expected, it was Sibyl – rather than Bob – whom the journalists contacted and whose replies were quoted. She had forgone the "dîme" during past years, she told them, in order to encourage better farming but no improvements had followed:

...There is no hardship in the tithes because farmers are not forced to grow cereal crops. Some of their land is left fallow and not even grazed. Somebody might as well get something out of it. The whole trouble is that islanders are too prosperous with visitors. They have become lazy and slack...

She had said pretty much the same about Sark's precious farming land years before and was to echo the same view many times afterwards. As for her own "feudal powers" she told reporters:

...It is untrue that I have power to turn an islander out of Sark. In fact, I have only one vote in the Court of Chief Pleas in which 485 people are represented by 52 men, the highest percentage in the world.

Referring to the financial aspect, she said:

As leader of Sark, I get no regular payment whatsoever, and no allowance for entertaining distinguished visitors. The money has got to come from somewhere...

For a while the bars and cottages of Sark were once again the settings for heated discussion but even those who claimed loudly that feudalism was outmoded could suggest no acceptable alternative. It always irritated Sibyl that islanders would talk outside Chief Pleas in this fashion and yet few would turn up at meetings

* The Privy Council Inquiry into the Constitution of the Channel Islands referred to by the farmer had been embarked upon the previous year and Sark's exclusion from the investigations – presumably because of its unique position as a Fief Haubert – had been the subject of some discussion.

to voice their opinions there. Even some of the elected Deputies of the People did not appear at the major gatherings during the year and there were many important schemes at that time under discussion which affected the whole island. She welcomed the comments of the Sark correspondent of the *Guernsey Press* early in October who urged islanders to make an effort to use their vote in the coming election for new Deputies: "The people themselves have the power to remove apathy, if they themselves are not apathetic." When Jehanne, her youngest daughter, who had always shown great interest in Sark's affairs, was one of those chosen to serve as a Deputy, Sibyl was delighted for she knew that Jehanne would be conscientious over any task she undertook.

Earlier in the year Jehanne had become engaged to an Englishman, Henry (Harry) Parkin Bell, whom she had first met before the war. The pair were planning to marry the following year and in the meantime were busy renovating the property they had bought – La Fripponerie, better known as the island "tenement" of Bel Air. Jehanne's first meeting as a Deputy was at Michaelmas and when a proposition was put before Chief Pleas that – there being no other form of motorised transport – tractors should be allowed to carry out heavy haulage work, she was able to speak with some authority on the problems of carting materials to and from the harbour.

The law as it stood at that time forbade any goods being transported by tractor unless the Constable's permission had been obtained or the consignment was for agricultural purposes. The Seneschal (William Baker) felt that if these permits were given to all tractor drivers the resulting traffic could become a nuisance, but another tenant said that he felt sorry for the poor horses that had to drag up the heavy loads. Jehanne agreed, saying that she thought everything over two tons *should* be carried by other means, having asked for heavy concrete blocks to be brought up by tractor and been refused. Sibyl's view was that the time would soon be coming "with rehabilitation work in progress" when heavy loads would be arriving even more frequently on the island and that the Constable should be given wider powers to grant permission for tractors to bring these up. In the years to come she was to wish, however, that stricter, rather than more lenient, measures had been taken with regard to these vehicles. A tenant's comment at this meeting, that a speed limit of three miles an hour would be "no use at all" because "as soon as the Constable's back is turned the drivers would go at fifty m.p.h. on roads not built for such speed", was to be proved right and the misuse of tractors generally was to become a major issue in future island affairs.

Soon after that lively Michaelmas meeting of Chief Pleas, Sibyl left for England, bound for yet another American lecture tour. This time she crossed the Atlantic alone, for Bob stayed behind to deal with any urgent matters that might arise out of the important schemes now afoot for the island. The tour was her most ambitious so far, for during the three months that she was to be away, she was booked to speak in places as far apart as Minneapolis and Texas, New York and California. Her lectures were this time on the Channel Islands as a whole, rather than on Sark alone, and she took with her several additional films of Guernsey and Jersey, which did much to increase the holiday traffic to those islands during the next few seasons.

She took the opportunity before she sailed home in March of collecting various items for Jehanne, which were still unobtainable at home, including the fruit and other ingredients for her wedding cake, yards of ivory satin brocade for a dress and other items for the trousseau and she boarded the *Queen Mary* accompanied by no fewer than twenty-seven bulky packages. At Southampton Jehanne was allowed on board as Sibyl had been suffering from a sharp bout of sciatica but, much to her daughter's amusement, this appeared to be swiftly and miraculously cured when – on discovering in the customs' shed, where she had been given preferential treatment because of her disability that she had left Jehanne's wedding veil under the bed in her cabin – she jumped smartly over the bench and sprinted back up the gangway in order to retrieve the precious article.

The wedding on 10th June, 1948, was a great occasion on Sark. It was the first to have taken place from the Seigneurie for over two hundred years and everyone was *en fête*, with island boats dressed overall and bunting everywhere – from the lighthouse at Pointe Robert to the smallest cottage. Charlie Perrée was put in charge of the seven carriages used to transport the main party to and from the church and he drove the bride in the same victoria in which he had taken Bob and Sibyl after their wedding twenty years earlier. At the island hall afterwards Jehanne and Harry cut the wedding cake and the four hundred assembled islanders and friends drank their health before the couple went on to another reception at the Seigneurie. Many went down to the harbour later to see them leave for their honeymoon in a white-beribboned speedboat on their way across to Guernsey for the first stage of their journey to England. Holidaymakers on the larger island caught some of the excitement on Sark that day as they watched the speedboat escorted into St. Peter Port by two similarly decorated boats.

It was, Sibyl told her friends afterwards, the kind of wedding she would have liked to have had herself but the happiness of the occasion was marred for her by the knowledge that Amice, her beloved eldest daughter, was desperately ill in a London hospital, having undergone a series of operations for cancer. Amice had not been well for some time but had always made light of her illness which Sibyl now knew was terminal. Shortly after the wedding she travelled to England to see her daughter and was appalled by what she found. The gentle Amice, for whom of all her children she had felt the greatest love, was unrecognisable from the buxom, healthy girl who had shared the happy days with her in Cologne and had returned to her farm in Guernsey only three years before with such hopes for the future. The thin, grey figure on the bed, obviously in pain, took her back to the time when her own mother had lain in a similar condition all those years before and she could hardly bear to see yet another much-loved person endure such suffering. She visited her frequently during the days that followed and each day on leaving the hospital made her way to a nearby church where – as she later admitted in a letter to her sister, Doris, she "*prayed* that Amice would not live through another night". She died on 8th July and at Sibyl's request was brought back to Sark for burial. Over ten years later, in recalling this period, she wrote:

> Amice's suffering and death caused me more bitterness of heart than anything that has ever happened to me. In many ways she was nearer to me than anyone else in the world . . . Of all the family she was the most beloved and outstanding personality. From the time she was a baby, she had the infectious gift of happiness which made everyone with whom she came into contact devoted to her. She never seemed to have a care in the world, and yet when I look at her photograph now I notice that although she was very pretty, there was something rather pathetic about her expression . . .

Sibyl's love for Amice carried over into that for her eldest daughter's two children – Peter and Sally – and after her mother's death it was usually to Sibyl that, as a schoolgirl, Sally went with her troubles, for she felt that her deep affection for her grandmother was reciprocated.

Bob comforted his wife as best he could but, as on so many other occasions in her life when she had had to face up to unhappy situations, she turned almost immediately to the solace of work and the plans for the island's future. At the next meeting of Chief Pleas in the autumn she strongly supported the motion that a committee be set up to deal with the "preservation of the island's beauty", claiming that if no restrictions were made "holiday camps and other eyesores could destroy Sark's beauty and all the nice tourists would stay away". The committee was duly formed and she agreed to act as its president.

Not discussed at the meeting but already under way were her plans for the opening of the almost complete La Maseline Harbour, which was to cost the island £52,000. She had, some months before, written to ask if the Duke of Edinburgh would consider making the official opening and was delighted when she was told that he had agreed and that both he and Princess Elizabeth would come to Sark in June of the following year. This projected visit did more than anything else to help turn Sibyl's thoughts away from the sorrow of Amice's death, for it had always been her ambition, since she first became Dame of Sark, to welcome a member of the Royal family to the island. Never before had such an official visit been made.

In her grandfather's time there had been hopes that Queen Victoria would come ashore during a tour of the Channel Islands in 1859, but bad weather had prevented a landing. On her orders, however, the Royal Yacht had been sailed as close to the coast as possible and the people waiting at the harbour had cheered and cannons on the clifftops had been fired, but this did not compensate for the islanders' bitter disappointment. They had gone to a great deal of trouble to decorate their houses and the entrance to the harbour with flowers and flags. A red carpet had been unrolled in readiness at the quay, where most of the population, headed by Sibyl's grandfather in full uniform of the Sark Militia, had waited patiently for several hours. A magnificent luncheon had also been prepared at the Seigneurie, but when the hungry welcoming party had returned they were in for another disappointment for the Seigneur's peacocks had got into the house, eaten all the food and created havoc among the beautifully laid tables. Princess Victoria, sister of King George V, had been the only member of the Royal family actually to set foot on Sark, in Sibyl's father's time, and this had been an unofficial visit. She had landed from a private yacht in 1902, intending to return the same day but owing to a sudden gale was forced to stay overnight. Sophia had received word that she was on the island and, respecting the Princess's wishes that she should remain incognito, tactfully sent flowers and a nightdress to the hotel where she was staying without divulging her identity.

There was therefore great excitement when the final plans were announced for the visit of the Duke of Edinburgh and Princess Elizabeth and everyone seemed determined that Sark should be shown at its best. June weather is usually good in the Channel Islands so there was an understandable apprehension when the morning of the visit, the 23rd, dawned with leaden skies and a choppy sea. These fears seemed justified when a message was received from the battleship HMS *Anson*, a mile or so off-shore with the Duke and Princess Elizabeth aboard, that it was proposing to sail on to Guernsey with its accompanying destroyers HMS *Roebuck* and HMS *Wizard*. Happily this message was followed shortly afterwards by another informing Sibyl and the assembled islanders that, after dropping anchor at St. Peter Port, the Royal couple and their entourage would transfer to two motor torpedo boats and return to Sark. This was duly accomplished but that treacherous strip of sea was still making matters difficult.

When the MTB pulled alongside the quay after what had obviously been a rough trip, Sibyl, Bob and the islanders watched nervously as the Princess made several attempts to step off onto the steep stone steps of the harbour. The wind blew around her as she tensed herself to jump but each time she tried the swell prevented her. There was a cheer of relief when, with Prince Philip's help, she finally landed safely, after one frightening moment when it had looked as if she had lost her balance and was about to fall. A Salvation Army band, which had come over from Guernsey for the occasion, struck up the National Anthem and Bob then read a Loyal Address to which the Princess replied. When the Duke formally opened the new harbour, he mentioned that this whole Royal visit to the Channel Islands had only come about through Sibyl's invitation to him, a comment which pleased her greatly, particularly as many Jersey and Guernsey officials were present to hear it. As the Duke unveiled the plaque the excited crowd surged forward to get a closer view and there was a roar of appreciation as he remarked, "I bet *you* were a handful for the Germans to keep in order."

The whole occasion was happy and relaxed and for the time being, at least, Sark's private feuds and bickerings were forgotten as everyone set about giving the visitors the island's own particular brand of welcome. The church bell was rung and bunches of flowers were thrown into the carriage, driven by a jubilantly proud Charlie Perrée, as the small procession made its way along the roads to the Seigneurie, escorted by the Constable, Frank Baker, and his assistant Henry Carré. As it turned into the drive to the house the Princess's personal standard was, on Sibyl's instructions, to be broken from the tower and the luncheon for fourteen, about which she had given considerable thought, was to be ready. As with the many similar visits that were to follow, everything appeared to go as planned. The party did full justice to the Virginia ham and its accompaniments – ordered by Sibyl from America specially for the occasion – the freshly-caught young lobsters, Sark-grown strawberries and thick island cream. It was only afterwards that she heard that the Princess's personal standard had been flown not only at half mast but upside down, an error pointed out, with some amusement, by the Duke to Harry Bell.

Afterwards, in the comfortable drawing room, the Princess recalled with pleasure the small terrier which had decided to break away from the crowd and make her acquaintance during Bob's speech of welcome at the harbour. She had given the dog a friendly pat, an act which had endeared her still further to the islanders. To Sibyl's consternation the Princess then asked if she might see Bella, the large, white poodle which had appeared so often in photographs with her mistress. Bella had been relegated to an upstairs room, as it had not occurred to Sibyl that the Princess might want to see her pet and, with so much to do during the past few days, she had not had time to attend to its grooming. The poodle was duly brought down and, in Sibyl's own words, did not "disgrace" her – in fact Bella's presence provided a homely addition to the relaxed and informal atmosphere of the whole visit.

Sibyl was very fond of her poodle bitches which she had kept and bred from for some years. She usually groomed and clipped them herself and managed to keep two throughout the war years by feeding them on scraps. An ordinance made by Chief Pleas in 1698 decreed that only the Seigneur could keep a bitch. This was designed to limit the number of dogs as the island was, at that time, being overrun by sheep-worrying strays. The Seigneur also had an exclusive right to keep pigeons, Droit de Columbier – which had originated from the old Norman feudal law and continued to be upheld on Sark to protect crops from too many scavenging birds. But it was over the ordinance relating to dogs that in the summer of 1950 Sibyl, quite unjustly, found herself once again at the centre of some unpleasant publicity.

Two years previously, a small terrier bitch, Jip, had arrived on Sark with her master, who had no knowledge of the island's rule. A dog tax was duly collected but no one thought of checking Jip's sex until the attentions of a number of island dogs made this only too apparent. As the old Sark law decreed that the bitch may either leave the island or be destroyed, the owner regretfully chose the latter. The newspaper stories about the incident once again made great play over Sibyl's "feudal powers" which, some claimed, had been responsible for the "tragedy", and much to her distress she received shoals of abusive letters and telegrams blaming her for what had happened. This episode also brought other repercussions for it led to further discussions within Chief Pleas on the future of "feudalism" on Sark.

The possibility of breaking away from "feudal rule" was made a great issue in the autumn election of twelve new People's Deputies and several candidates pressed for changes which would bring "closer ties to the British mainland". Only one of these "rebel" candidates, however, was elected. Though many claimed to support the campaign beforehand, when it came to the point few really wanted any changes made. Nor did they really want to risk displeasing La Dame. Whatever they might say about her behind her back, there was still a healthy respect for Sibyl among the Sarkese both in and outside Chief Pleas. A magazine article of the time quoted one as saying that before a meeting "members went into the bars for a drink to give themselves the strength to resist La Dame" and, after the meetings, "returned to console themselves because they hadn't been able to". Most realised that her eloquence with Chief Pleas and her powers of persuasion could more often than not turn the majority vote in her favour, yet few, since Albert Falle's outburst soon after the war, appeared to have the courage to question any of her actions. But there was one man now living on Sark who had no fear of questioning either Sibyl or Chief Pleas about matters which he felt needed further investigation.

Chapter 14

Henry Head was a Guernseyman who sat in Chief Pleas on his wife's behalf after she had inherited La Ville Roussel de bas, one of the original forty tenements. A fellow Guernseyman described him as being, a "tough, wiry little man with the curiosity of a magpie" and he was already known to many as the "Stormy Petrel" for his reputation of being able to stir up interest whenever he encountered apathy. He very quickly made it his business to look into some of the complexities of the Sark laws and, to everyone's consternation, towards the end of 1949 unearthed the disturbing fact that the last amended Constitution of 1922 had never been sent to the King for ratification and that to all intents and purposes Chief Pleas was therefore an illegal body. Sibyl was, naturally, as perturbed by this revelation as were the other members of Chief Pleas and after much hurried discussion between the Lieutenant Governor, the Bailiff of Guernsey and the Home Office, the Privy Council was obliged to issue a directive declaring the island parliament "legal" until such time as the matter could be cleared up and a new constitution, incorporating several other much-needed reforms, had been prepared and had received Royal Assent. But Henry Head's investigations no doubt prompted Sibyl at this time into seeing that her own affairs were also put in order.

For years she had flouted the rule that, as a married woman, she had no legal right to sit or speak in Chief Pleas. The drafting of the new Reform (Sark) Law of 1951 now gave her the opportunity to incorporate a clause giving her the legal rights she had so long assumed. When the new Constitution came up for approval at Chief Pleas, however, this clause was strongly opposed by those who felt that a married woman tenant, sitting in Chief Pleas in her own right instead of being represented there by her husband, "tampered with the legal position of the rights and laws of inheritance" and that these would also have to be altered to meet the new situation. The "Stormy Petrel", in playful mood, referred to a hundred-year-old law in the Greffe records, which the Seigneur of the time had drafted, decreeing that every woman tenant *should* be represented by a male. But the motion to reject the clause was defeated by an overwhelming majority. Did Sibyl sway the meeting in any way? No one admitted to this afterwards, but if the clause had not been allowed to go through, now that the subject had been aired, further questions about her own position would undoubtedly have been raised.

The *Jersey Evening Post* of 26th September, 1951, in an introduction to an article on the passing of the new Reform Law by Chief Pleas, clearly summarised her new legal position from that date and the situation as it should have been before:

> ... The Seigneur will have a voice and vote as Seigneur.
>
> The wife of the Seigneur, who is a Tenant (owner of one of the original forty farms) in her own right, may take her seat in the Pleas. Hitherto, La Dame de Serk has not had a voice and vote.
>
> All women owners of one of "The Forties", married or single, may now sit in Chief Pleas with voice and vote. Women had lost their rights to their husbands, who took control of all they surveyed, including the wife's right to vote.
>
> Should a husband and wife both own one of "The Forties", they may each take their seat in the Pleas.
>
> A woman, if she so desires, may appoint her husband to act for her and exercise her voice and vote ...

Another change was that the Seigneur's ancient right of veto on any Ordinance was now reduced merely to a delaying power of twenty-one days after which, if again passed by Chief Pleas, such Ordinance became law. Public accounts were now to be rendered annually, the "Corvée" was eventually abolished in favour of a household levy and the 1922 law relating to the election of People's Deputies was also clarified.

Shortly after this important session of Chief Pleas, while in London for a short holiday, Sibyl saw the preview of a film version of Jerrard Tickell's* novel *Appointment with Venus*, which had been made on the island earlier in the year. The plot, although entirely fictional, had been based on Sark (Armorel in the story) and told of how a prize cow was smuggled out during the occupation and taken to England. Sibyl had watched some of the filming and on several occasions had entertained members of the company at the Seigneurie. David Niven, who took the lead, was already

* A writer who had lived on the island for some years.

an old acquaintance for Sibyl had first met him in America before the war at the home of Bob's friend, "Lefty" Flynn. The film was directed by Ralph Thomas and the producer was Betty Box. Others members of the cast included Barry Jones, Noel Purcell, Glynis Johns and Kenneth More. With limited motorised transport the filming had not been easy – and thereby hangs a tale.

Sibyl and Bob were on holiday in Spain when the film unit was due to arrive and, Jehanne also being away, Dr. Hewitt, who had now retired as Medical Officer of Health, was acting as Deputy Seigneur in their absence. When Jehanne returned she was told by a worried Dr. Hewitt that Sark was in a ferment because her mother had written to the Seneschal saying that she had agreed to the unit bringing a Land Rover with them for the filming. As tractors were still the only motorised transport allowed – and even these were still a bone of contention in some quarters – her action would be strongly contested at the Chief Pleas meeting in a few days' time. It transpired that some weeks before, while at a dinner party in London given by Betty Box and her husband, Sibyl had agreed to the vehicle being brought in and since then preparations for the filming had gone ahead and the vehicle had been specially adapted to tow two generators. Without it, Betty Box informed Jehanne on the telephone, the film could not be made on Sark. As hotels had already been booked and all arrangements made for commencing work the following week, it was left to Jehanne to make excuses to Chief Pleas for her mother's action. This she did, with a certain amount of embarrassment, at the same time pointing out that if the vehicle was not allowed into the island at this late stage, Sark's hotels and others who stood to profit from the film unit's presence would almost certainly suffer. Fortunately for all concerned, Chief Pleas agreed to the Land Rover being brought over, but only on the firm understanding that such a concession should not create a precedent. Sibyl's excuse on her return, that she thought a Land Rover meant "some sort of senior Boy Scout", hardly convinced her daughter. But all ended well and many of the islanders enjoyed the excitement of having the film unit around, particularly as many took part themselves as extras.

During Sibyl's autumn stay in London she made yet another broadcast for *In Town Tonight.* She was now becoming a seasoned broadcaster for she needed little persuasion to agree to take part in a programme and was rarely nervous. On this occasion she became involved in another mix-up over transport, though of a rather different kind from the Land Rover affair. The

American film star, Danny Kaye, was also appearing in the programme and to avoid him being mobbed by fans – as was usual when he was in London – a plain delivery van was sent to bring him to a side entrance of the studios. By mistake, the van arrived at Sibyl's hotel and a Rolls Royce at Danny's. Quite unperturbed, she clambered in and enjoyed seeing the startled reaction of those meeting her at the other end.

By this time Sibyl and Bob were taking every opportunity they could to get away, particularly since they had bought an old Hotchkiss car which they kept garaged in France with the express purpose of using it to tour Europe, visiting friends. In the spring of 1952 during a tour of France, Luxembourg and Germany, Bob insisted on a nostalgic trip back to Laufen, where he had been imprisoned during the war, a morbid fancy, to Sibyl's way of thinking. To his surprise the *Schloss* had been converted into an old people's home with bright curtains and window-boxes full of flowers and was very different from the bug-infested prison he remembered. They also called on two former German officers whom they had first met during the occupation, Prince von Oettingen and Baron von Aufsess, who showed them round their historic homes.

After their tour of Germany, the Hathaways were back in Sark by May and Sibyl was busy dealing with applications for the post of vicar. In advertising the position she had asked for a moderate churchman, not less than forty-five years of age, with a broad outlook and real pastoral experience, who was willing to interest himself in all sections of the community – and appointed the Reverend Herbert E. Grant. Within four years, however, owing to ill-health he too had left the island and was replaced by the Reverend Philip Ellard-Handley, who was to remain for longer than any of his predecessors under Sibyl's patronage. But it was not long before their relationship deteriorated, for her attitude towards her incumbents – and theirs to her – had changed little over the years, and all the old arguments over the Church Contract and responsibility for repairs were resurrected with as much acrimony and as little result as before.

Meanwhile the "Stormy Petrel" was still making it his business to look into the obscurities of Sark's laws and although Sibyl often became impatient with his more extravagant statements, she grudgingly gave him credit for exposing much that had been unsatisfactory in island affairs. There were occasional verbal sparring matches between them in Chief Pleas and she once admitted to a certain amount of satisfaction from seeing a motion carried in her favour to which she knew he was opposed – and the larger the majority, the better she liked it for there was nothing she enjoyed more than a battle. But so did Henry Head.

During his term as Constable in the early 'fifties he once telephoned her at the Seigneurie to ask who should be responsible for or lay claim to wreckage washed ashore. Sibyl, thinking, as he had intended her to do, that something of value had been found, immediately claimed her rights. She was not amused, however, to learn that the "find" had been a large, very dead whale and that she now had the responsibility of disposing of it. But it was during this same period that she had cause to appreciate Henry Head's other side when he tactfully handled a more personal matter concerning Douce, who was by this time back on the island with her daughter. Waiting until Sibyl was away on holiday with Bob, he called on Jehanne and Harry Bell to tell them of his concern over the way Douce was taking her young daughter into the bars each night and that he intended to bring a Court order to prevent this. He knew that Douce's behaviour was already causing Sibyl embarrassment and did not want to add to this by taking such action while she was on the island.

Sibyl's private life in those early postwar years had not been easy. Since his return from Laufen, Bob had never fully recovered his health. He drank more than was good for him, was crotchety and petulant and took sudden, unreasonable dislikes to many of the visitors to the Seigneurie – including Sibyl's grandson and heir, Michael. Much of this dislike of Buster's son may have stemmed from Bob's often-declared wish that Jehanne, rather than Michael, should one day inherit the Seignory. Sibyl knew that Jehanne had always been Bob's favourite among the children and also was well aware of her youngest daughter's capabilities. She acted with great competence as Deputy Seigneur whenever they were away, understood the complexities of Sark's laws and knew and loved the island people. Michael had been brought up by his mother in London and although he was very fond of Sark, having visited it frequently since he was a small child, Sibyl could not help but agree with her husband that Jehanne might have more to offer the island. But Sark's laws of succession could not be manipulated and this aroused Bob's antagonism towards Michael even further.

Douce was another member of the family Bob refused to have at the Seigneurie but in this case, perhaps, there was more justification for his attitude, as this daughter had continued to be a source of worry and embarrassment to Sibyl. Despite several attempts to cure Douce's drinking habits by sending her to England for treatment, there had been no improvement and after one

Charlie Perrée driving Princess Elizabeth and the Duke of Edinburgh to the Seigneurie in 1949. Below, a meeting of Chief Pleas, Bob Hathaway left, with stick.

With David Niven and daughter, Jeha
during the film of *Appointmen with Venus.*

A visit from HRH Princess Anne in 1972.

The Seigneurie becomes a postage stamp.

much-publicised affair with a man in Guernsey, she had left the Channel Islands and, taking her young daughter with her, had spent the early postwar years in Europe with a variety of drinking companions. In deteriorating health she returned to Sark in the early 1950s at the invitation – misguided, Sibyl always thought – of a family friend and continued to frequent the bars there, letting it be known to visitors and residents alike that she was "the daughter of La Dame". The local people were kind to her for many remembered her interest in their island during the 'thirties and knew that she had a genuine love for Sark but some deplored the example she was setting her daughter. Sibyl did what she could for this young grand-daughter, helping to pay for her education away from the island and her mother, and providing a kindly ear for her many troubles. She also supplied pocket-money for school, though she sometimes suspected that this soon disappeared into Douce's purse and thence to the island bars. To many of Sibyl's friends, who did not know what went on behind the scenes, the treatment she and Bob meted out to Douce at this time seemed hard – and perhaps it was. On the other hand, stories often came back to them of the bitter, scandalous things Douce was purported to have said about them when drink had loosened her tongue and Bob would countenance no criticism of his wife from anyone.

In May, 1954, the pair took a touring holiday in France and Spain with Stewart and Helen Hathaway. On the return journey Bob became ill in London and the specialist attending him diagnosed the acute pain in his leg as being due to thrombosis and advised rest. Sibyl was concerned for she knew he would be busy that summer with a visit by the Duke and Duchess of Gloucester for the Cattle Show in July, the usual influx of official visitors and the wedding of Amice's son, Peter, in late August. After a few weeks back on the island, however, he seemed much better and enjoyed showing the Royal visitors round the Seigneurie gardens before driving with them to the show-field where the Duke, President that year of the English Guernsey Cattle Society, presented the cups.

Viewing the gardens was always an important feature of any visit to the Seigneurie, for Sibyl was very proud of what she had managed to achieve here over the years. She knew every flower that grew within the stone walls and always tried to ensure that something was blooming whatever the season. Most of the fruit and vegetables for the household were grown in the gardens and the centuries-old vine in the greenhouse usually yielded a good crop of grapes. In former times there had been cider apple trees in many parts of the island but although the old cider press still stood beside the Seigneurie, the trees had long since gone. But it was the flowers in her garden that Sibyl cared for most and which visitors usually remembered best. She invariably brought back some cutting or plant from her travels and a surprising number of these settled down happily in the Sark soil. Before the war she had brought violets from the Garden of Gethsemane, cacti from the Arizona desert, ivy from Mount Vernon and even a rare shrub from India and she continued to add to this collection over the years. Sometimes she gave away cuttings or flowers and after the Princess Royal had visited the island, Sibyl sent her some special blue violets and large primroses which the Princess had particularly admired. She was pleased to hear later that they were growing well in one of the rock gardens at Harewood.

A month or so after the Duke and Duchess of Gloucester's visit, Sibyl entertained Lord and Lady Oaksey and this was to prove another memorable occasion for her – though for rather different reasons. She had ordered a carriage to take her guests from the Seigneurie to the harbour and the driver was prosecuted later for having been "in a state of intoxication while in charge of a horse and carriage", which resulted in him being fined ten shillings and put on the Island's Black List – in force now for some years. Sibyl gave evidence before the Seneschal that the man had been "shaking about on his feet" when he had arrived to pick up her visitors and the fact that she had nonetheless allowed him to take them down to the harbour caused some comment and a certain amount of publicity in the local and national press. Cassandra of the *Daily Mirror*, one of Fleet Street's best-known columnists of the day, made a feature of the story and the tone of his article and that of another journalist in the *Daily Sketch* annoyed Sibyl. The result was an official complaint on her behalf to the General Council of the Press by Sir Thomas Elmhirst, then Lieutenant Governor of Guernsey, saying that there had been "several untrue statements" in the two articles and that the general tone was considered to be "pandering to sensationalism". The editorial director of the *Daily Mirror* dismissed the complaint as "entirely ridiculous" and the editor of the *Daily Sketch* contended that the article had not criticised either Sibyl or the Seneschal – if there was criticism at all it was of a satirical nature. The Press Council also decided to dismiss the complaint and notified the Lieutenant Governor that if the articles held Sibyl and the Seneschal up to public ridicule, the matter was one for a court of law. But Cassandra did not let the matter rest there and in a later column wrote:

> . . . I forgot that elderly ladies who rule islands where religion, agriculture, fishing, land and transport are completely under their thumb . . . may be inclined to export their ill-tempered and frivolous complaints to the mainland. I forgot that criticism – even if it is confined to a wry smile about cabbies and judges and bottles – is like a rude word in the visitors' book to those whose opinion of themselves is rarely exposed to the asperities of a larger world than a thousand acres and 500 people living in a toy kingdom . . .

From then on, Sibyl and her island were to find themselves the target for many other, often unfair criticisms from this master of the acid pen.

In the autumn Bob's leg became more painful and he consulted specialists in Switzerland and London but there was little improvement in his condition. Within a few days of getting home, although he was obviously far from well, he insisted on taking part in what he later said was one of the happiest occasions of his life – the celebration of his silver wedding, to which were invited "as many islanders as could crowd into the hall".

Over two hundred and fifty people took up the invitation and were greeted at the door on that cold November day, first by Sibyl and then by Bob. Present also was Mona Linton, the friend who had first introduced the couple twenty-five years earlier. After the presentation of gifts from the Sark people, toasts were drunk and Sibyl stood up to reply first, referring to the many changes there had been on the island during the past twenty-five years and to the fact that both she and Bob always felt part of Sark's "one big family". Then it was Bob's turn. Normally a man of few words, his warm, sincere speech came as a delight to all who heard it:

> I am not going to call you "Ladies and Gentlemen" but "My Friends" for that is what I hope you will always be . . . It has been said that there have been changes in Sark but I have not noticed any change of heart in the people of Sark. You have all made me most happy to be with you during those twenty-five years . . . My hope is to be able to do all in my power to make you kind and warm-hearted people happy . . .

There was no doubting the warmth with which his words were received and in the genuine feeling of harmony the petty squabbles between the various factions were forgotten. It was, indeed, like any large family gathering. At half-past five, Sibyl and Bob left their guests to continue their party and set off to visit, with wine and cake, those who through old age or illness were unable to attend. It was raining by this time and when they had completed their rounds, Sibyl could see that Bob was very tired and chilled. Despite his protests, she insisted that he should stay behind at the Seigneurie and rest, while she returned on her own to the dancing now rounding off the party at the hall.

After such a happy occasion it came as a great shock to everyone when, less than four weeks later, he again collapsed and although he appeared to make a slight recovery had a further relapse within a few days and died on the afternoon of 15th December.

Many islanders attended the simple funeral and his coffin was carried from the Seigneurie to the church by members of the Douzaine,* over whose meetings he had so often presided. The quiet, kindly American with the dry sense of humour had made many friends in his lifetime – not least among the Sarkese themselves – but Sibyl said afterwards that he would have been particularly pleased to have known of one letter which she received soon after his death for, like Sibyl, he had a great respect for the Royal family of the country to which he had given his allegiance.

Buckingham Palace
17th December, 1954

Dear Mrs. Hathaway,

The Queen desires me to tell you how very much grieved she was yesterday to learn of the death of your husband the Seigneur of Sark.

Her Majesty, who has the happiest recollections of her visit to Sark when she was Princess Elizabeth and of your kindness to her, sends you her deepest sympathy in your loss.

Yours sincerely,
M. E. Adeane.

It had never occurred to Sibyl, despite Bob's recent illness, that she might outlive him. He was only sixty-seven when he died while she, although she looked much younger, was already in her seventies. She had missed him greatly during the war when he had been deported and even during the difficult times with him since; his companionship, wise and often humorous counsel and unfailing devotion had been a very real support to her. His death meant yet another period of adjustment at a time when Sark,

* The island "cabinet".

with the rest of the world, was also experiencing its own upheavals. She felt that, for the time being at least, she must get away and she gratefully accepted the invitation of one of her oldest and greatest friends – Glady Francis (née Richardson) – to spend Christmas at her villa in Tunisia.

Part Four

Conclusion

Chapter 15

It was mid-February before Sibyl returned and she was pleased that Jehanne and her husband, Harry, were there to greet her at the harbour. They were living at L'Ecluse – a property adjoining the Seigneurie – and Sibyl was grateful for their daily visits and for the attentions of her friends during her first months back on Sark without Bob. She would never have admitted this at the time for she liked to appear strong and self-sufficient and indeed some of her friends were upset by the rather brusque way she spurned their well-meant offers of help. She could also be disparaging about their overtures of friendship – as illustrated in a letter to her sister, Doris, a few months later:

> ... J—— said that I must be very lonely and that he and his mother [a woman of similar age to Sibyl] would take care of me!!! You really would imagine I had no one of my own and not even a friend!! In fact it would seem I am very soon to be put in an old folks' home!!!

Yet many of her other acquaintances knew how kind she could be. When the husband of one of her oldest friends died suddenly at a Guernsey hotel, Sibyl took charge of all the funeral and other arrangements for her and stayed with her for several days afterwards until the initial shock was over. Another, whose mother had died unexpectedly as he was on his way to visit her on the island, also had reason to be grateful for Sibyl's kindness and forethought at such a time for, on a busy day, she had made time to meet him at the harbour and take him back to the Seigneurie first before gently breaking the sad news. But these seemingly contradictory attitudes were so typical of Sibyl.

Many on the island who saw only the tough, regal image that she liked to put forward, would have been surprised had they known of her generosity towards those Sarkese whom she felt to be genuinely in need. She frequently gave financial or other help towards the education and welfare of their children or arranged hospital treatment for those who were chronically ill – Sark having no free medical service – and gave practical encouragement to a variety of worthy causes. When a close friend who knew something of this once asked her why she was so reluctant to let these kindly actions become known to her critics, her answer was that she feared others might "take advantage" and this might result in a loss of respect for her position, the same reason that she gave for not becoming "too friendly" with her islanders.

She liked to assume a similar harsh façade in her dealings with her kinfolk, yet wrote to Doris one Christmas:

> . . . I do wish you and *all* the family the very best for the New Year. I am very family-minded, as you know, all the cousins meant so much in my young and rather lonely life . . .

Despite this, she often said that if she could have her time over again she would be a "barren woman" because of the troubles her children had brought her. But she was really very proud of being at the head of her ever-increasing flock – writing to a friend after the birth of a second great-grandchild – ". . . So you see I am fast becoming a matriarch – or rather an ancestress . . ." Years later, she told one of her grand-daughters: "Your next baby will be my *17th great-grandchild*! ! I feel like one of the Begots or Begats in the Bible." Although she had no time for them as babies, when her grandchildren – and later her great-grandchildren – became young adults, she usually enjoyed their company and they delighted in hers, though regarding her with some awe. She would sit with them in the drawing room or her study after dinner and make coffee over a spirit stove, which was always quite a ritual in itself. Afterwards she would work away at her petit-point or tapestry in its wooden frame, every now and then pushing her spectacles up onto her forehead as her shortsighted eyes peered more closely at the stitches, and regale them with stories. Sometimes these would be about Sark in her girlhood days or highly-coloured and amusing tales of her life and there was nothing she enjoyed more than passing on snippets of gossip she had picked up at the bridge table or on her travels.

She continued, after Bob's death, to take every opportunity she could during the winter months of getting away from what she once termed the "claustrophobic atmosphere" of the small island. After one holiday in Tunisia and Spain she wrote to her sister:

> I now feel I must make the very best of this trip as at my age there won't be many more, and so long as I get all this warmth

> I feel each time that I sort of "recover" from old age, while after a spell in Sark I begin to feel my body is like an old dress I want to cast off!!!

But Sark was still home and that is where she spent most of the year.

In 1956, the BBC decided to make its first television documentary about Sark and she was delighted to be asked to take part. Richard Dimbleby and his film unit arrived in mid-June to make the programme, which was scheduled for screening the following month and Sibyl wrote excitedly to Doris:

> ... It's a hell of a performance. They bring twenty men (producers, engineers, cameras etc) and eight tons of gear. The chapel is to be converted into the "television control centre" with miles of cables all over the house and a special type of aerial on top of the tower. On 27th it will be done all over again (same outfit but in French) so the house will be just impossible for about five days.

Despite these protests, however, it was obvious that she enjoyed every moment and that she took to being televised as easily and unselfconsciously as she had to every other public performance. The Seneschal (William Baker) and Greffier (Hilary Carré) also appeared, as did Charlie Perrée in his "number one" victoria, which now proudly bore the Royal Edinburgh coat-of-arms as a record of the occasion when the Queen as Princess Elizabeth and Prince Philip had been driven in his carriage at the opening of La Maseline Harbour. The following year the Royal visitors returned to Sark but Charlie, to his annoyance, was this time not called upon to drive them, for Chief Pleas had decided the honour should go to the prize-winning driver at the recent annual Horse Show.

When Sibyl first heard that Sark would be included in the Queen's 1957 official tour of the Channel Islands she was jubilant and described this first visit of a reigning monarch as the greatest event in the island's history. In her usual efficient manner she made sure that the committee appointed to organise the day had everything worked out down to the last detail, so that all would run as smoothly as possible.

As she waited at the harbour on that sunny day in July for the barge from the Royal Yacht *Britannia* to draw alongside, she told a member of Chief Pleas that it was an occasion to which she had looked forward for most of her life. To her mind it meant recognition of Sark's importance within the Commonwealth, small though it was, and the firm establishment of herself at its head. But the smallness of the island presented its own problems for the officials, who were scheduled to appear in several places within a short space of time without upsetting Royal protocol. Sibyl later described how she had been obliged to make an "inconspicuous dash" in her carriage from the harbour to the Boys' School, where Chief Pleas was assembled, in order to greet the Queen again as she arrived with the Duke of Edinburgh after a brief stop at St. Peter's Church to meet the vicar and his church wardens.

As the Queen entered the hall, the Prévôt, Philip Guille, announced: *"Sa Majesté La Reine et Son Altesse Royale"*. The Greffier, Hilary Carré, read the opening prayer and roll-call of Chief Pleas members and then it was the turn of William Baker, the Seneschal, to read and on bended knee to present the Loyal Address to the Queen. Unfortunately in his nervousness he extended the script to her upside down, realised what he had done and, greatly embarrassed, thrust it forward again correctly, conscious, no doubt, of Sibyl's barely disguised displeasure. But everyone else was sympathetic over his confusion for this was, after all, the first time any Seneschal of Sark had been called upon to present such an address to a reigning sovereign. The Queen made her reply and Sibyl then moved forward to pay her own formal homage as holder of the fief.

Anxious as always to be absolutely correct, she had sought the advice of the College of Heralds, for never before had such an oath of loyalty been sworn by one woman to another who was her over-lord. The oath, in its original form began, *"Sire, je suis Votre Homme"*, appropriate for her father when he had sworn it to King George V in Guernsey during the 'twenties, but hardly suitable for Sibyl to make to the Queen. It was decided that she should perform the traditional three obeisances then kneel at the Queen's feet, her hands raised palm to palm. The Queen would then enclose them with her own as Sibyl made her oath in Norman French: *"Ma Souveraine Dame, je Vous rends homage lige et vous sera foyale et loyale contre tous."* The Queen would then reply: *"Nous vous acceptons Advouant tous vos légitimes droits et possessions relevant de cette tenure de Nous, sauf pareillement à tous Nos Droits de Régalité."* After which Sibyl would rise, curtsy and resume her seat.

Everything went according to plan and Sibyl's very real fear – that with her uneven legs and in high-heeled shoes she might fall whilst stepping her paces backwards from the Queen – was to prove unfounded. The Queen asked the Greffier to say the closing prayer and was escorted from the building by the Seneschal, Sibyl following with the Duke of Edinburgh. She wrote soon afterwards that she had been most moved by the whole ceremony for it had confirmed:

> . . . the whole meaning of the charter conferred by Her Majesty's predecessor, Queen Elizabeth I in 1565, stressing a sense of continuity as well as providing a lively testimony to the fact that for 392 years Sark had weathered many storms and yet prospered and benefited by the system then granted to it . . .

From the Boys' School hall, Sibyl and other officials had once more to slip away unobtrusively in order to greet the Queen yet again at the Seigneurie field, where the Queen's cups were to be presented for the best bull and cow on the island. While some pedalled off hurriedly on their bicycles – still the most popular form of transport on Sark – and Sibyl took a short cut across a field, the Royal carriages went at a leisurely pace along the roadway. After the cups had been presented and gifts handed to the Queen for Prince Charles and Princess Anne, Sibyl took her guests through the garden to the Seigneurie, where the Royal party rested for a short while before journeying on to Alderney.

As on all such special occasions, Sark presented a united front for the visit but rumbles of discontent were just below the surface. The attraction of the island as a tax-free haven where alcohol, tobacco and other luxury items were relatively cheap was already bringing about major changes. An increasing number of Sark properties were being bought up by outsiders and by the late 1950s less than half of the forty tenements were still owned by Sark families. As these properties automatically entitled their owners to seats on Chief Pleas, the character of the island parliament was also undergoing a change. Some of the new members were not prepared to farm the land they had bought, nor to accept the ancient customs and laws by which the conservative Sarkese had always lived. As the value of property began to rise to a level far beyond the average Sark pocket, it was inevitably Sibyl who was made the scapegoat for allowing such a situation to develop and there was strong feeling in some quarters that she cared more about getting her "triezième" of the purchase price of the tenements, than about the calibre of the new owners. But once an islander had made up his mind to sell his property, there was little she could do to stop him, providing the purchaser qualified under the terms of the old charter. There is evidence too, although not generally known, of her trying to dissuade some Sarkese from leaving their farms and of reducing or even waiving her "triezième" to those who wished to buy tenements. She also refused to give her conge* to certain would-be buyers, whom she considered would be unsuitable residents.

Newcomers to Sark and its ways have always been amused and bewildered by the manner in which the twelve members of the Douzaine assess the island's Direct Tax, used for helping its poor. Each year an estimate is made of the amount needed and a specific sum fixed per "Quarter". Householders are then assessed by the Douzaine as to their capital worth in "Quarters", note being taken of their general appearance and standard of living. Although strange to those outside Sark, this system appears to work and if occasional mistakes are made, these are generally rectified by an appeal to the chairman of the Douzaine. If this should fail, the matter can then be referred to the Sark Court and thence to the Guernsey Court if the appellant is still not satisfied. It was largely as a result of a few such mistakes being made that Henry Head, supported by People's Deputy, Hubert Lanyon, endeavoured early in 1958 to get Chief Pleas to agree to a Royal Commission being appointed to look into the administration of Sark, with the system of direct taxation – "By guess or by God", as he termed it – high on the list of needed reforms. He maintained that the laws of the island were "wrapped up in cobwebs of decay" and would "bedevil any lawyer in office". Direct Tax, he claimed, was based on "whether your face fitted" and a fairer system should take its place.

There was much correspondence in the local press following his suggestion, and opinion in the island was once again divided. Sibyl made it quite clear that she was all for maintaining the status quo and was backed by a petition in the *Guernsey Press* to that effect, signed by a number of islanders including some newcomers. But there was also some backing for Henry Head and Hubert Lanyon with regard to their proposition. Eventually, on Sibyl's advice, Seneschal William Baker consulted Sir Ambrose Sherwill, Bailiff of Guernsey, and was informed that there could be no question of a Royal Commission being set up. But a smaller, Channel Island committee could, perhaps, on request to the Lieutenant Governor and the Secretary of State, be appointed to look into Sark's administration, if that was the wish of Chief Pleas. An extraordinary meeting was called in July, 1958, to approve a slightly re-worded proposition on these lines put forward by the

* Permission to purchase – another of her seigneurial rights.

"Stormy Petrel" and Hubert Lanyon but, despite having received assurances of backing beforehand, their motion was overwhelmingly defeated. As always, when it came to the point, it seemed that the Sark people preferred to go their own way and most of the newcomers also backed Sibyl against the investigation. It was said that she did her own "lobbying" outside Chief Pleas to ensure that the meeting was well attended and even telephoned to England to bring over those who might support her view. It is certainly a fact that many were present that day who normally did not bother to take their seats at meetings.

Afterwards Sir Ambrose Sherwill wrote to Sir Austin Strutt at the Home Office that he was convinced there was nothing seriously amiss in Sark but that there was, nevertheless

> ... room for a number of minor reforms which, I should have thought, would have increased the happiness and prosperity of that little community. Apparently, if one can judge by Monday's vote, the great majority of the inhabitants are quite content with things as they are ...

Undoubtedly Hubert Lanyon lost some custom at his bakery and general stores through his support for the "Stormy Petrel's" motion and both of them soon withdrew from Sark affairs. Henry Head left the island to live in Guernsey two years later, apparently still convinced that both Sibyl and the officials of Chief Pleas were to blame for the continuance of much that was unsatisfactory in the handling of island affairs. He wrote to a friend shortly before leaving:

> ... At present there are no Rules of Procedure at all, debates are carried out on a catch-as-catch-can basis and with the Dame sitting alongside the Seneschal behind a heavy cloth which drapes the table, hiding the leg-tapping and we are shouted down by the Seneschal as soon as we are on a topic disliked by the Dame or himself. I usually plod on regardless and having said as much as I can, report it in the *Guernsey Star* where the Governor can see it ...

Whether Sibyl really did go to such lengths to turn affairs her way seems unlikely but there is no denying that, even in her late seventies, her powers of persuasion both in and out of Chief Pleas were as effective as ever. She continued to assert in her press interviews that "those who wanted to discredit the ancient laws and customs would do well to reflect on the long prosperity of the past, which depended – and still depends – on the money brought to Sark by visitors who are mainly attracted by our different way of life". Few could deny that in this respect she was right and the proof was in the increasing number who came to the island each year. She put forward these views to the Home Secretary (R. A. Butler) and his wife when they visited the island two years later, in October, 1960, and the *Daily Mail* of 24th October reported her as giving him "a quiet lecture on how to be feudal and like it".

She was not, she was alleged to have said, a despot as people believed:

> ... We are one big happy family here. I am as much a subject of the laws of the island as everybody else. It is very democratic. Under feudalism you had serfs and things like that. Nobody here is a serf ... The house sales pay for the entertaining I have to do but that is all. I have nothing from the taxes that are collected on cigarettes and liquor ...

There *were*, she said, two men who wanted to alter the constitution "but they didn't get anywhere and now one has left the island and the other has lost almost all his trade ..."

Sibyl's entertaining was by now becoming more demanding both on her time and purse, for there appeared to be few official visitors to the larger Channel Islands who did not also ask if Sark could be included on their itinerary and this usually meant that she was called upon to give them lunch or some form of refreshment at the Seigneurie. These were all in addition to the regular visits of the Lieutenant Governor from Guernsey or others directly concerned with her island. But there is little doubt that she enjoyed such entertaining immensely.

Princess Margaret visited Sark in 1959 and Sibyl was delighted to receive an invitation the following year to her wedding. She wore, she wrote to Doris afterwards, "an Aage Tharup hat of palest pink ostrich feathers" given to her by an old friend and "had a wonderful seat in the Abbey in a box at the corner of the north transept and could see the whole chancel all the time ..." She always took great care over her clothes, hair and make-up and although she counted the dress designer Schaparelli among her friends, visiting her whenever she went to Paris, most of her clothes were bought at the large London stores "off the peg", rather than at the famous couturier houses.

At the January, 1961, meeting of Chief Pleas she proposed, as Chairman of the Publicity Committee, that more money should be voted towards publicising the island and this was carried unanimously. But the greatest publicity the island was to receive that year was through Sibyl herself, for in the February her autobiography was published – first in Britain and later in America. Sibyl had been working on the book since 1957 with two ghost writers, Jenny Nicholson and Peggy Graves. Jenny began the book but after Sibyl had refused to allow her to make any mention of her children beyond their dates of birth, there was a heated argument. Sibyl stood firm and Jenny decided to withdraw. It was then left to Peggy Graves, whose husband, Charles, was distantly related to the Beaumont family, to take over and produce the type of book Sibyl wanted.

It is not difficult to understand why she should have been reluctant to write of her children. So many had caused her embarrassment over the years and in at least two cases were continuing to do so. As it was, some of her more elderly relations took exception to the frank way in which she dealt with her father's misdeeds, despite a glowing tribute to him in her Foreword, in which she claimed that it was to him that she owed her "character and real interest in life". She wrote the book, she told her interviewers, primarily for her family, and, in particular, for her nine great-grandchildren, because she regretted so much that her own great-grandmothers had never kept diaries. One could have told so much of interest about the privateering days in Guernsey during the Napoleonic Wars and the other of life in Montreal during the war against the United States in 1812.

At the end of February, after no less than four live television interviews in England following the publication of her book, she left on the *Queen Mary* for her first holiday in the United States since Bob's death. This began in Florida with her brother and sister-in-law at Varo Beach, after which she went on to friends in Charleston, Boston, Savannah, Washington and New York, where she was interviewed on the radio before returning home in the *Queen Elizabeth* at the end of April. With her went a large, white poodle dog, a present from a member of the Poodle Club of America. In June she was at the unveiling of a plaque at La Coupée to commemorate the rebuilding of the roadway in 1945 but within a few days had returned to London for a dinner at the Savoy with the Canadian Ambassador. Then it was back to Sark again for the annual Cattle Show in July and more official entertaining for the rest of the summer, sandwiched between the usual island business meetings of the Douzaine and prize-giving at the schools.

To have undertaken such a demanding programme would have exhausted many a woman half her age, yet Sibyl, now in her seventy-eighth year, had a stamina and vitality that were quite remarkable. Her mind was as alert as ever and although to islanders she often seemed gruff of manner and stern of face as she passed them on her bicycle or in a carriage, inside the Seigneurie she relaxed and in the words of one friend, "sparkled with vivacity and fun". Except for a sharp bout of bronchitis in the late autumn of 1960 she had kept remarkably healthy over the years, troubled only by minor ailments and occasional arthritis. In the spring of 1962, however, she was admitted to St. John and St. Elizabeth Hospital in London for extensive treatment for sciatica after being, as she wrote to a friend, "suddenly seized up with it in a London store". She recovered a little after treatment but still found that her arthritis made it extremely painful for her to walk any distance or ride her bicycle. Because of this she decided to ask Chief Pleas if she might be allowed to have an electrically-driven invalid chair to help her get around the island to her meetings. She had used carriages occasionally but, as she never knew what time her committees would finish, this often created problems for the drivers over their horses. Chief Pleas approved this ordinance "as a special concession" but the matter was not to end there.

Shortly afterwards, Deputy Malcolm Robson, who had set up Sark's first electricity plant, was brought before the Seneschal's Court for driving the chair on the roads, "in contravention of the Road Traffic (Sark) Ordinance of 1956" and fined two pounds. He claimed that he had only taken the chair some two hundred yards outside his generating plant to test its batteries but the Deputy Seneschal told him that his action had been "utterly reprehensible" as a member of the legislative body of the island and a Deputy of the People. Being August and the "silly season" on Fleet Street, the story was given wide coverage, as was the Chief Pleas meeting a month later when – after considerable debate – the motion that this concession should be extended to include the use of chairs by other disabled residents was defeated by a single vote. Only Sibyl was to be allowed such use on the roads.

Two years later the matter came up again when a similar application for an invalid carriage was made to Chief Pleas on behalf of John Philip Carré – a former Deputy, pilot and fisherman – who now found it impossible to get about the island due to illness. Sibyl remained silent at the meeting but the Seneschal decreed that such a concession could not be granted unless the law was changed and it was decided to refer the whole matter to the Crown Officers in Guernsey. James Pettigrew, in a harsh article in the *Sunday Mirror* of 10th October, 1965, attacked Sibyl for allowing such a motion to be approved without interference from herself. Under the headline "This Old Queen Bee Must Have Her Sting Drawn", he wrote:

> It is disgraceful that Chief Pleas will not hear this plea. Or that the all-powerful Dame gave them neither a nod nor a wink in the right direction ... It is the prerogative of very old ladies, especially Dames, to be autocratic. But not if it is at the expense of the well-being of others ...

After outlining the "feudal conditions of Sark", which the writer criticised Sibyl for maintaining, he went on:

> Of course to some, Sark is a little bit of paradise – no crime to speak of, no fumes, miniscule tax, cheap drink, sunshine and a mild climate. But for others, like John Philip Carré, feudalism is no fun ...

It was, yet again, a cruel and completely unjustified attack upon Sibyl. But although it upset her at the time, she did not take the matter further because – as others were quick to point out – for every critic of her or her island there were many more ready to champion both, and for the very reasons James Pettigrew had also outlined in his article. The debate on the use of such vehicles continued for some time before approval was finally given and it was not until the Invalid Carriage (Sark) Law was approved by the Privy Council in late 1967 that invalids such as John Philip Carré were allowed to use their wheelchairs outside their own property.

For official visits, Sibyl found it more convenient to continue using a carriage, with the stick she had now adopted to assist her walking, and such was the case on 10th May, 1963, when Queen Elizabeth the Queen Mother visited the island. It was noticeable to some who watched the Royal progress around Sark that day that Sibyl appeared to be pale and – unusual for her on such occasions – under some kind of strain. In fact, she had fallen in her bath on the morning of the visit and badly damaged her shoulder. Each time she exerted pressure on her stick the pain was excruciating but she insisted on meeting the Queen Mother, as planned, as she landed from her helicopter and introducing her to the island officials, lined up to greet their Royal guest. Even mounting and descending from the carriage was painful for Sibyl but she persevered and went with the Queen Mother to the Boys'

School where members of Chief Pleas were also waiting with other islanders to be presented. However, after lunch at the Seigneurie, Sibyl regretfully had to leave Jehanne and Harry to escort her guests on the now customary tour of the gardens, resplendent at that time with spring flowers.

Shortly after this visit, Sibyl consulted a London specialist and, after a busy summer, returned once again to England in September in order to enter the King Edward VII Hospital in London to undergo an operation to replace part of the arthritic hip joint which had been causing her progressively more pain. Before leaving Sark she had an enjoyable reunion, over lunch at the Seigneurie, with Count von Schmettow on his first visit to the Channel Islands since commanding the German occupation force some twenty years earlier. The following year she was also to welcome back the kindly German army doctor, Dr. Wolfgang Schubert, who had tended the island's sick – herself among them – during the latter years of the war.

The operation on her hip was a great success but she had a violent reaction to a blood transfusion and Jehanne, who had been left in charge on Sark, was telephoned to say that her mother's life was in grave danger. Sibyl later confessed to Elmo Elton Shaver, an American friend, that she had "really felt very ill and like chewed string for some weeks afterwards". But, much to everybody's surprise, she made a remarkable recovery and those who visited her in hospital were unanimous in their praise at the way she tackled this, her first major operation – let alone its complications – at close on eighty years of age. Even when she must have felt at her worst, she never lost interest in all that was going on around her, or in what was happening on Sark in her absence, and was very touched by the messages of goodwill she received from the island people. The Prime Minister (Harold Macmillan) was in one of the adjoining rooms at the hospital and, much to her visitors' amusement, Sibyl tried to urge them to eavesdrop on the important deliberations over who was to be his successor, being carried on around her neighbour's sick-bed. Outside, in the corridor, politicians came and went and Sibyl could hardly contain her curiosity over the whole affair.

She returned to Sark in time for her eightieth birthday on 13th January, on crutches, looking thinner and with a nurse, but all set, she insisted, on attending the Chief Pleas meeting as usual at the end of the month. Much to her annoyance she had been obliged to suffer the indignity of being lifted on and off the boat and taken by the island's tractor-drawn ambulance to the Seigneurie. It was not, she protested, the way she would have wished her islanders to have witnessed her return. Before leaving Guernsey she had been interviewed by a local reporter at the Old Government House Hotel in St. Peter Port, where she usually took a room on her way to and from Sark, and was asked if she had any intention of retiring in view of her illness and advancing years. Her reply was an emphatic "No" and she gave a similarly definite answer when asked if she would prefer to live anywhere other than Sark. Such an idea, apparently, was unthinkable. The writer concluded: "While the titular rulers of Sark are personified in such persons as Mrs Sibyl Hathaway, its future, I feel sure, is in safe hands."

Most of Sark attended her delayed birthday party in the island hall, a few months later. Fifty-eight young Sarkese sat down to a birthday tea in the afternoon with, at Sibyl's suggestion, a conjurer to entertain them and in the evening there was a supper party for more than three hundred of the adult population. As so often had been the case in the past, whatever criticisms or disagreements there may have been between them all, outwardly it was another family occasion with many of its members, including its matriarchal head, speaking to each other in patois and apparently delighting in one another's company. Perhaps the predominant feeling for Sibyl may have been more one of respect than of love, but at that time most would have agreed with an old Sark man afterwards when he said that when she was away from it, the island was never quite the same.

She resumed her duties that summer with as much vigour as ever, carrying out all her usual official duties without complaint. In October she took a short holiday with friends in Italy and the South of France before flying to Paris where she had been asked to give a lecture in November to L'Association France-Grande-Bretagne at L'Hôtel des Ingénieurs des Arts-et-Métiers. She entitled her lecture, "*Une île féodale au XXe siècle*", and spoke in fluent French for about forty minutes before an audience of some four hundred people, which included the British Ambassador, Sir Pierson Dickson, and M. Jean le Paret, Président de Conseil Municipal. She was very pleased by the discovery that writer André Maurois, who acted as chairman, had read her book and was well informed about her island and by the number of questions from the floor after her talk. The proceedings were widely reported in many of the leading French newspapers and on television in many parts of Europe. Sibyl enjoyed it all tremendously and managed to fit in a visit to a theatre and an opera while in Paris: "... I can't say I like the new Chagall ceiling at the Opéra," she wrote to Elmo Shaver, "it does not go with the 1860 décor..."

She returned to Sark before the end of the year and was soon making plans for the very special celebrations that were to mark the 400th anniversary of the granting of the charter to Helier de Carteret by Queen Elizabeth I. As Chairman of the Quatercentenary Committee she suggested to Chief Pleas at its meeting in January that to commemorate the occasion a loyal address should be sent to the Queen – "... It need not be an elaborate address; just a simple affair with our expressions of loyalty..." Other suggestions she made were that a shelter should be built between the two harbours to avoid "waiting about in that terrible draughty tunnel" and that china mugs and sets of printed labels, showing views of Sark, should be sold to help defray some of the expenses of the celebration.

But in the midst of all these plans, she did not neglect her other island matters, such as calling a special meeting of Chief Pleas to rebuke those who were putting their horses to work during a "coughing" epidemic. "There has never been," she told the assembly, "an emergency quite like this, with nearly all the horses coughing and I have received complaints during the past few days that a number of affected animals are being worked." Some time earlier the island had received bad publicity because a complaint had been made of the horses being ill treated and although that had proved to be "frivolous" such bad publicity was not wanted again and she suggested that a veterinary surgeon should be brought over from Guernsey to decide which horses were fit to work.

At the beginning of July she was invested at Buckingham Palace as Dame Commander of the Order of the British Empire. In 1949, just prior to the Queen's visit as Princess Elizabeth, she had been awarded an Order of the British Empire for her services to the island and now, she wrote to her sister, "... It is rather fun being a double 'Dame' but not in the American sense!!" Two of her grandchildren, Sally Ward-Jones, Amice's married daughter, and Caroline Bell, daughter of Jehanne and Harry accompanied her to the Palace.

The Quatercentenary celebrations began on Friday, 6th August – the actual date of the 1565 Letters Patent granted to Helier de Carteret – and his descendant, Guy Malet de Carteret, Seigneur of St. Ouen, came over from Jersey to open formally the Memorial Shelter at the harbour. Sibyl presented him with a gold medallion to commemorate the occasion and the Seneschal then received from the Seigneur of St. Ouen his family's flag, donated to Chief Pleas in the hope that the assembly would fly it during meetings from their official flagstaff, and his village also gave the Seneschal a new presidential chair. The three days of celebration ended with a Thanksgiving Service at St. Peter's Church on the Sunday. The Bishop of Winchester (the Rt. Rev. S. F. Allison) preached the sermon and the Lieutenant Governor of Guernsey, Sir Charles Coleman delivered a message from the Queen in response to the islanders' loyal address. Michael Beaumont, Sibyl's eldest grandson and her heir apparent, and Guy Malet de Carteret read the lessons. A special choir which included choristers from King's College, Cambridge, sang the anthem – "O give thanks unto the Lord" – which had been specially composed for the occasion by Sir Arthur Bliss, Master of the Queen's Musick. For Sibyl, dressed elegantly in the cream and black candy-striped suit she had worn for her investiture the previous month, it was indeed a memorable occasion. Her one disappointment throughout the celebrations was that, although a television crew had filmed the Thanksgiving Service and French and American journalists had been on Sark to cover the weekend, no British newspapers had been represented. "They come soon enough," she later told a friend with some bitterness, "when there is the merest trace of any scandal."

One such example occurred within a few weeks of the Quatercentenary, when a "diary" note by Ephraim Hardcastle in the *Sunday Express* of 29th August revealed the painful situation that then existed between Sibyl and her youngest son, Richard. Under the headline "For me this son is dead, says Dame Sibyl" Hardcastle wrote: "The Dame thinks of her son with such bitterness that she tells people he is dead." Now married and with five children, Richard had returned to Britain after seventeen years in Malta and, according to the report, "while his wealthy mother rules the 500 residents on the Channel Island of Sark, Mr. Beaumont and his family have moved on to an uninhabited island on the River Trent – where they are existing on National Assistance". Sibyl was quoted as saying:

> ... I have not had any contact with him for a long time and have no wish to. He has been the cause of a lot of trouble to us in the past. I don't want to go into any details, but I repeat that I consider him dead.

The article continued with a statement by Richard:

> ... I last saw my mother in 1946 ... I never want to go back

to Sark. There has been a lot of trouble. I have suffered through being the son of such a famous woman. I am sick and tired of her self-aggrandisement and the way she has abandoned my family. All I want to do is live a quiet life. Since we returned from Malta, we have found it very tough going and I am very short of cash at the moment. We have had a succession of visits from education and welfare officers and from the NSPCC . . . I expect that when my mother dies there will be some sort of inheritance for me. But just how much could come to me I do not know.

Those of her family and friends who knew how much her youngest son had once meant to her – and something of her side of the story – were sympathetic towards Sibyl and understood her reluctance to enlarge on what she had already revealed to the newspaper. Others were startled by the harshness of her statement. She was so often carried away by the emotion of the moment that she would say things she later regretted and this was one such occasion. Writing at the time to her friend Comtesse Susie Lippens, she commented: "What people go through with their families is awful . . . So many have this hell made for them by their young . . ."

Chapter 16

After Bob's death, Sibyl occasionally invited Douce to the Seigneurie though her daughter's excessive drinking was still a great embarrassment to her. By the mid-'sixties, however, these visits became more frequent as it was apparent to Sibyl that, despite an operation for cancer, her daughter's health was rapidly deteriorating. "She does not know it," she wrote to Doris in June, 1966, "but the Deep Ray did no good at all . . ." and her concern for her daughter was obvious. "Douce gets about with a lot of pluck and talks very cheerily of having her check-up in September in London . . . but she is ghastly thin and weighs only 96 lbs . . ."

In October Douce was again admitted to a London hospital and three months later Sibyl wrote to her sister:

> Douce is far along the road out, they give perhaps six weeks . . . Both her daughters go and the sister-in-charge is a Guernsey woman and keeps in touch with me. It is such a hopeless thing as you so well know with Denys . . . [Doris's only son, who had died some years before from leukaemia.]

In conversation and in some of her letters at that time, Sibyl referred to her daughter's illness in what could almost be construed as casual terms and many friends and relations could not understand why she did not visit Douce in London when she knew the end was so near. What they did not know was that she had helped pay for the hospital treatment and fares to and from England for the previous two years and had written to Douce's younger daughter, Jane:

> . . . I imagine that the heroin gives her a sort of uplift so that when she writes or telephones she says she feels better but I have spoken to the sister and she promises to telephone if Douce would like me to go. I feel if I go unexpectedly she would *know* and get a shock so I keep quiet here . . . If you hear of anything I could do or send, do let me know and I will do it at once . . .

Douce died in hospital on 17th February, 1967, and the *Guernsey Press* recorded that Sark had "lost a good friend", for many admired the courage with which she had faced her long illness.

Cancer was a sickness that hung over her "like a cloud" Sibyl once told a friend. So many of her family and friends had suffered from it. Astley had already undergone an operation in Australia but was recovering, as was Doris, but Sibyl always had the fear that she might be the next to develop symptoms. She wrote to her sister at this time: "I hope you are having your proper check-up. I am going to see my surgeon when I come over, just to be sure . . ."

The deaths occurred that same year of two others who had been close to Sibyl for some forty years – her farm bailiff, Len Bishop and his wife, Jenny. Illness had forced them to retire from their work at the Seigneurie and return to Herefordshire but Sibyl had remained in close contact with them, for her links with the Bishop family dated back to the time Len's sister became Nanny to her children at Ross-on-Wye. Nanny had died before the war but Sibyl and her family still remembered her with gratitude and affection for she, too, had been very much a part of their lives for so long. "I do so miss them all," she wrote to a son-in-law, Christopher Briscoe.

One emotion that Sibyl never seemed able to conceal over the years was her jealousy of anyone who drew attention away from herself and an example of this occurred during the late 'sixties on one of Doris's rare visits to Sark. Although Sibyl wrote frequently to her sister, giving snippets of Sark news that she knew would be of interest and constantly urged Doris to take a holiday on the island at her expense, she was really very jealous of her sister's rapport with the Sark people. On this occasion they had shared a carriage with friends on their way to dine at one of the hotels and Doris had sat up on the box with the driver, chatting merrily in patois to him all the way – to Sibyl's growing pique. The fact that Doris could converse in the native language as easily as herself, had always been as much a source of irritation to her as her sister's obvious popularity with the islanders and, much to the amusement of her friends, who had been well aware of what had been happening, Sibyl insisted on riding with the driver herself on the return journey – something she would not normally have even considered.

She had always been proud of the island's carriages and horses and was delighted when, in the spring of 1967, she was made an honorary freeman of the Lorimer's Company. Writing to her American friend, Elmo Elton Shaver, she explained:

...It is one of the old City [of London] companies, dating since the fourteenth century, when the Lorimers were the sole makers of bits and stirrups and spurs for horses. All this in view of my island being a stronghold for horses...

During this period discussions were taking place on Britain's proposed entry into the European Economic Community and Sibyl took part in talks to decide whether or not her fiercely independent island would also join. A petition was forwarded by her to the Privy Council, bearing the signatures of all members of Chief Pleas, asking that the island should be excluded from any provisions resulting from the United Kingdom's membership and that "the ancient privileges and rights re-affirmed by Her Majesty the Queen in person in July, 1957, should continue in force without change or alteration". She wrote to her friend, Comtesse Susie Lippens, in Belgium:

...We here dread the Common Market. Everything about it would be our ruin. It's an uncomfortable world – China, Africa, Rhodesia and the Far East. I try not to think about it and concentrate on my garden...

She nevertheless studied all the relevant facts and figures, well aware of the islanders' main fears, that their entry into the EEC might bring unwelcome changes in their tax system or an increase in the price of tobacco, alcohol and the luxury goods sold on Sark. These and other points she discussed fully with one of the English tenants, Basil Allen,* who – as chairman of the Chief Pleas committee on the Common Market – was Sark's main representative in the deliberations between the Channel Islands and the Home Office.

In one of her Christmas letters to Elmo Shaver some years later she wrote:

Had a worrying year with the decision over the Common Market – which we do not really want – but we now have very much better terms than I ever hoped for, so we just have to go in, otherwise we would find ourselves out on a limb...

In the midst of her discussions on Sark's future in Europe, there were other, equally pressing matters requiring her attention. Not

* Deputy Seigneur to Sibyl from May 1968, after Jehanne's retirement due to ill-health.

least of these was a proposal, by Sark's Committee for the Preservation of Natural Amenities in January, 1967, that an over-all development plan be prepared by an outside expert to help safeguard the quality and nature of any future building on the island. It was also suggested that, as sixty-one per cent of the houses were now in the possession of "outsiders", some form of housing loan be introduced to enable Sark-born residents to build houses for themselves and so encourage them to stay on the island and preserve the traditional framework of the community.

Sibyl heartily backed the whole scheme, saying:

> ... In Guernsey and Jersey everything has grown up in a higgledy-piggledy way and the islands are spoilt. It would be a great asset to Sark to have its development controlled from the start. Do not let us leave it too late.

Chief Pleas agreed and a well-known landscape architect, Geoffrey Jellicoe, was commissioned to prepare the plan, which was laid before a special meeting of the island parliament the following August. He recommended that fewer houses should be built and those that were should be of a better quality. All future development should, he felt, be concentrated in a few well-defined areas, screened by trees. Other suggestions included better sanitation, a fresh water supply, a coastal path (one of Sibyl's favourite schemes) a new hotel of "international standard" and a nine-hole golf course. It was the last two which caused criticism, for many Sarkese felt them to be both unnecessary and out of place. They spent the winter discussing the whole project and when it came up for official approval at the Chief Pleas meeting in January, 1968, the plan was outvoted and abandoned. Although Sibyl was one who voted for its adoption, she later admitted that she had reservations as she felt the scheme embraced rather more than most people had envisaged.

Shipping was another topic which occupied her during the late 'sixties, for the service then operating between Guernsey and Sark had not been satisfactory and early in 1968 the island decided to form its own company with its own vessels and the president of Sark's shipping committee, Basil Allen, was entrusted with the negotiations. Sibyl, who was also on the shipping committee, found – as she had on so many occasions – the usual channels of communication too slow and, anxious to have a vessel at the island's disposal as soon as possible, characteristically took the matter into her own hands. During an official visit to Sark that summer, a Minister of State made a polite offer of assistance and

Sibyl needed no further prompting. Very soon he had received a personal letter from her giving a detailed specification of the kind of vessel Sark required and asking for his help in acquiring it. Her action resulted in some embarrassment for the Minister, for Chief Pleas had not yet met to discuss the matter and, up to that time, he had not received any official notification of what was needed through the Lieutenant Governor, the usual channel of communication between the United Kingdom government and Sark. Considerable diplomacy had therefore to be exercised on his behalf by Government Office in Guernsey in order to get him off the hook. Eventually a sum was voted by Chief Pleas to buy and refit suitable vessels, the necessary companies were formed and the m.v. *Ile de Serk* sailed on her maiden voyage under the Sark flag in the autumn of the following year.

When the m.v. *La Dame de Serk* went into service a few months later, Sibyl was both flattered and amused at the idea of a British boat being named after her. "For, after all," she joked to a friend, "I am now a Vice-President of L'Association des Descendants des Corsairs." She had been asked by the French association some years earlier if she would like to become a member and had been most indignant when it was suggested to her later that her privateering ancestor, John Allaire, had really been "on the other side". "Nonsense," she had retorted angrily. "My great-great-grandfather was quite impartial."

She began 1969 in a buoyant mood, writing on her birthday to Elmo Shaver:

> The telephone keeps ringing with congratulations – though I am not sure why it is a matter of congratulation for it is not by any merit on my part that I have lived so long! My doctors tell me that my heart and blood pressure are like a woman of less than 50, so I start my 85th year well . . .

During a stormy debate in Chief Pleas some days later she spoke with as much vigour as ever against a resolution of "no confidence" in the Natural Amenities Committee. To a proposal that the committee should consist only of members with ten years' continuous residence on the island, Sibyl replied, icily:

> . . . Do you think the people are going to come here and buy land then be excluded from all right of voting, which is what is implied in your memorandum? They won't come here on those terms . . .

But the more Sark became built over, she went on, the less day tourists and other visitors would want to come to the island:

> These are the people who bring money to Sark – not the people who build a little chalet then live elsewhere and let the chalet to summer visitors. These people are only taking money away from Sark hoteliers and guesthouse-keepers . . .

She knew, as usual, how best to sway the Sarkese into her way of thinking, yet at the same time retain the approval of those "English" members of the Committee who genuinely cared for the island and were doing their best to help preserve its charm. The resolution was, predictably, overwhelmingly defeated.

Sibyl also announced at the meeting that she had received notification that a Government Commission of Enquiry into the Constitution of the Channel Islands would shortly be visiting Sark. She had mixed feelings about this intrusion into her island's affairs. She wrote to Christopher Briscoe, early in January:

> . . . This d——d Government are having a Royal Commission to enquire into the Constitution of the Channel Islands. I loathe this battle for existence now. Men can take off for the moon but cannot be reasonable and leave people in peace in this world . . .

On the other hand, she had been aware for some time that there were certain island matters that were not being conducted as well as they might and that in some ways she was beginning to lose control over the changes that were taking place. Some laws were being flagrantly ignored – particularly those concerning tractors and drink licences – and the annually elected constables and their assistants (the vingteniers), who gave their services voluntarily, often found control difficult for in such a small community they were, as likely as not, related to the miscreants. Added to all this, a new tenant had arrived within the last few years, whose strong personality and presence had already created some disturbance within the island – mainly due to the unique nature of his tenancy.

Leonard Matchan, a wealthy businessman, had bought Brecqhou (the small island off Sark) in May, 1966, along with its tenant's seat in Chief Pleas, and shortly afterwards his use of a helicopter to take him to and from his "tenement" prompted a resolution in the island parliament questioning the legality of such action. "Any plane can land on a piece of land on Sark or Brecqhou," he told a startled Chief Pleas, "if the owner of the property gives permission." This had sparked off discussions and speculation over the right of other tenants to fly aircraft from their own land and when it was discovered some two years later, in the summer of 1968, that two landing strips had already been marked out on Little Sark, the whole matter was again brought before Chief Pleas. Although a resolution was passed seeking to "prohibit the landing of any aircraft of any kind anywhere in the island of Sark, the islets and rocks adjacent thereto and the territorial waters thereof . . ." a further clause was added, after a persuasive and skilful argument put forward good-humouredly by Leonard Matchan. This loophole – ". . . or otherwise by special permission, taking established usage prior to the date of this resolution into consideration . . ." – enabled him to continue using his helicopter to and from Brecqhou. His victory and its resultant publicity irked some islanders, for it was common knowledge that he already used a Land Rover and other motorised vehicles – quite legally, as they were only driven within his own boundaries – flew his own flag and appeared to be a law unto himself on his 160-acre island. On the two occasions that he had taken his seat in Chief Pleas he accomplished what he had set out to achieve and although Sibyl remained on good terms with her tenant, his success in the island parliament made her a trifle apprehensive.

Some weeks after this Michaelmas meeting of Chief Pleas, she went to Portugal for a holiday but it turned out to be less restful than she had hoped for while in the Algarve she experienced an earthquake. "There were some deaths and some houses down, but nothing to what I had in India in 1924," she wrote to a friend. ". . . All my things crashed down and slid across a marble floor. I was on the eleventh floor and it seemed these new buildings are safest as we saw much destruction of old houses all around . . ." By "we" she meant her old friend and former Sark Medical Officer, Dr. Hewitt who – now a widower – often holidayed with her. He frequently recalled afterwards how calmly she had accepted the situation, more concerned, it appeared, for his safety than her own.

While she had been away from the island, there had been some discussion in Chief Pleas about a complaint from the newly-appointed doctor that a bicycle was not sufficient to take him on his rounds in all weathers. Sibyl's spare invalid chair was suggested as an alternative but, as it was pointed out at the meeting, the law as it stood would prevent anyone other than those who were medically unfit using it. When the doctor resigned some weeks later, he was quoted as saying that he had decided to leave, owing to lack of suitable transport and essential medical equipment. Sibyl, as president of the medical committee, countered this by issuing a statement containing the doctor's actual letter of resignation, in which he gave his reasons for leaving as being "purely personal", and she claimed that the only request made by him during his brief stay had been for a portable X-ray machine, which her committee had already agreed to supply. The whole affair divided the island and received wide publicity with the usual caustic comments from some quarters directed at Sibyl, under such headlines as "The Dame's Carless Rapture . . ." Philip Perrée, a tenant hotelier and farmer of Little Sark, with whom Sibyl had already frequently clashed, collected signatures from more than half of the islanders for a petition to Chief Pleas asking that the doctor be dissuaded from leaving by allowing "the necessary changes to be made". It was over this matter and the approval of the Projet de Loi, entitled The Post Office (Guernsey) Law 1969, that Sibyl was to feel for the first time that her authority in Chief Pleas was being seriously challenged.

The island parliament had already approved the draft law the previous year, giving Guernsey, rather than the GPO, responsibility for its postal services, but when the law came up for final approval, at a special meeting on 7th July, Leonard Matchan objected to copies being circulated only three days beforehand which, he said, gave no time for its adequate consideration, particularly as many new items were included. Despite Sibyl's attempts to pass the law through, saying that "Sark might find itself without postal services by September if Guernsey were kept waiting too long", Matchan's suggestion that a committee should first be appointed to consider the full implications of the law was carried by a clear majority. He also intervened – "providing the sweet voice of reason", according to a *Guernsey Press* report – in the heated discussions on whether the doctor should be approached by Sibyl's medical committee to return. She had already told Chief Pleas that, petition or not, it was not up to her committee to ask the Medical Officer to withdraw his resignation, he must do it himself. "Obviously," said the tenant of Brecqhou, "the doctor knew the conditions before he came to Sark, but a man can change his mind and circumstances can change it for him . . . It is also obvious that neither can the committee nor Chief Pleas go 'cap in hand' to ask him to withdraw his resignation – but there is nothing to stop Mr. Perrée from asking him to do so." This was agreed and after acceptance of Matchan's further proposal, that the medical committee should be empowered to supply the doctor with "some form of conveyance, either a small tractor or an invalid carriage", he offered to provide a covered tractor himself. Although she thanked him for his offer, Sibyl was obviously not happy with the way matters had developed and as she left the hall she looked tired and every bit of her eighty-five years.

Six days later, she wrote to Doris:

> The Chief Pleas here is really hopeless. They were all led astray by Matchan the other day and voted 23 to 13 to refer the new Guernsey Projet de Loi for the Post Office to a committee. All because Guernsey did not allow Matchan to have stamps for Brecqhou! Now we may have NO Postal Service after 1st October. I am fed up and feel that this island should now be completely altered and run from Guernsey. I am ready to give up (I don't mean to sell but give my charter back to the Queen). I have to go over this week to Guernsey to meet Crowther* of the Government Commission that is going to sit later on . . .

She took the opportunity of this short visit to call upon the Lieutenant Governor (Vice-Admiral Sir Charles Mills), the Attorney-General (John H. Loveridge) and the Bailiff (Sir William Arnold). During informal talks with them she expressed her desire for some kind of constitutional reform for Sark, which would give the elected members of Chief Pleas a majority over the tenants and hinted at her fears that a "a rich and persuasive tenant could achieve a position of undue influence", should affairs remain as they were. She also wrote to Michael to tell him, as her heir apparent, something of her intentions, apprising him of the contents of a statement she proposed to make to Chief Pleas and of a list of suggestions for constitutional reform she said she had discussed with the Bailiff and Attorney-General during her talks in Guernsey (see Appendix Two). But it came as a complete surprise to her island parliament when, on 28th July, at a special meeting called to consider the findings of Matchan's committee on the Post Office (Guernsey) Law, and the possible reappointment of the doctor, she stood up and – unfolding a single sheet of paper – began to read the hand-written contents:

> As you know a commission has recently been appointed to review the Constitution of all the Channel Islands. It therefore seems to me to be the right moment to announce to you that I intend to hand over the administration of this island to the

* Lord Crowther, Chairman of the Royal Commission on the Constitution of the Channel Islands.

> States of Guernsey in somewhat the same way as the Hereditary Le Messurier Family did in Alderney. I have conferred with the Governor, the Bailiff and the Procureur and shall be sending representatives of this island to consult with them – the Procureur has agreed to preside at such a meeting. I have absolutely no intention of selling or leaving Sark. This is all I have to say at present.

It was an emotional moment – for Sibyl, as well as for most members of the shocked Chief Pleas, few of whom had ever seen La Dame display her feelings so openly. It brought tears to the eyes of some and many noticed that Sibyl's hands shook for several moments after she had resumed her seat in the Seigneurial chair. It was, perhaps, a little ironic that at the same meeting both the issues under discussion went in Sibyl's favour – the doctor would have to reapply should he wish to return, and the Post Office Law was approved without the amendments suggested by Matchan.

For the following few days Sark was in a ferment. As was to be expected, opinion was divided between those who appeared to favour her decision and the majority who seemed incensed that she should have even considered handing over the administration to Guernsey, their main fears being that this would mean the introduction of Income Tax and other restrictions alien to Sark life. "We don't want Guernsey bureaucrats governing us," Philip Perrée was quoted as saying and spoke of "UDI for Little Sark". But few thought to query whether, in fact, she could legally take the action proposed. A Home Office memorandum at the time makes the situation clear:

> It doesn't lie with the Seigneur of Sark to hand over the administration. Her ownership confers on her the normal rights of a freeholder (and much influence since she is the only freeholder) but it does not imply ownership of the administration. The constitution of Sark is provided by the Reform (Sark) Law 1951, to which the Chief Pleas owes its power to make ordinances for the maintenance of public order and regulations of local affairs in the island. The Seigneur has the power of veto but it is only of a brief suspensory nature. The island is a part of the Bailiwick of Guernsey and the Lieutenant Governor of Guernsey is equally the Lieutenant Governor of Sark. The Royal Court of Guernsey has the power to annul an ordinance of the Chief Pleas of Sark on the grounds that it is unreasonable or ultra vires but only in criminal matters can the States of Guernsey legislate

> for Sark without the consent of Chief Pleas which is otherwise a sovereign legislature, subject only to the Queen-in-Council. No alteration to this constitutional position could be decreed by decree of the Seigneur. The normal procedure would be by means of a projet de loi submitted by Chief Pleas . . .

For some days after her statement, Sibyl remained inside the Seigneurie refusing to discuss the situation, well aware that journalists were bombarding her Seneschal, William Baker, and others with questions they were unable to answer. A French photographer hid in the rhododendron bushes by her house, hoping to get a picture, but only her family and close friends were allowed in. "The ugly Victorian house," wrote Philip Howard in *The Times* of 1st August, "has an air of impregnability, suggesting the presence of lurking bowmen and buckets of boiling oil . . ."

In Guernsey the Bailiff, Sir William Arnold, was in a difficult situation, knowing that once again Sibyl had taken the law into her own hands but he quickly set about putting the record straight. In interviews with the national press he said that it was up to the people of Sark to decide and, knowing them, he thought they would wish to continue going their own way and Guernsey would do nothing to dissuade them. He admitted that the administration needed amending "but that is a far cry from saying 'take us over lock, stock and barrel' . . . It seems that this is La Dame's way of saying 'I want to get out but I do not want to leave any mess and this is why I want to hand over to Guernsey'." In the States of Deliberation – Guernsey's parliament – he made a statement to the effect that in her Guernsey talks, Sibyl had expressed no more than her *intention* to retire from public life:

> Few people are more justly entitled to that, after a long and arduous service of loyalty to the people she loves so well . . . But I think it should be said here, and known outside this House, that there have been no previous discussions about the merits or demerits, let alone the implications involved . . . Neither Sark nor Guernsey is committed to anything whatsoever and I can only say that if it is the desire of us all that the wishes of La Dame should be acceded to, then we in Guernsey, I am sure, would readily offer our services to Sark, now as always in the past . . .

He went on to correct another part of her statement which suggested that the Royal Commission would be reviewing "the Constitution of the Channel Islands". It had been appointed, he said, to see whether the constitutional and economic relationships between the islands and the United Kingdom need be changed and the Commission would be most unlikely to become involved in domestic inter-island relationships.

Sibyl issued a statement a few days later claiming that for the past two years it had been constantly in her mind that Chief Pleas needed considerable reform as it was now outmoded. A completely new, legally-constituted, administrative body with constructive legal guidance from Guernsey should replace it:

> I feel that it becomes unbearable when the very laws that are made by Chief Pleas are broken by the members themselves ... I can no longer publicise the island as a haven of rest when there are 42 tractors, few of which obey the traffic laws ... I am tired of having to call in the Guernsey police every few weeks because of complaints and the utter disregard of the licensing laws. I feel I can no longer put up with the perpetual complaints I receive as if I were personally to blame for everything that other people dislike for their own personal reasons ... After all, I have only one vote in Chief Pleas like everyone else and, contrary to what many imagine, I have no power to impose any views of my own. I did not even succeed in getting a district nurse appointed although I did get Chief Pleas to agree to paid hospitalisation for our sick poor and scholarships to Guernsey for our children's further education ...

She sounded what she undoubtedly felt at the time – a tired, elderly woman under a strain who was robbed, if only temporarily, of the sparkle most people associated with her.

But she had many sympathisers and the writer of an editorial in the Channel Islands' *Hotelier and Caterer* magazine in August was one:

> Too many people are too ready to blame all Sark's troubles onto the Dame. In fact for a long time now, she has been Sark's "Aunt Sally" and practically everyone has been shooting at her and with due respect to all concerned, I don't think those who should know better have shown her the due deference her age, her achievements and her over-riding love of Sark and its people merit ...

The writer could, he claimed, "enumerate a long list of laws" agreed to by Chief Pleas which had been flouted by the very people who made them.

But less than a month after her statement there were already signs of a general tightening up of regulations, both with regard to licensing laws and the use of tractors. The first evidence of this was on 12th August when two drivers were brought before the Seneschal's Court and fined three pounds each for "contravening Sark's Traffic Law" by carrying too many passengers in a trailer. This was one of the last courts to be presided over by William Baker, the man who had been Sark's Seneschal for over twenty-four years, for in September he, too, decided after talks with Sibyl that it was time for him to retire. He had worked as an official with her since her accession, having been appointed island Treasurer in 1925, during her father's time, and made Seneschal by her in 1945. One of her chief sources of power as Seigneur was that she could refuse to appoint a new Seneschal and in this event it would have been left to Guernsey to make the appointment. The island therefore watched and waited for her next move, not sure after her "abdication" what she might do. In the end she decided upon a Guernsey bank official – Bernard G. Jones – who, since his childhood, had spent many holidays on Sark. The fact that he was not island born, unlike most of his predecessors, was not well received in some quarters but others thought Sibyl had been wise to choose an outsider who could bring a more objective view to his position as island magistrate and president of Chief Pleas.

Early in September, before the appointment of the new Seneschal, Sibyl had summoned an island Deputy to the Seigneurie and the notes he made of this meeting provide an interesting insight into her plans at that time – and her personality also. He recorded that Sibyl had closed the sitting room door behind them in a conspiratorial manner and after offering him a drink had said she wanted to tell him something "very confidential". Sitting on the sill behind the drinks cabinet she had revealed something of her discussions with the Bailiff of Guernsey who had advised her that, in addition to a new Seneschal, the island needed a Clerk of Committees* to attend and record all committee meetings of Chief Pleas and asked her guest if he would be interested, should this office become established. She then told him of her plans for an open-air bus to be run in conjunction with the shipping service, whereby people needing transport could get a ticket with their boat fare. The Deputy's notes continued:

. . . She seemed annoyed that people should think she was auto-

* This post was, in fact, later established.

cratic and lacking in foresight. I told her that I thought she was very forward looking ... She also said with a laugh that her grandson had remarked, "for goodness sake Granny, don't you die yet!" He was absolutely in accord with all she was doing. He wanted to come and live on Sark but not until all these things were put right. She did not feel it fair to him to let the island go downhill. People from outside felt that it was doing this.

She said that no one could stop her from writing to the Queen and telling her that she no longer wished to have the Charter. She said that the Bailiff had apologised for his misleading statement to the press. She thought that the Douzaine should be abolished and taxes levied in a more even way. Her ideas on reform generally seemed very sound.

She said that she was tired of receiving letters from disgruntled visitors who thought she was responsible for the lax state of affairs. One wrote that she had enjoyed Sark but "why did she (La Dame) allow so much horse manure on the roads?" Dame Sibyl wondered whether she was expected to go round with a dustpan and brush and collect it!

She felt that it was because of her great interest in things that she had such an active mind and continued to seem young ... all her contemporaries were rather dull and slow and she felt more at ease with people in their sixties (she is eighty-five!).

The Deputy ended his notes by saying that he considered her to be "incredibly alert mentally" and that physically she "moved easily and with a certain grace".

By the late autumn, although there was much going on behind the scenes, no one on Sark had any clear idea of what Sibyl proposed to do. She had already resumed certain of her official duties and even took her place at the Michaelmas meeting of Chief Pleas without any comment being made about her "abdication". But it was not until the election of the new People's Deputies in December, that rumours began circulating of her intention to make an announcement at the next meeting in January.

Chapter 17

Soon after her eighty-sixth birthday, Sibyl wrote to Elmo Shaver of a friend's sudden death in her sleep and commented: "... a very happy solution to life. Hope I can get it but I fear I am a 'Tough Guy' and may have more worrying years ahead ..." Her appearance at this time certainly gave no signs of the tired, disenchanted woman of the summer before, who had spoken of handing over her island's administration to Guernsey. By now she had let it be known to most of her friends that the "abdication" statement had only been made in order to frighten the island into tightening up its laws, and gave no hint that she had, in fact, intended more than was legally possible. But subsequent talks with officials in Guernsey had helped her to determine her next course of action.

Early in January she called an unprecedented, informal meeting of all Chief Pleas members at the Seigneurie to discuss island affairs generally, listening to suggestions for possible improvements and putting forward several of her own. This gathering proved so successful that many felt for the first time that they were really members of the family Sibyl always claimed them to be and everyone hoped that the occasion might soon be repeated.

At the official meeting, some days later, her old vivacity seemed to have fully returned, bolstered by the obvious pleasure with which her presence was greeted after the get-together at the Seigneurie. She started by saying that she had given a great deal of thought to her decision to hand over her rights but had eventually been persuaded "by an enormous number of letters and requests" to retract what she had said. These words brought spontaneous and prolonged applause which prevented her from continuing for some minutes and she was obviously moved by their reception. She went on:

> ... But I do feel that I must have more help and that there must be a better spirit for the island coming from Chief Pleas. There must be a better pulling together and there must be more

unity by everyone to do what they can for the good of the island. Chief Pleas must not make laws and then go and break them ... There are so many of you who have good ideas that should be examined but you do not bring them to Chief Pleas ... There is no one except me at the moment that you can bring things to and I am getting old and cannot do everything, although I am willing to do whatever I can ...

She then suggested the formation of an Advisory Committee consisting of the Seigneur's own personal representative to act as Chairman and one Tenant and one Deputy of the People who would be elected by Chief Pleas. These three would be responsible for considering and reporting upon any project submitted to them for the good of the island which fell outside the scope of the usual committees. She went on:

... I would also like to suggest, being a woman myself and knowing that so many of you feel that the rights of women in Sark need revision, that the Tenant member of the new committee should be a woman while the Deputy could be a man ...

Chief Pleas agreed to everything she proposed and two Sark-born people – Florida Perrée and Lawrence De Carteret – were duly elected, Sibyl's current Deputy Seigneur, Basil Allen, being chosen by her to be the Chairman of the new committee. It was obvious to all that Sibyl had made a triumphant come-back and that her "abdication" had, as she had been telling her friends, "made the Sark people sit up and look into their affairs".

In March, the *Guernsey Press* commented that even committees which had not met "for weeks, or months, or years" had been holding meetings:

... whether this is due to the injection of new blood into Chief Pleas at the General Election of Deputies, or to La Dame's plea to the members of the assembly to work harder and more co-operatively for the good of the island is not known ...

One unofficial gathering on the island was that of several married women who, spurred on by Sibyl's backing, met to discuss their lack of rights under Sark law and to draft a letter to the new Advisory Committee asking that an improvement in their status might be considered. Their action triggered off a fresh spate of publicity and once again Sark was invaded by television teams and news reporters.

One article which appeared in a German magazine under the

heading, "This is the island of women without rights" carried the sub-title "The whip cracks often but marriages last a lifetime". According to the writer, the natives of Sark were wife-beaters, the law allowed it and wives enjoyed it. The article was illustrated by photographs of two Sark "wives" being beaten with sticks by their "husbands". All this arose from the old feudal law which gave men authority to chastise their spouses providing they broke no bones, drew no blood or damaged eyes. It was the sort of publicity Sibyl felt the island could well do without and, when she was asked about the article by a London newspaper, left no doubt as to her contempt for it, saying: "It is totally vulgar and totally untrue of anything to do with Sark. I do not suppose it is possible to libel an island but if it is, then this has certainly been achieved by this magazine." The "wives" turned out to be two London models and the "husbands" temporary waiters at a local hotel, who excused themselves to the island by claiming that the photographer had told them he was trying to depict "historic Sark customs".

Women's rights were not, however, discussed at the Easter meeting of Chief Pleas – attended on this occasion by the Lieutenant Governor of Guernsey, Sir Charles Mills, for other more pressing items were on the agenda. Sibyl was obviously in her element now that she felt she had regained her position with the islanders and several matters were raised as a result of her new Advisory Committee's investigations. When there was discussion over the employment of a police constable from Guernsey to assist the elected Constable and his Vingtenier in combating crime on the island, she told the assembly:

> I feel so strongly about the disorder that is going on that unless Chief Pleas agrees to the employment of a police constable, I am going to exercise my powers under the 1951 Constitution.* If I fail to do so it is the duty [she turned to Sir Charles with a smile] of the Lieutenant Governor to do so. We must have a policeman in Sark – if only for the summer . . .

As was to be expected, the assembly unanimously agreed with her suggestion and many of these Guernsey constables, who then came to Sark for fortnightly spells of duty, had reason to look back with pleasure on their first meetings with Sibyl, for she invariably invited them to the Seigneurie on their arrival and went out of her way to treat them with great kindness and hospitality when briefing them on their duties.

* A clause of the Constitution empowered the Seigneur to ask for the services of a Guernsey policeman whenever he deemed it necessary.

Before the Easter meeting ended and the Lieutenant Governor and his party adjourned to the Seigneurie for lunch, Sibyl announced that the Royal Commission on the Constitution would be visiting the island later that month. The six members arrived on 30th April and were greeted by a large audience in the island hall. Although she had taken part in earlier discussions with the Commission in Guernsey, Sibyl stayed away and left it to her new Seneschal, Bernard Jones, and other members of Chief Pleas to greet the Commission and answer their questions. Afterwards the *Guernsey Press* reported that "*Pas de change*" neatly summed up the attitude of those who had given their evidence to the Commission.

It was while she was in London, after returning from a holiday in Europe in December, that reports first appeared in the national press that her youngest son, Richard, had submitted a petition to the Privy Council claiming that she was not the legal ruler of the island. He was also quoted as saying that he wanted to "reform the island's constitution and turn it into a democracy rather than a feudal state". He had already been in correspondence with both the Government Office in Guernsey and the Home Office and now sought publicity for his "claim". His latest exploit was, in Sibyl's opinion, "quite ridiculous" for there was no basis whatsoever for his involved claim that Buster rather than she should have inherited Sark on the death of her father and that, Buster now being dead, Michael – his son and her heir apparent – should already have taken over. The Sark law of inheritance had always been one of primogeniture. She had been the eldest child of her father and, as such – because he had no son – was his rightful successor. Although she seemed to brush the whole affair aside, the matter was not settled for another year and she disliked the publicity it received. It was not until two years later that the Queen, on the advice of the Privy Council, dismissed the petition but it was evident from the reports that followed – such as that in the *Jersey Evening Post* of 10th January, 1972, which gave the full terms of the petition (see Appendix Three) – that Richard did not intend to let the matter rest.

Her domestic life at the Seigneurie continued to run as smoothly as ever. She was full of admiration, she wrote to Comtesse Susie Lippens, early in 1971, for the way her grandchildren managed to cope without servants and with children to be taken to and from school:

> . . . Quite marvellous, I think. I am so spoilt myself because I have had my cook for 39 years and the butler 16 years and one "daily" for 22 years so I need never worry about the household.

I find that it spoils the life of so many of my friends, the fact of no servants to be had and often in large houses . . .

She was certainly fortunate in her staff, for their loyalty and admiration were such that, until it was brought to her notice by Jehanne that their wages should be raised, none had complained that they were earning far less than they could have obtained years before, elsewhere on the island. It was not so much that she was mean, but that it did not occur to her that the amounts might be inadequate, so unaware was she of the changing values in modern society. Neither was she always an easy mistress – often sharp of tongue and pernickety over trifles – but she could be kind and thoughtful, particularly when they were sick or in trouble. The staff, for their part, helped to see that the house and the numerous official functions at the Seigneurie ran as smoothly as they knew Sibyl would wish them to be.

Cecile always prepared the superb meals her mistress chose to give her guests and some of the recipes used were those collected by Sibyl on her travels, the ingredients scribbled at the back of her current diary, along with telephone numbers, addresses and other jottings. By far the most popular dish was lobster – freshly caught by local fishermen and cooked to Cecile's own recipe – and the fame of "Sibyl's lobster lunches" soon spread to official circles, where they quickly became associated with a visit to the island. Jim Hamon, who had worked for a time in the Seigneurie gardens before donning his white jacket and black trousers as her butler, "had a way with flowers", according to Sibyl and when her arthritic hands prevented her from arranging the blooms herself he took over and ensured there were always attractive arrangements in the main reception rooms. Willy Carré, who had also worked for her since the 'thirties, was in charge of the gardens which thousands now visited each year.

In old age, bridge was still one of Sibyl's favourite pastimes, whether at home or away, for, she would say, it "exercised" her mind. If she took up a book it was generally a light novel, a crime story or one of her collection of Kipling's poems or stories, though for more serious reading she would turn to history. She also enjoyed listening to the radio, particularly to plays, but rarely watched television, except for the news programmes or those dealing with the identification of antiques. Her general lack of any kind of musical appreciation, however, presented her with quite a problem when, in 1971, she was asked to choose eight records for the BBC's "Desert Island Discs" radio programme. She found it so difficult that in the end most of the records of music she decided she would "like to have played on a desert island" were chosen because of their associations with people or places of her acquaintance.

Sibyl's close family and friends knew that she was now often in pain, despite her usual bright chatter and stoic endeavours to live up to the motto she kept prominently displayed in her bathroom: "Smile – dammit – smile." This could not have been easy for her to have adhered to at times and perhaps some of those who encountered her in her invalid carriage on the Sark roads during the early 1970s were not aware that her unsmiling countenance was often due to her very real physical aches and pains. She wrote to Doris at this time: "So glad you are better – but we both have to live with pain don't we? Pa used to say 'Don't fuss, you'll be worse before you die!' – how true!!"

As each birthday came and went she would tell Jehanne and those close to her that she did not really want any more and that she could not understand why she should be "*congratulated* on being so old", when the credit was due "more to God and doctors". She disliked being less able to cope physically with her self-imposed, demanding life and feared that she might become even more infirm as the years passed. Her one dread, she once told "Hewie", at one of the Sunday lunches they now regularly had together, was that she might have a stroke and be "left lying there, unable to move or communicate". Not that she showed this, if she could help it, to the world outside. In 1971, at the age of eighty-seven, she was "thrilled", she told Doris, when she was asked if she would like to take the wheel of an 800 h.p. launch, which was taking her to start a rowing race from Dixcart Bay. She excitedly accepted the invitation and took the launch for a run round L'Etac rock at thirty-two knots. "I've never been so fast on a small boat before," she told a visiting journalist. "I've always loved speed, whether in a car, on skis, skates or toboggan."

In spite of radio-active mud treatment in Switzerland in the autumn of 1971, the pain in her right hand, aggravated by its constant pressure on the stick she carried, became acute. Yet she appeared on television for her eighty-eighth birthday the following January, in what many considered to have been her best televised interview to date, the *Guernsey Press* commenting that "her sparkling intelligence, her clear voice and her attractive appearance make the thought of getting old much less disturbing". Three months later, however, she entered King Edward VII Hospital in London for an operation on her hand. This appeared to be successful but she developed bursitis in her left shoulder and although she admitted in a letter to her grand-daughter Jane to "incredible pain" and that she was "still dreadfully tired", insisted on returning to Sark within a month of the operation, in order to entertain Prince William of Gloucester and Princess Anne in late May. But she had by no means fully recovered and began to lose weight and develop bouts of intermittent fever which left her even more exhausted. After a courageous effort to cope with her usual seasonal activities, she finally succumbed to another bout of fever in September, which this time caused her to be removed by stretcher to Guernsey on the ambulance launch, *The Flying Christine*, and from there to London and another spell in King Edward VII Hospital for several weeks of tests and antibiotic treatment. In November, she wrote to her sister from London: "No wonder the papers are trying to make out I have abdicated. I am being very good and quiet – no theatres or anything . . ."

Her grandchildren in England all rallied round for, without exception, they had a great admiration for their indomitable "Granny". Peter and his wife, Patricia, took her to stay at their home in Hertfordshire for a few days, as did Michael and his wife, Diana, in Bristol, after which Sally took her to convalesce in Switzerland. "Swiss mountain air always does me good," she wrote to Jane, "and I feel as fit as ever now." Another grandchild, Caroline, a nurse at a London hospital, then joined her for a few days before accompanying her back to London.

Caroline, daughter of Jehanne and Harry, had been born in the Seigneurie and had lived most of her life at L'Ecluse – a stone's throw away – and so had seen more of her grandmother throughout her childhood and adolescence than the other grandchildren, but this spell in Switzerland was the first holiday she had spent with Sibyl alone, away from Sark, and she thought it worth recording. Soon after she arrived at Vevey, her grandmother gave instructions on how she should behave towards the other hotel guests, as Caroline noted:

> . . . We meet Adrienne Allen and the Count de Blomay, and view – with certain disdain and haughtiness – the rest of the hotel patrons. We go to the dining room and I am instructed to whom I may say "*Bon Soir*" in my best accent . . .

Sibyl hired a car for Caroline to drive them both about and her grand-daughter, whose French did not match up to that of her grandmother, had felt uneasy about Sibyl's whispered conversation with the car-hire representative and by the furtive way money appeared to change hands, for she felt sure, by her grandmother's manner, that something illegal was being arranged. It was only after she had got back to England, having driven several hundred miles around Switzerland, that she discovered she had not been qualified, either in age or experience, to have driven at all.

Caroline met, as did Dr. Hewitt when he accompanied Sibyl on her travels, so many people who appeared to be old acquaintances of her grandmother that she was quite bewildered by the end of the holiday – and a trifle exhausted. Except on her eighty-ninth birthday, when she had complained of not feeling well, Sibyl was always first up in the morning, eager to be off on another motoring trip, and her stamina appeared extraordinary for a woman of her age. By the time they returned to London in mid-January, however, she was again running a temperature and was forced to spend another few days in hospital before returning to the Channel Islands early in February. "Lots to straighten up here," she wrote to Doris on her return to Sark, already feeling much better. "If it wasn't for my hip I would be spry as a two-year-old." She wrote to Comtesse Susie Lippens:

> ... Spring is really here and I am having a lovely time with camellias and daffodils. I have just bought a *tiny* electric chair and I can run round all the flower beds and see what is going on everywhere ...

It did not take her long to become once again busily engaged, recording more radio talks, being interviewed by the national and overseas press, attending all the Sark functions and entertaining the usual quota of official guests including – for the first time – the Archbishop of Canterbury, Dr. Ramsey. It was over the Primate's visit that Sibyl demonstrated yet again that even at this stage in her life, she was unable to overcome her prejudices, for her running battle with the island clergy had not lessened with the years and she made it clear that she had no intention of inviting the Vicar of Sark to the Seigneurie to take tea with the Archbishop and her other guests – an omission that was noted with some embarrassment by the other clergy in attendance.

At Chief Pleas meeting in October she spoke fervently in support of the recommendations made by the island's committee on women's rights and revealed, for the first time to the majority of members, her own situation during the war when Bob was away and how she had later been obliged to straighten up her affairs at the Royal Court in Guernsey:

> ... This just gives you an example of what can happen when a married woman cannot act on her own. I am not in favour of any new law applying to property, but it is not right for a woman to be penalised when she marries. She should be treated as she was before and should be allowed to run a business and earn her money and have personal property. At present if a farmer is ill and incapacitated his wife cannot even sell a cow ...

She hoped that approval would be given to the committee's recommendations which would make it possible for a woman to have charge of her own personal property, run a business and legally sign a document. The proposition was carried some months later at an extraordinary meeting of Chief Pleas and the law was eventually changed. Almost ninety years of age she may have been, but her persuasive powers were, it seemed, as strong as ever.

Well before her ninetieth birthday in January, 1974, Sibyl had let it be known that she did not want any celebration. She wrote to Doris in the late autumn of 1973:

> ... I am being pestered by the press to make recordings for my birthday and I've told them all and my family that I can't stand a party – if I give one it's got to be everyone and really that means 200 at least and is a great waste, so I am telling them on *no* account send flowers but only donations to my fund for dental care for our children, who have to go to Guernsey and it's so expensive now for our poor. That lets everyone out and suits me!

Sibyl had for some years been secretly putting into this fund the money she received from her talks and writings, though few on Sark, with the exception of those who had already benefited from it, knew of its existence. The Sark correspondent reported Sibyl's request in the *Guernsey Weekly Press* of 30th November, 1973, and added:

> ... Perhaps never before has a good deed been kept so quiet! And yet we understand that quite a number of children have benefited from the fund. Apparently it usually works this way. The MOH makes regular inspections of the schoolchildren's teeth and eyes. If they need expensive treatment, out of reach of their parents, he knows where help can be obtained. What a nice idea. And what a much nicer birthday present than hundreds of bunches of flowers, to look at the balance credited to this very splendid fund!

Well over £1,000 was raised for the fund as a result of Sibyl's request – a sum which both surprised and delighted her.

She spent her ninetieth birthday quietly at the Seigneurie with a few friends and members of her family. "I received some 114 telegrams, 259 cards and countless letters," she wrote afterwards to Elmo Shaver. One of her most welcome and unexpected presents was the news that the well-known rose-growing firm of

Harkness had named a new rose after her, at the instigation of Edith Page (a former joint proprietress, with Frances Duckett, of the Dixcart Hotel), and three plants arrived on her birthday. When the rose, a flame-coloured floribunda, came on the market a year later, some more were sent for a bed Sibyl had already designated for them.

She greeted one of the many journalists who visited her for a birthday feature for their newspapers: "You haven't come to interview me for my obituary, have you? I know the man who's supposed to be writing it for one of the London papers . . ." Those who saw her at that time found it difficult to believe that she had, in fact, reached such a great age. Dressed in a neat suit with attractive hair and make-up, she could have passed as a woman twenty years younger. "Even her legs," recalled one journalist, "were well shaped and her brain was as alert as ever and well able to deal with anyone asking questions she considered 'out of line'." "Outside pressures today do make it more difficult to keep our character [on Sark] unchanged," she told Willa Owen, who interviewed her for *The Times*, but she was confident that Michael Beaumont, her heir-apparent, who loved the island as she did, would see that "the Seigneurial tradition and the tranquil, unspoilt ways of Sark" were kept safe.

She had for some years done what she thought was necessary to prepare Michael for taking over the island on her death, inviting him for some of the Royal visits and making a point of introducing him, when she could, to government officials from England and the other Channel Islands. He had also attended meetings of Chief Pleas when on holiday from his job as a design engineer. Latterly she had been concerned as to how he would manage financially, for what money she had to leave was mainly in trust for other members of the family. She made several suggestions to him, including that of converting the rambling old Seigneurie into apartments that could be rented for the summer months and tried to be helpful over anything he wished to know about the island. His great difficulty was, however, that he could never "tie her down" long enough to answer all his questions in the short time he and his family usually had on Sark. Her chatter would often run on to include so much else that the original query would remain unanswered – lost in all that followed.

Michael had met his wife, Diana, on Sark, for she also had spent many holidays there since infancy. Her grandmother had lived on the island for a number of years and her father, John La Trobe Bateman, had also settled there after retirement and taken an active part in Chief Pleas as a People's Deputy. Both Michael and Diana knew that at one time Sibyl would have preferred others to succeed her as Seigneur and until only a few years before, Michael had still not been sure of his grandmother's intentions, but she now gave no hint that she was other than delighted that the island would be left in his care. "He and his brother, David," she had written some years earlier to Christopher Briscoe, "are both very stable, I am glad to say."

Sibyl had been upset when Cecile, her faithful cook and companion for some forty-five years, had been admitted to hospital in the February for a mastectomy. "At her age, it seems so awful," she wrote to Doris. She was having a bungalow built in the Seigneurie grounds for Cecile, though initially, as she told Elmo Shaver, it would "house my huge family who often want to come over in a crowd – I really can't cope any more with teenagers and they are too much for my old cook . . ." But her main reason, she told Cecile, was to ensure that her companion would have somewhere to live after she, Sibyl, had died. "You gave up your home," she told her, "to come and live with me here at the Seigneurie and it is only right that you should be adequately provided for."

The summer season of 1974 promised to be as busy as ever for Sibyl. She was hoping to meet in July the actress, Celia Johnson, who was to take the lead part in *The Dame of Sark*, a dramatised version of Sibyl's war years on the island, adapted from her autobiography. She had been flattered when the playwright, William Douglas Home, had approached her at the beginning of the year to ask if he might have her blessing on such a project and, after some thought, had agreed to her name being used for the play's main character, rather than one that was fictitious. She had read and approved the script and was looking forward to the visits of those connected with the production and the play's first performance at Oxford in the autumn.

Sibyl had also been asked to name a new launch in June for the Sark Shipping Company, the first custom-built vessel to be used for the Sark–Guernsey crossing. Watched by a large crowd of visitors and islanders at Creux Harbour, she drew a Red Ensign from the bows of the new boat, naming it, as she did so, *L'Etoile de Serk* and in a short speech told of how, when she was first brought to the island at a few weeks old, the voyage had taken several hours: "We now have a boat which will do the journey in less than an hour." She then went aboard to make an inspection of the vessel and to drink a toast to it in champagne.

But the wind had been cold at the harbour and she caught a chill which prevented her from attending several other functions, including the mid-summer Flower Show a few weeks later and the Cattle Show on 10th July, two events she always enjoyed. The islanders did not pay too much heed, for she had made such surprisingly quick recoveries from her illnesses in the past that few doubted she would soon be on her feet again, and as involved as ever in all that was going on. This optimism seemed justified when they heard that she had insisted on the Lieutenant Governor of Guernsey, Sir Charles Mills, and Lady Mills staying overnight at the Seigneurie after the Cattle Show. A few days later, however, on 14th July, Sibyl complained of slight pains in her chest and back but put these down to the same "indigestion" that had been troubling her for the past two days. "I don't want much breakfast," she told Cecile, who had brought her an early morning cup of tea, "just a cup of hot milk and some bread and butter." Concerned that Cecile should not do too much, for she had insisted on resuming light duties at the Seigneurie after her return from hospital, she added: "But get Jim to bring it up, you must not carry the tray." Jim Hamon, the butler, took this to her at twenty to nine and had barely returned to the kitchen when her bell rang. Cecile answered it, thinking perhaps that her mistress had spilt the milk, but found instead that she was slumped unconscious over the tray in her big, four-poster bed.

Jehanne and the doctor were hurriedly sent for but although she came round sufficiently to apologise to Dr. Somers for bringing him out on a Sunday, she died peacefully a few hours later, at a quarter to twelve. That she could think of others rather than of herself during those few minutes of consciousness was a measure, the doctor said later, of the caring woman he always felt her to be, despite the harsh front she so often showed to the outside world. She had outlived two husbands, many of her closest friends and all but two of her children, Astley having died of a heart attack in Australia the previous November.

The news of her death came as a great shock to Sark. Most islanders had known her all their lives and it was difficult for them to grasp that she would no longer be there at the Seigneurie. Even those who had been her severest critics felt the loss of her strong personality which had imprinted itself upon the island so indelibly for forty-seven years. She had told a visitor to the Seigneurie some years before, with a twinkle in her eye, that the Sark people had become so used to her that "they think I will go on for ever or be taken up like Enoch!" Judy Court, wife of a former island Medical Officer, echoed the thoughts of many at that time when she wrote to the family:

> ... Somehow I always looked upon her as lasting for ever. I know it sounds silly but when a person with such personality and vitality, guts and courage, to whom one has looked up to

with admiration for so long is suddenly wiped off the earth – it *seems* almost impossible . . .

Many had thought that Sibyl was all set for her century but on her ninetieth birthday she had told "Hewie" that she did not much care for the thought of reaching her hundredth year. "All I want," she had said, "is to live for another three years so as to have been Dame of Sark for fifty years."

All her affairs were in order for she had made her preparations for dying many years earlier. One of her requests was that a letter which she had carefully prepared and written in her own hand, should be stencilled and sent to all her special friends. It read:

I have always felt that it should be my privilege to thank all my friends for making my life so full of interest and happiness –
People have meant everything to me and I am grateful for the help & friendship they have brought me –

Sibyl Hathaway

The curtains of her bedroom, she had instructed Jehanne, were not to be drawn when she died nor were the lights to be turned off for, she told her, "I shall be in the dark long enough".

She had also left instructions for the funeral which was to be conducted by the Dean of Guernsey, the Very Rev. F. W. Cogman:

I love flowers. The funeral must be very simple and Sark-like with no sort of Elegy or Talk. Psalm 91. Verses 2, 5, 10, 11 and 16. Hymn: "O God our help in Ages Past". Music: "Spring" (Elegiac Melodies) by Grieg.

Her requests were carried out to the letter. The coffin was taken to the church on the evening before the funeral by horse and cart, escorted by her grandson Michael Beaumont, now the new Seigneur, members of the Douzaine and Harry Bell, Jehanne's husband, who had acted as Deputy Seneschal for the past eighteen years and who, together with his wife, had helped Sibyl with so many of her affairs since Bob's death. The bell of St. Peter's Church tolled ninety times – once for every year of her life, for such was the custom on Sark – and the islanders, Home Office, Guernsey and Jersey officials and other representatives of the many associations to which she had given her allegiance, took their places inside the church with members of the family. The coffin, draped with Sibyl's own personal standard, the Cross of St. George with two leopards of Normandy in one quarter, was surmounted by a mass of flowers, picked the previous day from the Seigneurie gardens, for Sibyl disliked formal wreaths. Four Sark-born members of the Douzaine – Ensor Baker, Philip Perrée, Reginald Adams and Lawrence de Carteret – bore the coffin on their shoulders into the churchyard after the service and Sibyl was buried beside Bob, Amice and her father and mother, in the simple square that was the family grave. It had been suggested that, rather than flowers, subscriptions might be sent – as on her ninetieth birthday – to her Children's Fund but wreaths and flowers from islanders' own gardens covered the ground by the church. After the funeral schoolchildren were taken to see the grave and when one small boy decided to gather some wild flowers to put upon it, the others spontaneously followed suit, a gesture that no doubt would have touched Sibyl.

Now that the initial shock caused by the suddenness of her death was over, the general feeling pervading the day was not so much one of sadness but of acceptance of the passing, after a long, eventful and fulfilled life of a remarkable woman. Sark once again had a Seigneur and a new chapter of island history had begun.

Did she care more for being Dame of Sark than for Sark and its people – or are the two indivisible? She certainly enjoyed her unusual position of authority – not an easy one for her to carry, on an island which for so many centuries had been male-dominated – yet few, surely, could have sustained it with greater aplomb. Although the decisions she made were not always popular, she never failed to have the confidence in her own judgment which is the mark of true leadership, and there were few occasions when it could be said that she had been swayed from any of her proposed courses of action. But inevitably she made her mistakes, both in Sark's affairs and in the way she sometimes conducted her personal relationships, and today, several years after her death, the Sarkese are as divided as they have always been in their assessment of her character and her contribution to their island.

For those who complain that her personality and her lecture tours, television, radio and press interviews brought in more visitors and residents than Sark could adequately handle, there are as many more who continue to welcome the prosperity such fame and advertisement have brought to the small community. Those who sometimes encountered the harsh, often vindictive side of her nature find it difficult to accept that she could also be the kindly woman to whom others took their troubles and received practical, often financial help.

As far as Sibyl was concerned, Sark was always a family and she adopted the same attitude towards the island people as she did to her own children. She believed it to be her duty to look after their welfare – good and bad alike – to cuff them when necessary, praise or help them when she thought fit. Yet at no time did she find it easy to demonstrate her affection for them. Consequently, though many held her in high regard, few would admit to feelings of love. But who amongst them all could honestly claim that they had no respect for the keen sense of humour and sterling qualities that enabled her to overcome her many physical and emotional set-backs throughout her long life?

Was her urge to put her imprint on the world, her arrogance, her desire to lead and her competitive spirit born out of her need to prove herself to those who, in her youth, had made her aware of a deformity that did not match up to her basically perfectionist ideals? So many questions remain unanswered, for few, if any, of her family and many friends were ever privileged to know the real Sibyl who guarded her innermost thoughts as jealously as she did her position as Dame of Sark.

But perhaps these lines of Kipling, which she jotted down in her diary of 1924 while in camp in Kashmir, give some insight into what motivated, if only in part, this complex, interesting woman who never lost her zest for living:

It's like a book, I think, this Blinkin' world
Which you can read and care for just so long
But presently you feel that you will die
Unless you get the page you're reading done,
Or turn another, likely not so good.
But what you're after is to turn them all.

Appendixes

Appendix One

LETTERS PATENT OF 1565

Elizabeth, by the Grace of God, of England, France and Ireland Queen, Defender of the Faith etc. to all to whom these presents shall come greeting.

WHEREAS our Island of Sark, situate near our Islands of Guernsey and Jersey, within our Duchy of Normandy, is now and hath been for a long time past, void, waste, uninhabited and not cultivated, manured or occupied by any of our subjects – during which time not only We and Our Progenitors have lost the ancient and accustomed profits, rents, revenues, incomes and emoluments, from thence long since, and of old time, due to our Progenitors and Precedings – neither has any of Our beloved and liege subjects for many years past, had any advantage, emolument or profit from thence upon that account, but also the same Island, by reason of its being waste and deserted, that, therefore, during the same time been and still is, in time of war, a convenient place, access and cover to conceal and confederate Our enemies, attempting hostilities on Our said Islands, and others of Our Dominions; and in time of peace, pirates, thieves and such like, endeavouring to lay wait for and plunder Our beloved subjects, inhabiting Our aforesaid Islands of Jersey and Guernsey and others adjacent to them, frequenting them or trafficking among themselves to the great harm and no small damage of all Our subjects inhabiting the aforesaid Islands, to Our certain knowledge:

WE, therefore, maturely consulting and providing for the safety and tranquillity of the State and weal-public of the aforesaid Islands, and also, greatly weighing and pondering all things and circumstances to be considered in that behalf, are persuaded that nothing will be more proper or more expedient for the subduing, expelling and rooting out such enemies, pirates and thieves from the aforesaid Island of Sark than, as much as may be, to order, take care and provide that Our above-mentioned Island of Sark be, for ever in time to come, occupied, possessed, and inhabited by Englishmen and others of Our natural subjects.

KNOW YE, therefore, that We, as well for, as in consideration of the sum of fifty sols of good and lawful money of England, beforehand well and truly paid at the receipt of our said Island of Guernsey into the hands of our well beloved subject, Nicolas Carey, Esq., our Receiver-General in that Island, by Our beloved subject Helier de Carteret, Esq., Lord of the Seignory and Fee Haubert of St. Ouen in the said Island of Jersey, of which we acknowledge ourselves to be fully satisfied and paid, and that the said Helier de Carteret, his heirs, executors and administrators, are acquitted and exonerated thereof and of every parcel thereof, give and grant by these presents for Us, Our Heirs and successors, unto the aforesaid H. de Carteret, Esq., Seigneur of St. Ouen in Jersey, or by whatever other name or surname he may be called or known, all that aforesaid Island of Sark, with all its rights, members, liberties and appurtenances, and all and each of its castles, fortresses, houses, buildings, structures, ruined or collapsed with age, lands, meadows, pastures, commons, wastes, woods, waters, water-courses, ponds, fees, rents, reversions, services, advowsons, presentations, right of patronage of rectories, vicarages, chapels and churches of every kind, and also all manner of tithes, oblations, fruits, obventions, mines, quarries, ports, shores rocks, wrecks of the sea, farms, fee-farms, knight's fees, wards, marriages, escheats, reliefs, heriots, goods and chattels waived, goods and chattels of felons, fugitives or pirates, felons, outlaws and the forfeited or confiscated goods of persons condemned or convicted in any other way whatsoever; also all forfeitures, rights of pannage and warren, courts leet, views of frank pledge, assizes and assays of bread, wine and beer; all fairs, markets, customs, rights of tolls, jurisdictions, liberties, immunities, exemptions, franchises, commodities, profits, emoluments, and all the Queen's heredits whatsoever with every of their appurtenances, situate within the seas or sea-coasts contiguous or appertaining to the Island or within its shores, limits or precincts, and whatever were held, known or accepted as members or parts of the Island of Sark.

WE grant and concede by these presents to the said Helier de Carteret, and to his heirs, the aforesaid Island with all its rights and privileges (as listed above) in as ample a manner and form as any of Our Progenitors, Kings of England, or any other having possession or seized of the said Island, ever lawfully had, held or enjoyed, to have, to hold and enjoy for his sole and personal use "in capite" for ever for the twentieth part of a Knight's Fee, and by paying for the same annually on the Feast of the Archangel St. Michael to Us, Our Heirs and successors, fifty sols of good and lawful money of England to Our receipt in the Island of Guernsey:

PROVIDED that if the said Helier de Carteret, his heirs or assigns, do not cause or procure the said Island within two years, and so hereafter from time to time to be continually inhabited, dwelt in or occupied by forty men at least, our subjects, or such as shall oblige themselves by oath to Our Captain of Our Island of Jersey or Guernsey that they will be faithfully true or obedient to Us, the Queen, Our Heirs or successors, the said Helier de Carteret, his heirs or assigns shall forfeit to us by way of punishment or penalty ten pounds, to be taken and levied out of his lands, tenements and goods by an order of seizure from the Governor of Our Island of Guernsey or his duly authorised representative.

AND if after such first default, and after an admonition given the said Helier de Carteret do not within six months then next following make up the aforesaid number of forty men at least he shall forfeit twenty pounds . . . The next forfeit after a further six months shall be forty pounds.

AND if a third admonition be not obeyed, then these the Queen's Letters Patent shall cease and be void, and it shall be lawful for Us, Our Heirs and successors, to re-enter in the said Island of Sark.

THE SAID Helier de Carteret and his heirs or assigns shall not give, sell or alienate all his whole Estate without the express licence of Us, the Queen, or Our Heirs and successors. At the same time by Our will and good pleasure We grant to the said Helier de Carteret or his heirs and assigns that it shall be lawful for him and them at all times, for the future, or from time to time, for ever, during the force and virtue of these Our Letters Patent, at his or their pleasure, to lease, grant and farm some parts or parcels of the said Island of Sark, by indentures to be sealed with his seal or theirs, for term or terms of life, lives, years, for ever, or otherwise in as ample and in the like manner and form as the said Helier de Carteret or his ancestors or any others, seized in fee simple, or other lands held of Us in capite, have made use to lease, grant or farm. Such leases and letting out to farm to be made under the seal of the said Helier de Carteret, to be as equally valid, firm and effectual in law as if they were made or granted under the seals of Guernsey or Jersey.

WITNESS Ourself at Westminster the sixth day of August in the seventh year of Our Reign (1565).

Appendix Two

SUGGESTIONS FOR CONSTITUTIONAL CHANGES MADE BY THE DAME OF SARK IN 1969

1. The Chief Pleas as such to be replaced by a system such as Alderney.
2. The Seneschal and the Seigneur to be replaced by a paid official who is made authoritative by being appointed by Guernsey and with some legal training so as to obviate the constant use of the already overworked Crown Officers. This official could also act as Magistrate with 4 Jurats chosen by the States but residing in Sark.
3. A Greffier as at present.
4. A reduction of the number of Committees (at present 20) and a paid clerk appointed to attend on these to take minutes and tighten up procedure.
5. Alter the tenants' right of voting. Too many of these are now only absentees and play no part in island affairs unless for some very personal motive.

The present form of taxation by the "douzaine" is all wrong. This should be done away with, and replaced by a small finance committee two of whom should be appointed by Guernsey with the official who replaces the Seigneur and Seneschal.

The Island is at present financially sound and self-supporting, therefore alter the present pattern of finance as little as possible.

I seek much professional investigation in this field. There should be Health, Pensions and unemployment contributions and some taxation and restriction regarding companies operating from Sark.

POLICE. The provision of police from Guernsey paid by Sark and replaced at intervals is of the utmost importance. Law enforcement is at the lowest ebb, there is a complete disregard of licensing laws, traffic control (there are now over 40 tractors) and sanitation.

The Seigneur would voluntarily relinquish his tithes etc. etc. and become merely the holder of a fief as in Guernsey and Jersey.

Appendix Three

Jersey Evening Post, 10th January, 1972

QUEEN DISMISSES PETITIONS TO UNSEAT DAME OF SARK

PRIVY COUNCIL ADVISES NO ACTION

The Queen, on the advice of the Privy Council, has dismissed the petitions of Mr. Richard Vyvyan Dudley Beaumont concerning the succession to the Seigneurie of the Island of Sark and other matters.

Mr. Beaumont, son of Dame Sibyl Hathaway, Dame de Sercq, by her first husband, Mr. Dudley Beaumont, contested the right of his mother to be Lord of the Manor of Sark under the terms of an Order-in-Council of King James II of 1611, which, he claims, provides that the Seigneurie and seignorial rights are indivisible; that the Seigneurie descends to the eldest son or one of his descendants in the male line, or, in default of the eldest son and any issue thereby, to the second son, etc.; and that only in default of any such issue can a daughter inherit.

The last but one Seigneur of Sark was the late Mr. W. F. Collings, who only left two daughters, one of whom was the present Dame de Sercq, born on 13th January, 1884. But there was one other issue of Mr. W. T. Collings, father of W. F. Collings, and such male heirs existed in the person of the late Dr. Charles Collings, of Guernsey, and other members of the Collings family, who, so Mr. Richard Beaumont contends, should have had precedence over the daughter of the late W. F. Collings.

THE HEIR

He further argues that his nephew, Michael Beaumont, whose father, killed in 1941, was the eldest of the three sons of La Dame and Dudley Beaumont, should now be the Seigneur of Sark and not just heir to the Seigneurie, on two counts: Because he is of the male line of both W. F. Collings and W. T. Collings, Seigneurs of Sark, and on account of the *"Droit du mari a cause de sa femme"* (the right of a husband through his wife), as this would have passed the accession to the Seigneurie to Mr. Dudley Beaumont from his wife and thence to their eldest son and so to Mr. Michael Beaumont (Mr. Dudley Beaumont being deceased when Mr. W. F. Collings died and Mr. Beaumont's eldest son being killed in 1941).

Apart from claiming that Dame Sibyl Hathaway should not have inherited from her father, as there was male Collings issue who took precedence, Mr. Richard Beaumont drew attention to further complications in the tangled web of the inheritance to the Seigneurie of Sark. After La Dame had married Robert Woodward Hathaway, she proclaimed him Seigneur of Sark by the *"droit du mari"*. The 1611 Order-in-Council provides that it is the "Seigneur's lawful heirs" who become heirs to the overlordship of Sark, and Mr. Robert Hathaway's next of kin are his brother's children who are in America. Thus they would also appear to have had a prior claim to the Seigneurie before La Dame.

HOW?

But how, asks Mr. Richard Beaumont, as the Seigneurie and seignorial rights are indivisible and could not have belonged to Sibyl and Robert Hathaway at the same time, could Robert Hathaway have become Seigneur when the right of inheritance had already passed to Dame Sibyl's first husband and so to their issue? And further, Mr. Beaumont argues, how did Dame Sibyl again become Dame de Sercq after the death of her second husband, Robert Hathaway, Seigneur, when no charter or Order-in-Council provides for any reversion of the inheritance of the Seigneur or of seignorial rights to the Seigneur's widow. In fact, says Mr. Beaumont, the *"droit du douaire"* (widow's portion) provides for the Seigneur's widow as to life enjoyment of one-third of his immovable property and (according to an 1872 Order-in-Council) as to one-third of his movable property.

Mr. Richard Beaumont also claims that one of his sons, if Mr. Michael Beaumont had succeeded to the inheritance and was now Seigneur, would have been within the seventh degree of accession and would have a *"droit de retraite"*, i.e., that if Mr. Michael Beaumont had wished to dispose of the inheritance, his cousin could have intervened.

Further contended by Mr. Richard Beaumont is that, under the 1872 Order-in-Council, which divides the "disponible" property of a deceased into one-third going to the husband or wife surviving, one-third equally among the children, and one-third disposable by will, he had received his lawful inheritance insofar as his father's estate stood at the time of his death in 1918, but that the petitioner was also entitled to his one-sixth part of one-third of £133,147 10s. This, by a settlement of 1899, fell into his father's estate on the death of his father (petitioner's grandfather) in 1926, and which he claims, he has not received to date.

The Privy Council statement said that the Lords of the Committee of Council for the Affairs of Guernsey and Jersey "have taken the said petitions into consideration and do this day (22nd December 1971) agree humbly to report, as their opinion, that it would not be appropriate for Your Majesty to issue any directions in the matter and that, accordingly, the said petitions ought to be dismissed".

Mr. Beaumont claims, however, that it should not be assumed that because his petitions have been dismissed that they have failed for the Privy Council's decision does not state that there are no grounds on which to make a direction. He is now considering whether he can take any further action.

Bibliography

Bibliography

Blakemore, Trevor, *Elementals* (1935)
Poems and Ballads (1912)
Poems (Neville Spearman, 1955)
"Sark" (unpublished mss.)

Cachemaille, J. L. V., *Historical Sketch of Island of Sark* (1874)

Clark, Leonard, *Sark Discovered* (Dent, 1956)

Cruickshank, Charles, *The German Occupation of the Channel Islands* (O.U.P., 1975)

De Carteret, A. R. and Ewen, A. H., *The Fief of Sark* (Guernsey Press, 1969)

Falla, Frank, *The Silent War* (Leslie Frewin, 1967)

Hathaway, Sibyl, *Notes on Feudal Tenure* (Sark, 1928)
Maid of Sark (D. Appleton-Century, 1939)
Dame of Sark (Heinemann, 1961)

Hawkes, Ken, *Sark* (David and Charles, 1976)

Le Huray, C. P., *The Bailiwick of Guernsey* (Hodder and Stoughton, 1952)

Marshall, Michael, *Sark* (Guernsey Press, 1961)
Hitler Invades Sark (Guernsey Press, 1963)

Peake, Mervyn, *Mr. Pye* (Heinemann, 1953)

Platt, Ernest, *Sark as I found it* (John Long, 1935)

Schmettow, Rudolf Graf Von, "Channel Islands before and during invasion to surrender, May 1945" (mss.)

Stevenson, Sylvia, *Tethered Dragons* (Rich and Cowen, 1932)

Swinburne, A. C., *Collected Poems*

Tickell, Jerrard, *Appointment with Venus* (Hodder and Stoughton, 1951)

Toms, Carel, *Hitler's Fortress Islands* (New English Library, 1967)

Toplis, W. A. and Oxenham, J., *The Book of Sark* (Hodder and Stoughton, 1908)

Watney, John, *Mervyn Peake* (Michael Joseph, 1976)

Wood, Alan and Mary Seaton, *Islands in Danger* (Evans Bros., 1955)

Guernsey Press and Star, Jersey Evening Post, Societé Guernesiase Review

Index

Index

Adams, Reginald, 244
Advisory Committee, Sark, 232
Alderney, 15, 135, 205, 226, 250
Alexandra, Queen, 45
Algarve, 223
Allaire, John, 17–19, 25, 35, 72, 221
Allaire, Marie (see Collings)
Allen, Basil, 219, 220, 232
Allen, Col., 166–7
American Weekly, 169
Anne, Princess, 205, 237
Anson, HMS, 185
Appleton-Century, D. (Publishers), 115
Appleyard, Maj. J. G., 153
Appointment with Venus (film), 189
Arnold, Sir William, Bailiff of Guernsey, 225, 227, 229
l'Association des Descendants des Corsairs, 221
l'Association France-Grande-Bretagne, 213
Atlanta, USA, 118
Aufsess, Baron von, 191

Baker, Ensor, 244
Baker, Frank, 185
Baker, William, Seneschal of Sark, 181, 203–4, 206, 227, 229
Bateman, John La Trobe, 240
BBC, 115, 124, 149, 163, 203, 235
Beaumont, Basil Ian, 49
Beaumont, Bridget Amice (see Cantan)
Beaumont, Cyril John Astley, 46, 67, 69, 71, 102–3, 171, 218, 242
Beaumont, David, 241
Beaumont, Diana (née La Trobe Bateman), 237, 240
Beaumont, Douce Alianore Daphne (see Briscoe)
Beaumont, Dudley John, first meeting, 34–5; engagement, 36–40; wedding, 40–1; background and early marriage, 42–6; social life at Ross-on-Wye, 49–50; move to Sark, 51–3; war service, 54–6; illness and death, 57–9
Beaumont, Enid (née Ripley), 71, 73, 102–3, 120
Beaumont, Francis William Lionel (Buster), 43, 45, 47, 60–1, 66–9, 71, 73, 85, 87, 93, 102–3, 105–6, 110, 115–16, 119–20, 158–9, 164, 171, 192, 234
Beaumont, (née Cooper), 42–3
Beaumont, Jehanne Rosemary Ernestine (see Bell)
Beaumont, John Michael, 85, 102, 182, 215, 225, 237, 240, 244, 251–2
Beaumont, John Thomas "Barber", 42
Beaumont, Mary (née Lawson), 116, 119, 144
Beaumont, Nora, 41
Beaumont, Rachel, 41

Beaumont, Richard Vyvyan Dudley (Tuppenny), 55, 67, 72–3, 93, 98–9, 101, 103, 105, 109–11, 119, 171, 215, 234, 251–3
Beaumont, Trust and Estate, 59, 60, 82, 87, 93, 97, 119
Beaumont, William Spencer, 42–3, 60, 73
Bec du Nez, le, 57
Bel Air Hotel, 38, 147
Believe it or Not, Ripley, 117
Bell, Caroline, 214, 237
Bell, Henry Parkin, 181, 186, 192, 201, 212, 214, 237, 244
Bell, Jehanne (née Beaumont), 60, 67, 72, 84, 101, 106, 110–11, 116, 131–2, 144, 158–9, 163–4, 172, 177, 181–2, 190, 192, 201, 212, 214, 219, 235, 237, 242–4
Biberach, 158
Bicknor, Gloucestershire, 45–7, 49
Bicknor House, 49
Bishop, Gertrude (Nanny), 49, 55, 61, 64–5, 67, 72, 81, 93, 112, 119, 218
Bishop, Jenny and Leonard, 81, 146, 149–50, 156, 163, 218
Blakemore, Trevor, 56
Bliss, Sir Arthur, 215
Boston, USA, 125
Bouget, Cecile, 136, 144, 165, 235, 241–2
Box, Betty, 190
Brache, Harold, 166
Bradfield College, Berkshire, 103, 105
Brecqhou, 97, 99, 222–5
Briscoe, Christopher (letters to), 218, 222, 241
Briscoe, Douce (née Beaumont), 49, 54, 67, 84–5, 101, 105–6, 110–12, 116, 119, 129, 131, 134, 144, 171, 192, 217–18
Brittania, Royal Yacht, 203
Brock Road (see St. Peter Port)
Browning, Robert, 49
Bulldog, HMS, 168, 171
Burma, 116
Butler, R. A., 208

Cachemaille, Rev. J. L. D., 123
Campbell, John, 112
Cantan, Bridget Amice (née Beaumont), 43–5, 47, 56, 61–4, 67, 69, 71, 73, 85, 102, 105, 120, 132, 138, 144, 158–9, 172, 183–4, 193
Cantan, Harry, 71, 73, 132, 138, 158–9, 161–2
Cantan, Patricia, 237
Cantan, Peter, 85, 87, 102, 183, 193, 237
Cantan, Sally (see Ward-Jones)
Carey, Edith, 107
Carey, Nicolas, 248
Carey, Victor, Bailiff of Guernsey, 170
Carré, Henry, 185
Carré, Hilary, Greffier of Sark, 203–4
Carré, John Philip, 210–11
Carré, Philip, 136
Carré, William, Seneschal of Sark, 129, 134, 136
Carré, Willy, 235
Carteret, Lord John, 17
"Cassandra" (William Connor) (*Daily Mirror*), 194
Ceylon, 70–1
Ceylon News, 116
Chamberlain, Neville, 126
Champéry, 72
Charles, Prince, 205
Charleston, USA, 209
Cheesewright, Ethel, 108, 114
Chicago, USA, 125
Chief Pleas, 8, 15, 74, 79, 83, 85, 87, 90, 94, 104, 107–8, 113, 119–20, 125, 129, 133, 137, 140, 145, 168, 173–5, 178, 180–2, 184, 186–91, 204–8, 210–12, 214, 219–34, 238–40, 250

Church Contract, Sark (1823), 122, 191
Churchill, Winston, 81, 166, 179
Cleveland, USA, 178
Cloud of Witness, 29, 31, 37–9, 48–9, 57, 59, 73
Cogman, Very Rev. F. W., 244
Coleford, Gloucestershire, 46
Coleman, Sir Charles, Lt. Governor of Guernsey, 215
Collings, Dr. Charles, 251
Collings, Doris (see Verschoyle)
Collings, Marie (née Allaire), 18, 19, 22
Collings, Sophia (née Moffatt), 22–6, 28–31, 33, 35, 37–8, 41, 45, 47–8, 51, 184
Collings, Thomas Guerin, 19
Collings, William Frederick, 21–31, 33, 35, 37–40, 44–5, 47–52, 60, 68, 74, 251–2
Collings, Rev. William Thomas, 18–22, 252
Collins, Stanley, 100
Cologne, 61–2, 64, 71, 112, 133, 183
Colombo, 71, 116
Columbus, USA, 117
Connaught, Duke of, 44
Constitution of the Channel Islands, Royal Commission on, 222, 225, 227–8, 234
Cooper, Frank Cadogan, 84
Cooper, Joseph, 42
Corvée, 130, 189
Coupée, la, 173, 209
Cour de Longue, la, 138, 172
Courier, SS, 47
Court, Judy, 242
Creux Harbour, 34, 89, 90, 116, 120, 131, 136, 150, 241
Crosby, Bing, 178
Crowther, Lord, 225
Cruickshank, Dr. Charles, 139
Cruises, to Canary Isles, 69, 93; Greece, 72; Mediterranean, 73, 82; Norway, 65
Daily Express, 124
Daily Mail, 81, 208
Daily Mirror, 51, 194
Daily Sketch, 194
Dallas, USA, 118
Dame de Serk, m.v., 221
Dame of Sark (play), 241
Day, James Wentworth, 113
Death Valley, USA, 118
de Carteret, Frederick, Seneschal of Sark, 79, 108
de Carteret, Guy Malet, 214–5
de Carteret, Helier, 16, 17, 21, 132, 214, 248–9
de Carteret, Lawrence, 232, 244
Delevigne, Sir Malcolm (see Home Office)
Derrible Bay, 57, 153, 162
Desert Island Discs, 235
Dickens, Charles, 21
Dickson, Sir Pierson, 213
Dilke, Sir Charles, 44
Dillon, Francis, 123–4
Dimbleby, Richard, 203
Direct Tax, Sark, 206
Dixcart Bay, 153, 236
Dixcart Hotel, 153, 175, 240
Dixcart Valley, 153, 162
Douglas Home, William, 241
Douzaine, 196, 206, 209, 230, 250
Droitwich Spa, 57
Duala, Cameroons, 55
Duckett, Frances, 240
Dugmore, Major W., 97–8, 102
Dugmore, A. R., 124

East Orange, USA, 106
l'Ecluse, 201, 237
Edinburgh, Prince Philip, Duke of, 184–6, 203–5
Edward VII, King, 45
Edward VIII, King, 116
Elizabeth College, Guernsey, 66, 132

Elizabeth II, Queen, 196, 203–5, 214, 234, 251; as Princess Elizabeth, 184–6
Elizabeth, Queen Mother, 211; as Queen Elizabeth, wife of George, VI, 170
Ellard-Handley, Rev. P., 191
Elmhirst, Sir Thomas, Lt. Governor of Guernsey, 194
English Speaking Union, 118, 125
'Eperquerie, Sark, 25, 90
l'Etac, Sark, 236
l'Etoile de Serk, m.v., 241
European Economic Community, 219
Evening Standard, 169

Falla, Raymond, 141, 161
Falle, Albert, 175–6, 187
Fief Haubert, 17, 82, 180, 248
Flaherty, Robert, 115
Flying Christine, 237
Flynn, Maurice (Lefty), 118, 190
Foreign Office, 56
Foreign Policy Association, USA, 125
Fort Worth, USA, 118
Francis, Gladys (née Richardson), 116, 123, 159, 161–3, 197
French Riviera, 69
Fripponerie, la, 181

George III, King, 17
George V, King, 116
George VI, King, 118, 170
German Occupation of the Channel Islands, The, 139
Giffard, Agnew, 21
Gloucester, Duke and Duchess of, 193–4
Gloucester, Prince William of, 237
Gloucester, USA, 125
Gloucester Regiment, 54–5
Gosforth, SS, 21–2, 35
Grant, Rev. Herbert E., 191
Granville, 140, 160
Graves, Charles and Peggy, 209
Greenhow, Rev. E. N., 74, 89, 92, 95, 121, 123
Grune, Philip, 169
Guernsey, 15–18, 20–1, 23, 25, 29, 32, 35, 37–8, 40, 47, 51, 57, 60–2, 65–7, 69, 71–5, 80, 83–4, 87, 90, 96–7, 100, 106–7, 112–14, 117–18, 121, 131–2, 152, 155–6, 160, 164, 166–8, 170–3, 179, 182–3, 185, 193, 201, 204, 208–9, 220, 224–9, 231, 232–4, 237–9, 244, 247
Guernsey, Office of the Lt. Governor, 97, 99, 121, 221, 234; States Emergency Committee, 130; States of Deliberation, 227
Guernsey Evening Press, 154
Guernsey Press, 81, 83, 92, 123, 174, 181, 218, 224, 232, 234, 236
Guernsey Star, 207
Guernsey Weekly Press, 86, 239
G.U.N.S., 163
Guillemette, Louis, 132, 134, 156–7
Guille, Philip, Prévôt of Sark, 204

Hamon, Jim, 235, 242
Hamon, John, 28
Hamon, Nanette, 164
Hardcastle, Ephraim, 215
Harkness, rose-growers, 240
Harvard University, USA, 117
Hathaway, Cynthia, 115
Hathaway, Helen, 104, 126, 193
Hathaway, Robert Woodward, first meeting, 104; engagement and wedding, 105–6; background, 106; early marriage, 106–110; accompanies Sibyl on lecture tour to USA, 124–5; meeting with German occupying forces, 136–7; deporta-

tion, 155–7; internment and coded letters, 158–64; home-coming, 170–1; first post-war speech to Chief Pleas, 173; last illness and death, 193–6
Hathaway, Stewart, 104, 158–9, 193
Hathaway, Val, 126
Hays-Hammond, Jack, 125
Hayter, Cecil, 34
Head, Henry, 188, 192, 206–7
Healy, Tim, 82
Herm, 15, 21
Hewitt, Dr. N. S., 177, 190, 223, 236, 238, 243
Hickey, William, 124
Hinkel, "Papa", 161
Hirzel House, Guernsey, 25
Hog's Back, Sark, 162
Hollywood, USA, 118, 178
Holy Trinity Church, St. Marylebone, 105
Home Office, 96, 98–9, 121–2, 135, 159, 168–9, 176–7, 188, 219, 226, 234, 244; Sir Malcolm Delevigne, 87; Martin Jones, 107; C. G. Markbreiter, 86, 96–8, 159, 177; Sir Austin Strutt, 207
Hope, Bob, 178
Horan, Pat, 158
Hotelier and Caterer, Channel Islands, 228
Howard, Philip, 227
Hüffmeier, Admiral, 165–7
Hugo, Victor, 21, 116
Hutton, Baroness von, 115

Igls, Austria, 67
Ile de Serk, m.v., 221
India, visit to (1924), 70–1
Instone Airways, 64
In Town Tonight, 115, 190
Ireland, 73
Islands in Danger, 120
James, Douglas (Jimmy), 85, 87–8, 90–4, 101
Jaspellerie, la, 153
Jellicoe, Geoffrey, 220
Jepson, Selwyn, 116
Jersey, 15, 16, 28, 30, 38, 51–2, 100, 113, 135, 144, 160, 179, 182, 185, 220, 244, 247, 249–50
Jersey Evening Post, 189, 234, 251
Jethou, 15, 17, 18, 35, 47, 72
Johns, Glynis, 190
Johnson, Celia, 241
Jones, Barry, 190
Jones, Bernard G., Seneschal of Sark, 229, 234
Jones, Martin (see Home Office)
Judkins, Mrs., 34, 40

Kashmir, 69, 70, 245
Kaye, Danny, 191
King Edward VII Hospital, London, 212, 236–7
Kipling, Rudyard, 235, 245

Ladd, Alan, 178
Lane, Lady Augusta, 44, 60, 69
Lane, George, 44
Lane, Sir Ronald, 44
Lang, Anton, 64
Langtry, Lillie (Le Breton), 22
Lanyon, Hubert, 100, 163, 267
Lanz, Maj. Albrecht, 136–7, 140, 143
La Patourel, H. A., Attorney General of Guernsey, 117
Laufen, 158, 165, 170–1, 191–2
Lawshall, Suffolk, 43–5
Lawson, Mary (see Beaumont)
Le Feuvre, Philip, 153
Le Paret, Jean, 213
Le Pelley family, 17, 19, 20, 28
Letters Patent of 1565, 16, 249
Liddell, Alvar, 163
Liliuckalani, Queen of Sandwich Isles, 28
Linton, Mona, 104, 195

Lippens, Comtesse Susie, letters to, 216, 219, 234, 238
Liverpool, 144
Lorimer's Company, 218
Los Angeles, USA, 117–18
Loveridge, John H., Attorney General of Guernsey, 225
Lovibond, George, 50
Lukis, Frederick Corbin, 20, 32
Lukis, Francis, 32
Lukis House, 32, 35
Lukis, Louisa, Elizabeth, 20
Lukis, Mary Ann, 32

Maas, Dr. 136–7, 140, 143
Machon, Charles, 163
Mackenzie, Compton, 72
Mackenzie King, 129
Macmillan, Harold, 212
Maid of Sark, book, 115
Man of Aran, film, 115
Manoir, le, 17, 94, 121, 123, 162, 167
Marden, Capt. E. G., 101
Margaret, Princess, 208
Markbreiter, C. G., (see Home Office)
Marmoutiers, Sacre Coeur Convent, 30
Martel, Philip, 138–9, 158
Maseline Bay, 52, 120
Maseline Harbour, 184, 203
Matchan, Leonard, 222–6
Maurois, André, 213
McCormick, Rev. Eaton, 40
McGonigal, Lt. A. J. M., 162
McLaglen, Clifford, 116
Meek, Ralph, 158–9
Mills, Vice-Admiral Sir Charles, Lt. Governor of Guernsey, 225, 233, 242
Minneapolis, USA, 182
Moffatt, Hon. George, 22
Moffatt, Sophia (see Collings)
Moinerie de Haut, la, 99
More, Kenneth, 190
Montreal, 22–3, 178, 209
Morrison, Herbert, 168–9
Mortimer, Berkshire, 55
Mulholland, Desmond, 138–9, 158
Müller, General, 155
Munich, 64
Mürren, 50

NBC, 117
National Geographic Magazine, 112
National Geographic Society, 124–5
National Provincial Bank, 177
National Service League, 44, 49
Neame, Sir Philip, Lt. Governor of Guernsey, 178
News Chronicle, 179
New York, USA, 104–6, 117, 118, 124–5, 178, 182, 209
New York Sun, 105
Nicholson, Jenny, 209
Niven, David, 118, 189

Oaksey, Lord and Lady, 194
Oberammergau, 63–4
Oettingen, Prince von, 146, 191
Old Government House Hotel (see St. Peter Port)
Owen, Willa, 240

Page, Edith, 240
Palm Springs, USA, 118
Pannier, Pierre, 115
Paramount Studios, Hollywood, USA, 118
Paris, 71, 125, 158, 213
Pasadena, USA, 118, 178
Patagonia, USA, 125
Peake, Mervyn, 114
Percy, Saville (Esme), 62
Perrée, Charlie, 107, 182, 185, 203
Perrée, Florida, 232
Perrée, Philip, 224, 226, 244
Perronerie, la, 17
Pettigrew, James, 210–11
Phillips, Rev. R. H., 123
Pierre Percée, la, 60, 65

Pittard, Dr. 123, 125, 146, 153
Pittard, Frances, 153, 155
Platt, Ernest, 41, 68, 81
Pointe Robert, Sark, 106, 182
Port du Moulin, Sark, 20
Port Gorey, Sark, 113
Press Council, 194
Princeton University, USA, 117
Privy Council, 87, 95–6, 180, 188, 211, 219, 234, 251, 253
Purcell, Noel, 190

Ramsey, Dr. Michael, Archbishop of Canterbury, 238
Reading, Berkshire, British Dairy Institute, 53
Reform (Sark) Law, 1951, 188–9
Rink, Jane (née Briscoe), 129, 134, 217
Ripley, Enid (see Beaumont)
Roberts, Lord, 44
Robson, J. Malcolm, 210
Roebuck HMS, 185
Roosevelt, President F. D., 179
Ross-on-Wye, Herefordshire, 46, 49, 50, 52, 55, 63, 100, 218; Edde Cross House, 49
Royal Aeronautical College, 113
Royal Ontario Museum, 178
Royal, The Princess (sister of George VI), 194
Royal Sark Militia, 20, 22, 184
Rundstedt, Field Marshal von, 165

Sackville West, Major General Sir Charles (later Lord Sackville) Lt. Governor of Guernsey, 18, 71, 75, 96, 98–100; Lady Sackville West, 73
St. James's Church, Piccadilly, 40–1, 59
St. John and St. Elizabeth Hospital, London, 210
St. Magloire, 15
St. Maur, Betty, 54
St. Neots, Huntingdonshire, 36
St. Ouen, Jersey, 16, 214–15, 248
St. Peter's Church, Sark, 91, 107, 121, 204, 215, 244
St. Peter Port, Guernsey, 25, 32, 51, 60, 65, 67, 90, 131, 135–6, 150, 156, 166, 182, 185, 213; Brock Road, 65, 68, 72, 80–1, 84–5, 89; Old Government House Hotel, 213
San Francisco, USA, 118
Sark Shipping Company, 220–1, 241
Savannah, USA, 209
Schmettow, Col. Graf von, 144, 165, 212
Schubert, Dr. Wolfgang, 163–4, 212
Seichan, Rev. L. N., 23, 27
Seigneurie, la, 17, 20, 24, 26, 28, 32, 34–9, 48, 51, 68, 72, 74, 80–2, 84–5, 89, 91, 93–4, 100–2, 107–9, 111–13, 116, 129, 131, 135–8, 140–7, 149, 151–3, 156, 160, 163–4, 166, 173, 179, 182, 184–5, 189, 192–4, 196, 201, 205, 208, 212, 217, 227, 229, 231, 233–5, 237, 239, 240–2, 244, 251
Sempill, Lord, 112–13
Sharp, Mrs. 150
Shaver, Elmo Elton, letters to, 212, 214, 218–19, 221, 231, 239
Sherwill, Major Ambrose (later Sir Ambrose, Bailiff of Guernsey), 139, 158, 206–7
Skelton, Major John, 142, 149–52
Skelton, Madge, 142, 151–2
Snow, Brigadier, 167
Societé de Geographie, 125
Somers, Dr. R. B. Usher, 242
Spartanburg, USA, 118
Speke, Mrs. Lily, 104
States of Deliberation (see Guernsey)

States Emergency Commission (see Guernsey)
Stock's Hotel, Sark, 175
Stover Park, Devon, 54
Strachey, John, 179
Strutt, Sir Austin (see Home Office)
Sunday Dispatch, 121
Sunday Express, 115, 215
Sunday Mirror, 211
Swinburne, A. C., 15, 21
Switzerland, 50, 72, 195, 237

Texas, USA, 182
Tickell, Jerrard, 189
Thomas, Ralph, 190
Times, The, 51, 81, 90, 172, 227, 240
Toilers of the Sea, 116, 119
Toplis, William, 21, 114
Tryon, USA, 118
Tunisia, 197, 202
Turner, J. M. W., 115

United States of America, visits to, 1929, 104–5; 1936, 117–18; 1938, 124–5; 1946, 178; 1947, 182; 1961, 209

Valette de Bas, la, 52, 55, 59, 60
Vega, SS, Red Cross ship, 165
Varo Beach, USA, 209
Vermeil, M. and Mlle., 27
Verschoyle, Denys, 217
Verschoyle, Doris, (née Collings), 26–8, 31, 38, 45, 48–9, 51–2, 177, 183, 201–3, 208, 217–18, 225, 236, 239, 241
Verschoyle, Henry, 52
Vévey, 237
Victoria, Queen, 27, 44, 184
Victoria, Princess, 184
Voluntary Aid Detachment (Red Cross), 50, 54

Ward-Jones, Sally (née Cantan), 183, 214, 237
War Emergency Committee, Sark, 129, 137, 140–1
War Office, 55, 91
Washington, USA, 117, 125, 209
Welcome to Sark, BBC documentary, 124
Wengen, 50
Whitehall Court, London, 57
Wizard, HMS, 185
Women's Press Club of America, 125
Wood, A. and M. Seaton, 120

Yale University, USA, 117, 125
YMCA, 61

Zukor, Adolph, 118